Fear, Faith, and Moving Forward

Natalie J. White

Fear, Faith, and Moving Forward

ISBN 978-1-7350707-0-4

Library of Congress Control Number: 2020925261

Publisher: Grace Ridge Media, LLC, 3535 8th St E, West Fargo, ND 58078

Layout and design: Copyright © 2021, How 2 Creative Services of Audubon, Minnesota

Back cover photo by Becca Albertson, other photos by Patrick Yeagle and Natalie White.

This book is dedicated to Lydia, with Love.

Dedication

For Lydia, with love

"I sought the Lord, and He answered me;
he delivered me from all my fears."
Psalm 34:4

CONTENTS

Author's Note

This book represents the author's personal experiences and viewpoints. While it may serve as a guide for some, the knowledge, circumstances, resources, and inherent privileges discussed here are unique to the author. Each person should make their own healthcare and financial decisions with that understanding. This story remains true to the original intent and chronology, though many parts were condensed in order to improve readability. Therefore, this is a snapshot of all that happened within a two year period. The names of all medical personnel have been changed or eliminated for privacy. Any similarities are purely coincidental. The medical facilities and other entities are not specifically identified. Names of friends and family are real; however, only first names have been used.

Prologue

"Even though I walk through the valley of the shadow of death, I will fear no evil, for you are with me; your rod and your staff, they comfort me."
Psalm 23:4 ESV

In late April of 2012, I dreamed of a frightening tornado looming straight over our house. It was the biggest I had ever seen. Thick and black, the funnel cloud hung ominously, circling only about twenty feet above our house. I woke up in a cold sweat because my nightmare seemed all too real. Subconsciously, I knew this wasn't just any storm. It was evil.

I jumped out of bed and ran to peer out the bedroom window. I called out to my husband, Dave, but he didn't wake up. Then, I quickly checked the weather on my cell phone; there were no alerts. The night was calm, yet I felt uneasy as I walked into the kitchen. I turned on some lights and listened for anything unusual. As I raced around, making sure the house was secure, I prayed. "Lord, what does this mean?" Trying to get rid of my fear, it seemed natural for me to turn to God. But, even then, I didn't have peace.

My family was asleep, and nothing seemed out of the ordinary. Dave had been working so hard to provide for us that I decided not to wake him needlessly. Yet, I could not shake the sense of dread which gripped my heart. That spring had been full of storms and tornado watches and warnings, so I was already on high alert. Only a few nights before, the tornado sirens had sounded in the middle of the night. Dave and I had grabbed our five-month-old daughter, Lydia, and headed to the basement to watch the weather update. We spent the rest of the night sleeping in the downstairs guest room, just to be safe.

Since Lydia had been born, life had been a blur. She had only started sleeping through the night two weeks earlier, and I was still so exhausted. As a result of meeting her needs, I had gotten out of my old routines. I had unintentionally neglected my habit of spending time with the Lord and reading my Bible every morning. It was difficult for me to find regular time with Him.

Anxiety crept in as I thought about my nightmare. I had tried to do my best, but I didn't feel as close to God as I usually did. Suddenly, I wondered, "If I haven't been doing my part lately, is God mad at me? Could I rely on Him if something were to happen? Would He come to our rescue?" Filled with fear and doubt, I prayed, asking the Lord to forgive my errant heart.

Because there seemed to be no immediate threat, I decided to go back to bed. I walked around the kitchen island, toward the hall to our bedroom. I paused to turn off the kitchen lights when, suddenly, the sense of foreboding returned. Time stood still as I glanced down the hall toward the two bedrooms. Lydia was asleep in the room on the right, Dave in our bedroom on the left. Instinctively, I felt something was going to happen. But what? And behind which door? Somehow, I knew whatever was coming was a test.

At the time, I had no idea what this all meant, though I would find out soon enough.

Part I

Facing Fear

Chapter 1

"For we walk by faith, not by sight."
2 Corinthians 5:7 NKJV

My first Mother's Day as a mom was on May 13th, 2012. I had been looking forward to celebrating that day; however, it didn't feel special after all. We had planned to participate in a dedication ceremony at church, when families presented their children to God and committed to raising them to know Him. Instead, I was tired and frustrated because my husband had been sick in bed all week. Dave loved his job as an engineer for Caterpillar, so missing work was very unusual for him. Yet, he could barely move without pain and discomfort.

Since Monday, his gut had been making loud, disturbing sounds. I could hear air grumbling through his intestines from over ten feet away. In addition to the strange bowel sounds, Dave had no appetite and reported losing several pounds. Despite eating hardly anything for days, he kept telling me he felt uncomfortably full.

These issues concerned me as both a wife and as a registered dietitian. After several unsuccessful days of coaxing Dave to drink fluids, I was at a loss for how to help him. I had insisted he see his doctor, but the physician didn't know what was wrong. All week, I had kept the curtains in our bedroom drawn shut so Dave could rest.

As time went on, I began to think that maybe Dave was overreacting, though it was unlike him to complain. I had grown impatient because it was challenging to keep everything quiet, including Lydia. She and our needy golden retriever, Britain, required my full attention. That week, I also worked my two part-time jobs at a nursing home and a walk-in clinic. Half-jokingly, I told a coworker Dave must've had 'man-flu.'

Then, at around 9:00 a.m. on Sunday, Dave called me into our bedroom, saying, "Natty, come here! You'll want to take a look at this." He sat hunched over on our bed, his head halfway into a large bucket. When I saw the black tarry fluid, I grew alarmed. It seemed that all the pressure building up in Dave's gut over the last week had forced waste products out the wrong end. The putrid smell made me want to vomit, too! Instead, I offered Dave some water to swish around in his mouth.

Then, I calmly said, "We need to get to the hospital right away. Can you get into the car, or do you need help?" Dave started retching again, so I waited until he finished. I emptied the bucket before deciding to bring it with us in case he threw up in the car.

Meanwhile, Dave moved down the hall and slowly made his way down one flight of stairs. I helped him into the car before returning inside for Lydia. I took her from her crib and strapped her in her car seat. Then, I drove as quickly as I could across town.

We zigzagged our way to the hospital, which was twenty minutes away, thankful for minimal traffic at that hour. We didn't get to that part of town often, so it was somewhat unfamiliar territory. However, this was our second time in twenty-four hours taking this route. At 2:00 a.m. on Saturday, Dave had finally agreed to go to the emergency room. To my dismay, after five hours, we had been sent home with anti-nausea medicine and without any answers.

Returning to the hospital made me uneasy, in part because I feared the extra jarring from the car would somehow burst Dave's gut open. I was also reluctant to interact with the staff again as they had been rather curt earlier. Specifically, they acted like Lydia's stroller was such a bother to walk around. It was a smaller, lightweight model, and I hadn't expected to receive snarky comments about it. I thought the staff would be understanding, given the circumstances.

Thankfully, this time around, we were admitted to the medical floor right away. Dave was placed in a double room, though the bed next to him was empty. I chose to bypass the stroller and carry Lydia instead. I didn't anticipate we would be there for several hours with nowhere to put her. To relieve the tension from my shoulders, I periodically placed Lydia on the spare bed next to Dave. But, she didn't stay put for long, recently having learned to roll.

As I held our squirmy baby, Dave's nurse came in and asked him questions, including what brought him in for care that day. He didn't feel like answering, so I spoke on his behalf. "Dave came home early from work on Monday, not feeling well. He's been in bed since then, except for Thursday when I took him to his doctor and yesterday morning in the ER."

The nurse asked for his emergency contact information. "Well, that would be me; we don't have any family nearby. We moved here in the summer of 2010 from Illinois for Dave's work at Caterpillar. Our nearest family is about ten hours away." The nurse continued to ask questions—and then Dave threw up again.

Dave was very weak, though I had been pushing fluids, such as water and those containing electrolytes. He had not eaten much, nor had he had any bowel movements for a week. Within minutes, a nasogastric tube (a small tube that goes through the nose into the stomach) was placed to relieve some of the pressure off Dave's gut. Right away, two liters of black fluid came out of the tube.

Dave then tried to drink some contrast solution for a CT scan, but he couldn't keep it down either. Finally, he said, "I'm sorry, but I can't drink any more of this. Can you please just do the test?" Thankfully, the physician agreed to attempt the CT scan.

While Dave was gone, I went to the waiting room with Lydia. At five-months-old, she had just started eating solid foods, like rice cereal and applesauce. I sat down and propped her up on the couch. She could sit up on her own but was still somewhat wobbly. I fed Lydia some pureed fruit before changing her diaper.

I looked around for a bathroom or changing table but couldn't find one. So, I put Lydia on the waiting room floor, using a little mat from the diaper bag. I could have used the couch but didn't want to risk it getting dirty. I was doing my best to clean up when an older nurse with graying hair shuffled by us. She looked like she couldn't wait to be done with work that day. When she saw us, she paused. Being in the hospital on a special holiday, I hoped for compassion.

Instead, the nurse raised an eyebrow and said, "I wouldn't put her on the floor if I were you. It's dirty, and there are a lot of germs. You never know what she might get." Maybe she was trying to help, but I grew defensive at her snide comment.

"Well, my husband is here sick. We are waiting for him to get back to his room after a CT scan. Obviously, I don't want her on the floor, but I couldn't find anywhere else to change her!" I was furious. I wanted to add, "Thanks a lot. Kick me while I'm down!" I had always relied on my ability to let things go, yet that week, my patience had grown surprisingly thin.

Eventually, I found a bathroom where I tossed the diaper and washed my hands. Then, about fifteen minutes later, two men from our church found me in the waiting room. With a big smile, Pastor David greeted me and introduced his friend, Tate. "We came to check on Dave and encourage you!"

"Oh, thank you so much," I replied with a sigh. I was relieved to see a friendly face. "After a challenging week, it's so good to see you guys. Dave's downstairs for a test, so Lydia and I are just waiting."

Pastor David and his wife, Pastor Ischee, were good friends of ours and knew we had been looking forward to dedicating Lydia at church that day. Though, because Dave felt so weak, we had decided to cancel. I was disappointed to miss the special occasion, but it was the best decision.

As I chatted with the two men, I didn't mention how emotionally exhausted I was. At the time, I was just trying to hold myself together. They didn't get to see Dave before they left, but Pastor David offered to pray for us. As we stood in the waiting room, he laid his hand on my shoulder. He said a simple prayer, requesting wisdom for the doctors, healing for Dave, and peace for me as I waited.

After being gone for an hour, Dave was returned to his room. I had wondered if he had a small bowel obstruction, based on my education and professional experiences, but I was not prepared for what the CT scan results suggested. Within half an hour, a tall, dark-haired physician came to discuss the CT scan results. Dr. James was a general surgeon who didn't waste time with small talk. After he introduced himself, he sat on the side of Dave's hospital bed. I stood at the foot of the bed and held Lydia on my hip.

Dr. James said, "Mr. White, I hate to tell you this, but based on your CT results, it looks like you have colon cancer."

"What?! How is that possible?!" I was stunned. Dave's reaction was subdued.

Without any emotion, Dr. James said, "Dave appears to have a blockage. His labs, his dark emesis (vomit), and the CT scan are all characteristic of someone presenting with colon cancer." He continued, "We will need to do a colonoscopy and, most likely, an operation to remove the blockage, or tumor. Unfortunately, this could result in a colostomy." (A colostomy yields a 'stoma' where the end of the remaining healthy colon is pulled through the abdominal wall. Then, a colostomy bag is attached externally to collect waste products.)

"What?! No!" I gasped in disbelief. All week, while Dave was sick at home, I had been considering worse case scenarios. Yet, a colostomy had never crossed my mind. Angrily, I thought, "Dr. James is suggesting Dave has cancer and needs a colostomy?! What nerve to tell someone you just met all the things that could go wrong!"

Dave didn't know what a colostomy was, though I had dealt with them as a dietitian. While they can be a necessity at times, I didn't want Dave to feel degraded or embarrassed.

I pleaded with Dr. James. "Please do everything you can to avoid a colostomy. I don't want Dave to have to go through that."

I was upset and spoke up, but Dave just listened—all he wanted was for his pain to be resolved. Looking back, I realize it probably troubled Dr. James to have to tell us these things. After all, he was doing his job in giving us this news. Although I felt he was insensitive to suggest cancer with a colostomy, it was my emotions that were out of control.

Later that afternoon, we saw a gastrointestinal (GI) specialist. Dr. Warren was a kind, older man with a warm smile. He gave us a sense of confidence. He attempted a colonoscopy to see inside Dave's gut, yet he couldn't get very far due to inflammation and the blockage. So, we agreed to wait until a special mesh stent arrived later in the week. Meanwhile, the medical team had ordered several medicines, including stool softeners and laxatives, with hopes of getting Dave's bowels to move.

On Sunday evening, I called Dave's mom, Cynda, and my parents to tell them what was going on. When I explained that Dave hadn't been feeling well, I avoided the word 'cancer' because I didn't want to upset anyone. Cynda was concerned because she had visited the previous weekend, and Dave had seemed fine then. We agreed I would keep in touch with her once I knew more. I hated keeping the information from her, but I wanted to have a better idea of what we were dealing with first. (Dave called his dad to update him a little later.)

When I called my family, I discovered my parents and three siblings were all camping in a remote area with poor cell phone reception. They were surprised, yet no one suspected anything was really wrong. Dave was young and strong—no big deal. Then again, perhaps I tried to sound extra cheerful. They were having fun, and I didn't want them to worry. At some point, we notified Dave's supervisor at Caterpillar to give him a simple update, too.

Soon, Dave was transferred to a room on the surgical floor. The upcoming procedure was scheduled for Wednesday, so we had to bide our time until then. On each of the next three mornings, I took Lydia to daycare so that I could visit Dave. However, because we used a drop-in daycare with a four-hour limit, I had to monitor the clock closely.

I was torn between caring for Dave and managing everything else. After picking up Lydia, I would drive home to feed her dinner, feed and walk our dog, answer mail, and do other household tasks. Then, Lydia and I would return to the hospital until approximately 9:00 p.m. so we could be with Dave. During those long hours, I tried to keep Lydia quiet so he could rest. Other visitors came, but Dave felt so miserable he didn't feel much like talking.

On Wednesday, May 16th, I took Lydia to daycare for Dave's afternoon procedure. Soon after I arrived at the hospital, he was taken to the operating room (OR). True to form, Dave consoled me and encouraged me to leave and take time for myself. I decided to go to the local mall in the center of town, about ten minutes away. Often, I like to walk or pace when I process a situation, and I hoped to gain clarity on recent events.

As I roamed the mall, I prayed, "God, help the stent to work; give the doctors wisdom." However, I had difficulty focusing on my surroundings because I was so upset. Craving privacy, I saw a sign for a bathroom in the basement and ducked down the stairs. "Lord, please don't let it be cancer."

The gravity of the procedure going on a few miles away left me feeling helpless, lost, and afraid. With tears welling in my eyes, I washed my face in the bathroom sink. I noticed a sitting area and sat on a couch as I started weeping.

"Father, I don't know what to do."

I had grabbed several tissues and used them all.

"God, we need Your help."

After a little while, I calmed down and decided to walk through some of the mall shops. To distract myself, I tried on some clothes. I was in the fitting room when Dave called unexpectedly. I hadn't even been gone for an hour.

I answered the phone, hesitantly. "Hi, Babe, you're already done? How did it go?"

Dave calmly mentioned the stent had been unsuccessful. He explained, "The doctors said the last option is surgery, which they are preparing for right now. I asked them to wait for you to arrive, but they said you need to hurry. It's an emergency."

My stomach lurched as I stood in the fitting room. "Oh, no," I said quietly. "I'll grab Lydia at daycare, and then we'll be right there. I love you, Dave!"

After we hung up, I panicked. I got dressed, left the mall, and raced to daycare, which was located across the street from the mall. The time limit was almost up, so I needed to pick up Lydia anyway. When I walked into daycare, I started bawling. I was so distraught and could barely explain the situation. Kindly, the worker said I could leave Lydia awhile longer and arrange for someone else to pick her up. I was so grateful she bent the rules for me in this situation. I left Lydia at daycare and called Dave to get his input on what to do.

We had never been apart from our sweet baby overnight. Together, we decided Dave's coworker, Dean, and his wife, Jackie, were our best option.

We had grown familiar with them and felt comfortable leaving Lydia in their care. Dean and Jackie quickly agreed to help. When I arrived at the hospital, I notified the daycare of our plan and called Jackie to explain everything we needed her to do. I notified our families that Dave was going into surgery, too.

Dave had recently installed a garage code keypad, and it proved quite helpful that day. Three ladies went to our house, separately, to help us with various tasks. After I talked with Jackie, she went to our house to grab our extra car seat, clothes, and other items for Lydia. We found out later that Wednesday was Dean's birthday; he missed out on cake that year because Jackie didn't have time to make one. We were so grateful they altered their plans for us.

I also called my friend, Meredith, a dietitian serving with me on our local dietetic board. I was supposed to lead a meeting that night but asked Meredith to fill in for me instead. She was more than capable, though I apologized for the change in plans. It was unlike me to not follow-through. Meredith went to our house to pick up a few items for the meeting.

Finally, I called a close friend, Sara, from church. I had decided to spend the night at the hospital but didn't have time to go home first. Sara went to our house and picked up some toiletries, a change of clothes, and a few other items. She brought the items to the hospital and offered to sit with me during the operation. I appreciated all these friends who helped us on short notice. Without family nearby to help, it brought much comfort to know we were not alone.

At 5:00 p.m., Dave was taken to the OR. He didn't seem worried but instead looked forward to getting some relief. When it was time to say goodbye, I kissed him and said, "I love you." Then, I walked into the surgical waiting room. What would happen next?

Chapter 2

"Have I not commanded you? Be strong and courageous.
Do not be afraid; do not be discouraged, for the Lord your God
will be with you wherever you go."
Joshua 1:9 NIV

That evening, as I waited anxiously in the surgical waiting room with Sara, we mulled over the sense of unfairness which results when bad things happen to good people.

"How could God let this happen? What is His purpose in this?"

"What if Dave has cancer? How will we get through this?"

Naturally, Sara and I didn't have all the answers, though it felt good to discuss what was happening. The surgery took a long time, and it grew late. It was a blessing to have Sara there with me as I waited for news about my dear husband.

I was in the bathroom when Dr. James came to give an update. Of course, he didn't share any information with Sara but told her where he would be waiting for me. When I found Dr. James, he took me to a small closet-sized conference room. There were two chairs and a table with a lamp; nothing else could have fit. Dr. James's demeanor was somber, and I could not tell what he was thinking. I sat down, hoping for good news. Instead, he confirmed my worst fears.

"I'm sorry, Mrs. White. Your husband has cancer." I stared in horror at Dr. James. I was twenty-nine years old, hearing my husband had cancer. Dave was only thirty-three years old. My heart raced as snapshots of our life together flashed before my eyes. Had I heard correctly?

Somehow, all I could say at first was, "Okay." I couldn't think straight and needed to know more information. "Did you get it all?" I asked.

Dr. James explained, "We got everything in the surrounding area, all that we could see, including some lymph nodes. But, because it spread through every layer of the colon to the lymph, it has likely spread farther." My heart sank as he went on. "Typically, it spreads first to the liver and then to the lungs. We will have to do a PET scan in a few weeks to know if that has happened."

As if that wasn't bad enough news, there was more. Dr. James continued, "Also, Mrs. White, I had to do the colostomy procedure. It went as well as could be expected, and the stoma looks good. It should heal well and…."

Dr. James might have kept talking, though, at that point, my mind was a blur. This surgeon had just saved Dave's life, but I struggled to make sense of everything. When I heard about the colostomy (the one thing I wanted to avoid!), I was sad for him. I feared the changes that cancer and a colostomy would bring for us.

I was mentally, emotionally, and physically drained. Everything I had prayed not to happen, had happened. Dave had cancer, and he would be walking around with a colostomy. It was shocking. I felt so many emotions in a short period. I felt anger at the injustice of it all. How could such a good person as Dave get cancer, and worse, a colostomy?! I felt myself going into protection mode. I wanted to see my husband and know it was all going to be okay!

I retreated wordlessly to the waiting room while Dr. James returned to the OR, where his colleagues were finishing up the procedure. I explained the situation to Sara and asked her to keep it in confidence because I wanted Dave to hear the results before everyone else. Together, we tried to process this dismal news, to find a way to have it make sense. Then, six hours after Dave's surgery started, around 11:00 p.m., I received notification he was back in his room.

It was time for me to go in to see my sweet husband and to let Sara go home. I hugged her goodbye and thanked her for coming. Before going up to Dave's room, I texted our families to tell them he was out of surgery and that we would update them the next day. Then, I went to see him. I was unsure of what I would find. How would Dave appear? Would his wounds be evident? Would he be awake? I tried to anticipate my reaction, but I didn't know what to expect.

When I arrived, I walked cautiously into Dave's room. I was hesitant and wanted to be in control of my reaction. To my surprise, Dave appeared normal. He was quietly resting and didn't seem uncomfortable. Typically, the bright fluorescent lights at that time of night would have been annoying. But now, they only highlighted Dave's smile. I moved past a few machines and gave him a gentle kiss on the cheek.

"Hi, Babe, are you feeling alright?" He said he felt better than he had in days.

Dave was groggy after his surgery, so I didn't want him to find out about his cancer and colostomy until the anesthesia and pain medications wore off. Dave was a very easy-going person, and I wasn't sure if he would want to fight it out or understand the implications under the influence of potent drugs. I spent the night with Dave on a small couch in his hospital room, and Lydia spent her very first night apart from us.

Almost six months earlier, I had been the patient while Dave was on the couch as we waited for Lydia's birth. He had held my hand and coached me through labor and delivery. Now, with the tables turned, I yearned to shield Dave from the outcome of his surgery and diagnosis. It was a long night with the nurses checking on Dave each hour. I barely slept.

The next morning, Thursday, the medical residents came early to complete their rounds. Dave was still unaware of his diagnosis. He knew about the colostomy because the nurses had to monitor it, and he felt so much better having relief from all the gas and abdominal pressure. But when one resident started to mention the word 'cancer,' I interrupted her with an intense look that signified her to stop. Taking my cue, she asked to speak with me outside the room, where I explained that Dave still didn't know. When I walked back into the room, he could tell my countenance had changed.

"What's wrong, Natty?" he asked.

I was quiet for a moment, thinking about what to say and how to deliver this unbelievable news. I decided to be straightforward.

Tentatively, I asked, "Do you really want to know?"

Dave nodded, yes.

Taking a deep breath, I said, "You have cancer."

"Oh," Dave said softly. "Okay." His reaction was understated compared to mine. He didn't appear to experience the pendulum of emotions I had felt. We both looked at each other silently. In an instant, I felt decades older than I was.

Then, filled with immense gratitude for all he was to me, I sat on his hospital bed and grabbed his hand. "Dave, what are we going to do?! I can't bear the thought of losing you."

Being ever so practical, Dave replied, "Well, if I die, you'll do just fine without me because you are strong." His confidence in my ability moved me, but I could not envision my life without him! Dave also reminded me he had life insurance through his work, which would be a benefit if anything happened to him.

Tearfully, I whispered, "You've always taken such good care of me."

Within moments of hearing the diagnosis, Dave seemed to come to acceptance. He understood the reality—he could die. But instead of feeling sorry for himself, Dave brought up those end-of-life matters no one in their twenties or thirties should have to address.

Dave was a kind man with a servant's heart. He was pragmatic and unselfish. As usual, his deepest concern was for my well-being and Lydia's welfare. Together, we wondered how a future without Dave might look for Lydia and me. We talked about what to tell Lydia if he should die. We also considered practical topics, like how to handle discipline and schooling.

Dave and I discussed how to share this bombshell with our family and friends. Then, we discussed our cancer game plan and brainstormed some questions to ask regarding treatment options. Dave decided he wanted to fight it until it was unreasonable (i.e. no chance of survival). We weighed quality of life issues, such as when to stop chemo or 'pull the plug' if needed. We also reviewed financial matters, such as our budget, health insurance, and life insurance.

Then, I asked Dave if he had any funeral wishes. We didn't expect him to die, of course, but we added that to the list of heavy topics. Dave had no preferences other than to be cremated, and he said I would do fine arranging his funeral if it came to that. Finally, he broached the topic of me possibly remarrying in the future.

Dave said, "If you have the opportunity to get remarried, do! Don't worry about me! I want you to be happy. And besides, I will be in Heaven." From the beginning, Dave was confident, regardless of the outcome, I would be able to handle it.

I was not so sure of myself.

Looking back, I am amazed we had the presence of mind to discuss all we did at the time. Some people might postpone these tough conversations, but we took advantage of the time we had together. We remained optimistic as we weighed each possibility. As thorough planners, Dave and I were known for being prepared for just about anything. But as we soon found out, not everything in life can be planned or predetermined.

And, as we sat together on Dave's hospital bed, we reviewed our relationship from when we first met in college at Northern Illinois University (NIU), until now. We never dated back then but had been casual friends. When Dave moved three hours south to Decatur, Illinois, to work for Caterpillar, we lost touch for a couple of years. Then, in July 2005, we ran into each other at a wedding in our college town of DeKalb, Illinois. I was a dietetic intern working toward my Master's degree.

Dave and I grew in friendship for the next year and a half. Eventually, we started dating when I moved downstate for my first full-time clinical position at a local hospital. I lived with my parents and commuted to work. But because Dave lived about an hour away, we were able to see each other often. We were married about a year later in early 2008. Though we'd known each other for nearly twelve years, our time together suddenly seemed so short.

Later, on Thursday afternoon, our parents called to check in after Dave's surgery. We had decided not to say anything about cancer until we knew a little more about the prognosis. We only confirmed that we were waiting for the pathology report for the tumor. This bought us a little time, though we hated not telling our families the full story.

A local race occurred the first weekend after Dave's emergency surgery. That Saturday, I drove with Lydia, asleep in her car seat, to the hospital for what already felt like the thousandth time. I drove east, expecting to turn onto the road leading to the hospital. However, it was closed for the race. I was unfamiliar with how to get to the hospital parking lot from a different direction. Each street I turned onto was blocked, causing me to be even more disoriented. I drove on as hundreds of runners raced by, clueless to my frustration.

Finally, I rolled down my window to ask a traffic cop, "How do I get to the hospital?"

"Ma'am, you have to keep moving," he said, motioning me to turn left.

With hot tears rolling down my face, I shouted out the window, "My husband is sick in the hospital—I'm trying to get there to see him! Whose idea was it to shut down the main roads near a hospital for a race?!"

I didn't wait for the policeman's response. I turned left onto a street that appeared to be a dead end. I grew more upset but kept driving, trying to figure out where I was.

A few minutes later, I discovered I had been redirected around the backside of the hospital. Still irritated, I looked for parking. Then, I placed Lydia's car seat in the stroller, and we hurried inside to visit Dave. While I typically don't overreact so quickly, in many ways, this situation brought out my worst traits.

I was falling apart, but Dave was emotionally steady, cheerful as ever. I wondered how well he grasped the weight of his diagnosis, or if it had sunk in. I was the one with a healthcare background, not him. In my nutrition career, I had seen terminal cancer and other serious illnesses regularly. Perhaps Dave was overwhelmed with all the medical terms and medical staff?

After I had calmed myself down, I sat on Dave's bed with Lydia and told him, "You know, Hon, we would all understand if you wanted to yell, or get upset, or even throw something." That's what I would've wanted to do! His reply surprised me.

Dave said, "Yes, I thought about that. But, then I decided I can still be kind to the nurses when they have trouble finding my veins or as they are changing my dressings. And, I can still be loving and gentle with you and Lydia."

With no hesitation, Dave continued, "I'm going to live my life, whether I have one day, one year or seventy left. Cancer is not going to rule my life!"

Even amid his physical pain, Dave was joyful and focused on living his life to the fullest. He realized none of us have a guarantee in life. Everyone dies, and each day is a gift.

The pathology report came sooner than we expected. Thankfully, we didn't have to wait long for someone to explain the results. That weekend, we met with an on-call oncology hospitalist. Dr. D'Mico was warm and hopeful, though not misleading. He told us the cancer was at least stage III, but probably stage IV, since cancer cells can travel more easily once lymph is involved. He explained how colon cancer spreads throughout the body and what we might expect.

Dr. D'Mico stated that the tumor was low-grade, which meant this cancer grew slowly. However, low-grade tumors could also be more resistant to treatment. Then, he reviewed several treatment options, expressing his hope that Dave would do well because he seemed otherwise healthy. The treatment would be based on the results of the PET scan, coming up in a few weeks. Our main priority, for the moment, was for Dave to heal from surgery.

Dr. D'Mico also clarified some confusing terms, such as the word 'cure.' This term means a patient reaches the five-year mark after the last treatment with no recurrence. He warned us that a cure was not too promising for colon cancer, but that there were multiple treatment options, including surgery and chemotherapy. Dr. D'Mico also explained that at the end of the day, it was not really about cancer, whether it was present or not. It was about how Dave felt day to day and his quality of life.

After our meeting with Dr. D'Mico, many of my initial fears subsided because he was so encouraging. He helped us understand the cancer process, and it felt good to have solid information and answers to some of our questions. Yet, this feeling of peace didn't last for long. My battle against fear was only just beginning.

Dr. James also stopped by a few times to check on us. He genuinely seemed to care about Dave, and so my attitude toward him changed. As the days wore on, I gained a lot of respect for him. He had known what was wrong and had done what was needed. I was still not thrilled about the colostomy, however.

Dr. James wished us the best, telling us in effect, "Maybe it will be a bad couple of weeks, or a difficult six months—or even a rough year—but maybe you'll be able to look back on it and find the good. In my experience, this happens to the nicest of guys."

That May, I spent a lot of time in my navy blue, Hyundai Santa Fe driving back and forth between home, daycare, the hospital, and my two part-time jobs. Short prayers like "God, why is this happening? What do You want us to do?" were all I could manage.

My car radio was tuned to the local Christian station, as usual, because I found it encouraging. As I listened to the songs, I often gleaned hope from the lyrics. The music bolstered my faith.

One afternoon, as I drove home with Lydia, I heard a new song called "All This Time," by Britt Nicole. It was upbeat, and the lyrics reminded me that God was always with me, even in tough times. I was comforted but didn't have a clue how this was going to play out. Suddenly, I sensed God speak to my heart, "I'm going to use this to show you just how much I love you."

I was incredulous. I thought, "What?! How does cancer show me God's love? This is the worst thing I can imagine! If God really loved me, how could He let this happen?"

It seemed odd at the time, given all that had already happened. Life had given us lemons, but how were we supposed to make lemonade out of this?! Fear was running rampant through my mind. I had questions without answers, in an endless stream of worry and doubt. Yet, intuitively, I knew the words I heard addressed my fear. Somehow, God was going to teach me to trust Him at a deeper level.

A few days later, a Bible verse came to mind. 1 John 4:18, says, "There is no fear in love. But perfect love drives out fear, because fear has to do with punishment. The one who fears is not made perfect in love." I believed God *could* do mighty things, such as healing Dave, but *would* He?

Thankfully, Dave felt so much better after his first surgery. As time went on, his color returned, along with his sense of humor and some of his physical strength. Despite the extensive surgical wounds and the colostomy, he took it all in stride. We learned how to care for the colostomy, and Dave grew stronger day by day. Physicians and medical staff came in at all hours to check on him.

We both valued our privacy, and suddenly we felt very exposed. We quickly had to get over that. For example, I had to become comfortable with nursing Lydia even when someone walked in the door unannounced. Our friend, Jackie, was quite generous to watch Lydia as much as she could, but sometimes I needed to have her with me.

While Dave was in the hospital, we told our families, coworkers, and local friends about the cancer diagnosis. Everyone was shocked, but Dave maintained his positive outlook. In some ways, it seemed to help everyone else adjust. His supervisor, Paul, was very gracious and told us not to worry about his job. He just wanted Dave to heal up and feel better.

After about a week in the hospital, a group of three couples from our small group at church all came to visit us one night. Our lead pastor at the time, Pastor Bob, also came. Everyone gathered around Dave's hospital bed. Each couple offered to help with something, such as watching Lydia, taking care of our dog, Britain, or mowing our lawn.

We continued to make small talk about the last several days' events. Our friends just thought it was a simple illness, and Dave would rebound in no time. Soon, the conversation grew quiet, and he spoke up.

"Well, since you are all here now, you might as well know our news. The pathology reports show that I have colon cancer."

Everyone was silent. To me, it felt like the air went out of the room.

We didn't want to burden anyone, but I was relieved to put it out there finally. It was comforting knowing we didn't have to bear the diagnosis alone. We ended the visit with a prayer for healing and wisdom on the course of treatment. Everyone left with whispers of shock.

Then, after ten days in the hospital, on May 22nd, 2012, Dave was released to go home. We were a little nervous about all we needed to do. Overall, Dave was in a good mood but needed help showering and changing his surgical dressings twice a day. He was adjusting to his colostomy but sometimes needed help with that, too.

Bringing Dave home post-surgery felt similar to when we brought Lydia home after she was born. In both cases, I felt anxious because each of them was so fragile. Six months earlier, I sat with Lydia on her first ride home while Dave drove. I had wanted to be close so I could comfort her if she cried. Now, I was the driver and was trying my best to hold our family together. I didn't know it then, but in the weeks and months to come, I would be the driver in more ways than one. This time, when Lydia wailed in the back seat, I had to ignore her cries.

Even though the surgeons had done an excellent job sewing up Dave's incisions, I felt uneasy. In my mind, it seemed like his guts might accidentally fall out! During the operation, Dave had been cut from sternum to groin. On our way home, I drove slowly and frequently switched lanes to avoid potholes and bumps. Even so, the tiniest of bumps made Dave uncomfortable.

"Ooooh, that hurt. Can you please be more careful, Natty?"

He must have been in considerable pain because, when it came to vehicles, Dave loved muscle cars. He was all about speed and power. So, what usually would have been a twenty-minute drive probably took thirty. It was a tense trip across town, and I was relieved when we finally made it home.

Now we could begin the process of healing.

Chapter 3

"Do not be anxious about anything, but in every situation, by prayer and petition, with thanksgiving, present your requests to God."
Philippians 4:6 NIV

After we arrived home from the hospital, I first carried Lydia inside for a nap. Then, I went back out to the car for Dave. I helped him slowly walk up the eight stairs of our split-level home. An open floor plan, the upstairs contained our dining area, living room, and kitchen, as well as a bathroom and two bedrooms down the hall.

"Dave, would you like to go rest in our room?" I asked. But, he preferred to sit on the love seat, which was nearby. The walk to our bedroom seemed too tiring.

So, we turned toward the living room area. Dave rested there with his back to the television, while I unpacked his supplies at the kitchen island. As I kept my eye on Dave, I organized pain medications, gauze, and colostomy pouches into piles

"What am I going to do with all of this stuff?" I thought. "These items don't belong here!" Then, I realized I would have to make space for Dave's supplies, whether I liked it or not. I put everything in the bathroom for the time being.

I checked on Dave, but he didn't need anything. While he rested, we discussed how to tell our extended family and friends. We decided to call or email key groups of people before posting the news online to social media. With Dave's permission, I wrote to the wives of Caterpillar friends we knew in Illinois; they soon passed our news on to their husbands.

I also wrote to my dietitian friends in Illinois, sharing about similarities between my professional work history and our new reality. For instance, during this first hospital stay, Dave had needed nasogastric (NG) tubes, total parenteral nutrition (TPN), and extensive GI surgery. These were all relatively routine situations in my training and work experiences. But on occasion, I would have a patient with complex medical issues that did not follow the textbook medical course.

In the past, I had sometimes felt overwhelmed and stressed with the level of responsibility for those particular cases. I would leave work, questioning myself. "Did I recommend enough protein for wound healing?" Or, I would spend time reminding myself of the tasks I needed to do the next day when I returned.

Now, with Dave's cancer, I considered all those previous experiences, including meetings with patients, their families, and medical staff. I started wondering if perhaps God had used all those years to prepare me for "such a time as this" (from Esther 4:14). It brought me comfort because I could ask relevant questions, and I understood the medical terminology regarding Dave's case. Also, I was glad I could advocate for him, but even that would soon be tested.

Dave spent his first night back home on the love seat in the living room because it was more comfortable to him than our bed. At six-foot-two, he preferred the love seat to even the longer couch because he could prop up his back and legs. The next morning, Dave needed help getting ready for the day. I had to choose between caring for him and Lydia, as he needed a hand with his colostomy. He had to empty it periodically, and it was rather messy.

"Uh, Natty, can you help me?" he asked.

"Sure, Hon. I'll be right there." I was in the middle of feeding Lydia breakfast.

A moment later, I left her to help Dave. Lydia was safe in her high chair, but the sudden interruption to her meal upset her! Over the next several minutes, we listened to Lydia scream while I helped Dave clean up in the bathroom. Deciding who needed help first was very stressful for me. At that moment, it was clear Dave needed me more.

As Memorial Day weekend began, Dave still had no appetite. He was not drinking much either, and as a result, he had low energy levels. He spent a lot of time on the love seat, which was very rare when he was healthy. Another problem was Dave's surgical incision, which had re-opened and had started oozing fluid.

Having previously worked in a hospital, I knew holidays and weekends meant some services would be unavailable with fewer medical staff. With the long weekend ahead, I suggested we return to the hospital, preemptively. It was good we followed my intuition because Dave was readmitted with a post-operative infection. He was dehydrated and received IV fluids, in addition to an antibiotic and more pain medication.

Just a year before, I had been pregnant with Lydia, and we had traveled to Colorado and New Mexico to visit extended family. Then, life was full of promise. Now, the hospital was starting to feel like a second home. With Dave hospitalized over the holiday weekend, there was not much we could do to celebrate. So, we watched marathon episodes of food shows on cable.

After the long weekend, Dave returned home, and I spent the beginning of June helping him recover from his surgery. He needed to heal and regain some weight and strength before chemotherapy. Though Dave was eager to get back on his feet, he understood he needed to rest. The previous summer, we had been joyfully preparing for Lydia's birth, and now we were preparing for PET scans for cancer.

That summer, Dave spent all of the holidays—Memorial Day, Fourth of July, and Labor Day—in the hospital getting IV fluids, antibiotics, and pain medications. During those times, I was also scheduled to work at the nursing home. My supervisor, Lisa, had taken those days off to care for some family who lived out of state. She was sympathetic to our situation and let me alter many of my hours as needed, but the holiday hours were less flexible. As bad as she felt, there wasn't much she could do about it because she was in a similar situation with her family.

Even before cancer, I would arrive at work around 9:15 a.m. after dropping off Lydia at daycare for four hours. At my lunch break, I ate quickly at my desk, before driving over to pick up Lydia. The drop-in daycare rules meant I had to take her out of daycare for one hour before I could bring her back for another four hours. To stay close by and not waste time, I'd take Lydia to the mall directly across the street to nurse her in a family bathroom.

It was certainly not ideal, but I chose to make the best of it. After an hour, I took her back to daycare and tried to finish my work in the allotted time. Then, I would pick her up once more and head home to walk the dog before dinner. If Dave was in the hospital, we visited him, too.

Thankfully, my other part-time job was very flexible. My supervisor at the walk-in clinic let me rearrange my days there as needed. So, I balanced a complicated work schedule with Dave, Lydia, and everything else. By the end of August, I considered resigning from my position at the nursing home. However, at the time, Dave's cancer seemed stable, and I thought I could handle everything. Yet, stress would continue to add up as Dave's condition slowly deteriorated.

While Dave reacted calmly to his diagnosis and recovery, I was often an emotional wreck. At first, I tried to rationalize his cancer diagnosis, but I only grew more distraught when I considered he could die. In my despair, small pieces of information took on amplified meaning. For example, "What will the PET scan show?" soon became visions of Dave's organs riddled with cancer. I was scared to lose him and feared, because she was so little, Lydia would not remember him if he died.

With my turbulent emotions, it was difficult to calm down or find consistent peace. For instance, when Dave was feeling well, I also felt stable because it seemed like things were returning to normal. But when he was ill from chemotherapy or needed to be in the hospital, I was agitated, and everything felt like it was falling apart.

Over the summer, I had to adjust my routine and expectations. In June, I started rising at 4:00 a.m. to get everything done. I stayed up late to catch up, too. Once Lydia was up, the day flew by. There seemed to be no end to the tasks on my to-do list!

I wrestled with the 'what ifs,' and felt overwhelmed with all the added appointments and responsibilities. But, as time went on, I took my cues from Dave. People often asked how we managed it all. With God's help, we did the best we could.

One day, I asked him again, "Hon, how are you doing with all of this?" I gave him the opportunity to talk about whatever was on his mind.

Dave shrugged and reiterated that he was going to live each day to the fullest, regardless of the outcome. He was adamant that cancer was not going to rule his life.

After that, I decided, "Well, if Dave isn't going to worry about his cancer, why should I?" Dave's response may not be typical, but he was unequivocal. As much as it was up to him, cancer wasn't going to hold him back. This might have been admirable, but at the time, we didn't understand just how formidable it would become.

With everything going on, I had very little time to myself. I did what was necessary, but that often meant a deferment of self-care. One morning in early June, I took the dog for a walk while Dave rested on the love seat and Lydia napped in her crib. Generally, we aimed to get Britain outside for at least twenty minutes, twice a day. But that morning, I decided to go for a longer walk.

It was a beautiful morning with a slight breeze. White, wispy clouds hung against the bright blue sky. I relished the fact that no one needed me and took my time scouting out new houses in our area. I also took note of the landscaping other families had done. I meandered with Britain for about forty-five minutes, savoring the quiet moments to myself.

As we walked, I reflected upon all that had happened since we moved to the Fargo area two summers before as a result of a work promotion. Dave and I had been excited to start a new life in North Dakota. It was bittersweet leaving our families, but we felt God had called us to an adventure with Him. I'm glad we said 'yes' to God, but had we known what that adventure entailed, perhaps we would have stayed put!

We had fun experiencing all our new community had to offer. We joined a local church, made friends, and grew in our careers. Then, in late 2011, Lydia was born. Becoming parents was a huge change, and it took us a little while to adjust. Being so far from family was a challenge as we entered into the sleepless nights of parenthood.

Lydia started sleeping through the night when she was four-and-a-half months old. We had about two weeks of everyone getting adequate sleep, and then Dave's sickness pushed everything into high-gear, like never before. In June, Lydia was six-months-old and needed me for, well, everything. Dave and I usually split household duties, but when he got sick, his tasks became my responsibility, too.

Britain and I walked further through our neighborhood, and I continued reflecting upon the previous few weeks. It felt surreal, like a nightmare that couldn't possibly be true. Then suddenly, I remembered the actual nightmare I had shortly before Dave became ill. Worried there might be a connection between this and his cancer, we raced back home.

When we returned, Dave was in Lydia's bedroom, singing to her and trying to calm her down. She had awakened while I was gone and was screaming mad that Dave was unable to pick her up. He had a ten-pound lifting restriction, and Lydia exceeded that. She calmed down as soon as I pulled her from the crib.

After I put Lydia on the rug to play, I stood in the kitchen and began to cry. Dave came over and asked me what was wrong. Then, I told him about the nightmare I had just before cancer invaded our life. Intuitively, I had felt the dark, menacing cyclone looming directly over our house was an omen because the tornado was so threatening. I had been disturbed by the nightmare, yet I failed to mention it to Dave when it happened.

Trembling, I said, "I can't help but think this is my fault somehow. Maybe it could have been prevented if I had warned you in some way."

Adding to my inner turmoil, I recalled how in January 2008, two weeks after we had gotten married, Dave had a similar bout of sickness. He was in bed for four days and barely ate or drank anything during that time. One night, I heard a thud in the bathroom, racing in only to find Dave on the floor with his eyes rolled back in his head. He was out for about thirty seconds, becoming alert just as I was preparing to call 911. Weak and feverish, Dave chose to stay on the cool floor overnight. Worried, I brought his pillow and a blanket to make him more comfortable, but I didn't know what else to do.

Back then, Dave's doctor surmised he had the stomach flu. He finally felt like himself after a week, and things returned to normal. Yet strangely around that time, I had a persistent feeling that maybe he should get a colonoscopy. Perhaps it had been divine insight, yet, I did not speak up. Logically, there was no real reason for the test, and I second-guessed myself. How would I convince Dave to get a colonoscopy when I didn't think anyone so young would have problems? My feeling seemed ridiculous; therefore, I ignored it. Even then, fear had its grip on me.

Now, as I stood in the kitchen with Dave, I wondered if perhaps his sickness roughly two years before had triggered the growth of a tumor. (Of course, there is no way to know. Cancer cells can grow for years undetected.) I shared this with Dave while he listened silently. At first, he was serious, but then, a few moments later, he brushed it off.

He hugged me close and said, "No one causes cancer. It's not your fault, Natty. Do you understand? We'll get through this." Dave took it in stride, and he continued to face his trials bravely. The conversation didn't faze him one bit, and we never discussed it again.

Dave's PET scan was on June 4th. I had taken Lydia to daycare so that I could stay with Dave during the testing. While I waited, I tried to read a magazine to distract myself. People texted encouraging messages, but I still felt sick with worry and couldn't concentrate. "What if Dave's cancer has spread?"

A couple of days after the PET scan, we went to the clinic to review the test results. It was our first time meeting with the oncologist assigned to Dave's case. Dave sat closest to the physician's desk. I held Lydia on my lap and sat next to him while we waited.

I asked Dave, "Are you nervous to hear the results?"

He shrugged and said quietly, "Not really, no."

He seemed ready to take the news head-on, but I was anxious and hugged Lydia close.

We had brought her with us because we didn't expect the meeting to take very long. We preferred saving daycare time for when we had no other options, but child care had been a challenge from the start. Full-time daycare seemed expensive and unnecessary since I now only worked part-time.

Even though I had two jobs, my hours varied each week. Occasionally, I worked forty hours a week, but usually, I worked less than twenty hours. Without family nearby to help, the drop-in daycare was a reasonable option for us. It provided flexible hours with no contract or reservation.

When Dave got sick, however, everything became more difficult. I tried to gauge each week's daycare needs ahead of time, but our schedule was often up in the air because of Dave's illness, treatments, and appointments. Sometimes, I missed out on an important medical conversation at the hospital because I had to pick up Lydia.

Often, I had to choose between working and visiting Dave. Either way, I still had to consider our child care options and what to do with Lydia. The four-hour time limit became inconvenient, but there was little we could do. Friends offered to watch Lydia periodically, however, we didn't want to take advantage of anyone and used daycare much of the time.

Looking back, full-time daycare might have been a good idea. I didn't realize it then, but overnight, cancer became like a full-time job. Babies are also unpredictable at times, and both Lydia and cancer threw us curve balls regularly. For example, while we sat in the consultation room, Lydia needed an emergency diaper change.

Frustrated, I blurted out, "Are you kidding me?! Of all times to have a blowout!" I looked for a bathroom down the hall to change her diaper and outfit. We had brought the stroller and diaper bag, but managing all the baby gear added to the stress when I was already on edge.

Luckily, I didn't miss any of the consultation. Lydia and I returned to sit with Dave just as Dr. Lloyd, his oncologist, entered the room, slowly, with his head down. He shook Dave's hand, but not mine, before sitting. I don't know how Dave felt, but I was nauseous as I listened to Dr. Lloyd explain the PET scan results. The news was not good.

The cancer had already metastasized, making Dave's cancer stage IV. The scan showed one small spot on the dome (top) of the liver, but nothing in the lungs. The surgeons had not seen it because of its size and location. Dave didn't seem too concerned, but I was disheartened. It seemed like the situation kept growing worse, and this physician didn't give us any hope.

Soon, I started dreading our appointments with Dr. Lloyd because he often seemed to be the bearer of bad news. Each time we saw him, he gloomily walked into the room with his head down and shoulders slumped. Sometimes, I would skip the appointment if it was only a brief check-in to review labs. I often had to work anyway. On those occasions, Dave would give me updates later after we both got home.

Dr. Lloyd's pessimism wore me down. He didn't sugar-coat the information, nor did he hold our hand during the ordeal. It could have been due to his personality or the grim nature of his profession, but it felt like our oncologist proclaimed probable defeat from the start. No doubt our situation was dire, but I would have appreciated it if he had smiled on occasion!

Chapter 4

"The Lord is my strength and my shield; my heart trusts in him, and he helps me. My heart leaps for joy, and with my song I praise him."
Psalm 28:7 NIV

Dave and I met my freshman year of college in the fall of 2000. My sister, Livi, also attended NIU, but she met Dave before me because she was one year ahead of me in school. She always spoke highly of Dave and even now teases me that she met him first. Livi and I hung out together as much as we could, so many of her friends became mine, too.

During my first semester, I often stayed on campus between classes. I was studying with friends at a small church nearby when Dave roared into the parking lot in his maroon 1970 Chevelle. As he drove past the windows, what I call a 'gaggle' of girls all exclaimed with one voice, "Oh Dave's here, Dave's here!" Then, they all ran out to greet him. I had never seen anything like it! Naturally, this piqued my interest, and I casually watched to see what happened.

A few minutes later, Dave strolled in wearing a black leather jacket and a big smile. He appeared to be the epitome of cool with about seven girls ushering him inside! Everyone was laughing, and Dave's presence immediately boosted the atmosphere. I was talking with one of the only girls who didn't run outside, and I asked her who he was. She told me he was an engineering student who had been doing a co-op, which meant he alternated between being on campus and off-site working to gain experience in his field.

I noticed Dave's confidence and cheerful attitude right away. As cool as he looked, I quickly learned how down-to-earth he was. That day, I observed Dave taking the time to talk with each girl. Some were perhaps more popular than others, but it made no difference to him. He treated them all with respect and kindness. I was impressed that he talked with me as well.

I wasn't looking for a boyfriend at the time, but immediately, I knew Dave was someone I could marry one day. I dismissed the idea quickly because I had only just met him, and I knew I should stay focused on my course work. I was pretty shy back then and never admitted how much I liked him. However, my sister heard me talk about him all the time!

Over the next few years, I noticed Dave always looked for ways to help others. He loved volunteering with Habitat for Humanity, and one year, he and a group of friends helped build a house over spring break. Three vehicles made the long trip to Oklahoma. But, on the way back, a minivan full of students broke down. Out of necessity, they all crammed into the other two vehicles, including Dave's Chevrolet Blazer. Then, he and a few other engineering students rigged up a system so he could tow the minivan home!

I always looked forward to seeing Dave on campus. It didn't happen often, but he brightened my day whenever we ran into each other. Sometimes, he would see me walking to my classes. Instead of driving past, he stopped and offered to drop me off. He graciously listened to me talk about my school work. To my great relief, he never said I looked funny in my chef's uniform, which was a requirement for my food science classes!

When it came to helping others, Dave gave of his time, money, or service naturally. He took the initiative and was skilled at seeing what people needed. Now with cancer, the tables were turned. Dave and I were amazed by the level of generosity people showed us. In time, I realized I had a lot to learn. I often doubted my ability to meet the needs around me. I did what I could, but always questioned my effectiveness. However, our cancer experience completely changed how I perceive giving and serving.

People blessed us in such creative ways, and I saw there is no perfect way to be generous. For example, one evening, I arrived home from a full day of work and felt stressed about what to make for dinner. Then, my friend, Katie, called me to say she had ordered dinner for us—from her house in Montana. Upon delivery, even the tip was paid!

My heart opened a little more each time someone did something kind for us, such as walking our dog or sending a card or gift. I started giving God credit for His kindness and faithfulness to provide for us. Over time, I saw that doing something was better than doing nothing at all. Regardless of the gift—whether big or small—we were so thankful that people thought of us. We had often been the ones to help people, but when Dave got sick, we had to learn how to receive help from others. It was humbling.

Generally, Dave was very determined and didn't like being inactive. But with cancer, he had to make concessions. In Fargo, with no family nearby, we depended on the practical support of our church, coworkers, and neighbors. We soon realized we could not do everything on our own, and people were eager to help us. Four men, including three of Dave's Caterpillar coworkers, mowed our lawn all summer into the late fall. They set up a weekly rotation for mowing and other outside chores.

A few friends also helped Dave with our deck, which he had started in April. The men helped carry large boards and lift heavy beams, but it was impressive how much work Dave was able to do. He got as far as he could on the deck, but once chemo started in late June, his pace slowed down again. The project was on hiatus again until the fall.

Like Dave, I also had to learn to ask for and receive help. Three ladies, in particular, were a blessing to me. Jackie often volunteered to take Lydia for an afternoon, so I could work at the clinic or spend time with Dave. My friend, Sara, lived just down the road from the nursing home, which was even closer than daycare. Lydia stayed with her several times during the summer when I worked full days. I would spend my lunch break with Sara while nursing Lydia and playing with her. It was a relief and comfort to have such helpful friends.

My neighbor, Elissa, also was a support and confidante. Elissa watched Lydia and listened as I discussed Dave's cancer treatments and my battle with fear. Sharing my concerns with Elissa was helpful because it gave me time to gather my thoughts. I was able to process what was happening and how I felt about it. In some ways, our conversations helped me formulate prayer requests to later share with others.

The remainder of June went by quickly, with many activities jammed into a short time. We celebrated Father's Day on June 17th by going to lunch with a small group from church. In Fargo, many of our friends also lived far from their dads, so Dave, who was the only father present, became the 'token dad' for all of us that day! We enjoyed celebrating Dave, and it made him feel special, too.

By mid-June, Dave's strength was returning, and he felt well enough to resume some of his house projects. He enjoyed using tools, and perhaps the strenuous physical activity helped him to recapture his sense of normalcy. While he rested on the couch, Dave used our laptop to design a flower bed to run along the front of our house. Then, he dug out the area and started putting it together. Brick by brick, it was a labor of love.

Dave took more breaks than usual, but even so, he didn't stop much. I helped carry bricks, clear sod, and kept an eye on Lydia. Then, while we were planting the flowers, Dave removed his shirt when he grew hot in the summer sun. I was surprised that he wasn't bothered by his colostomy, which was hanging above his shorts. Since Dave and I were typically private people, I asked if he minded someone seeing his colostomy bag. As he sat down on a folding chair in the driveway, he shrugged and said, "No, the neighbors can think whatever they want!"

Dave also returned to work at Caterpillar as soon as he was cleared medically. Everyone was glad to have him back, and he was pleased to feel productive again. Caterpillar was expanding its facility, and Dave was responsible for certain aspects of the project. He led his team, reorganized workflow, and purchased enormous cranes for the remodel, among other tasks. His surgery had delayed his progress, and he was eager to get back.

Paul, Dave's supervisor, had been concerned when he became ill and had visited us in the hospital. He graciously understood Dave's need to attend doctor appointments and sit down occasionally to rest. Dave notified his team when he would be gone and worked ahead when possible. Even at Caterpillar, he took on an 'it is what it is' attitude. He made the best out of embarrassing situations, like when his colostomy made gassy noises during important meetings.

During this time, Dave also received his port placement for chemotherapy. A port is a small device inserted strategically into a central vein near the heart. A port provides access to the larger blood vessels without requiring a needle to be reinserted every time there is a chemo treatment. In this way, it helps minimize blockages or damage to smaller, peripheral veins. The chemo would go into Dave's port, located on his chest below his left clavicle.

Having the port made blood draws easier because the nurses wouldn't have to access the veins in his arm. Certain medicines could also be provided via the port. Professionally, I had seen many patients with ports, but seeing one under my husband's skin hit home that Dave was sick. There was no denying his condition was serious.

Dave's first chemotherapy treatment was scheduled for Tuesday, June 26th. Our goal was to fit three or four chemo sessions in before my sister's wedding in August. The chemo regimen took about forty-six hours, starting on Tuesday. Dave received chemo every two weeks as long as his labs were good. Some of the drugs were administered in the cancer center.

Then, Dave continued his treatment at home. He wore a small portable pump that delivered the rest of the infusion. He worked at Caterpillar nearly every day, as much as he could, even during chemo. On Thursdays, Dave returned to the cancer center—usually before he went to work—so the pump could be detached.

The side effects of Dave's treatment lasted for several days after the pump was removed. They included fatigue, decreased sense of taste, and lack of appetite. The side effects were worse during chemo week. Dave ate very little then. But, by the end of the following 'recovery' week, his appetite would return, and he would eat more. He was mostly back to being himself just before the next chemo session.

For his chemotherapy, Dave received a standard combination of drugs called FOLFOX. As it built up in his body, his energy plummeted. He was nauseous and spent much of the time on the love seat at home. Still, it seemed Dave's main side effect to the FOLFOX was extreme intolerance to cold temperatures, which is very common with this drug regimen.

For Dave, the cold sensitivity showed up within minutes of receiving the first treatment. We had left Lydia with Jackie so I could be at the cancer center to support Dave. He sat in a chair while the oncology nurses started the process of attaching the IVs to the port. As soon as the drugs began coursing through his veins, Dave requested a blanket. He was offered some water, too, but rejected it because it was so cold.

A few hours later, Dave left the cancer center wearing the portable pump with the infusion that would drip in until Thursday. Then, we stopped for lunch at Qdoba, a Mexican-style restaurant. It was around 1:00 p.m., and I was ravenous. After we sat down with our food, I started eating right away. I noticed Dave didn't.

"Hon, aren't you going to eat something?" I asked with concern.

Dave just picked at his food, "No. Sorry, but my burrito doesn't even look good." He paused for a moment, thinking. "I guess I'll just get something to drink," Dave said as he walked to the beverage station.

When he came back, he took a drink. Reeling back in shock, he said, "Wow! That is so cold!" He couldn't drink his beverage with ice in it and had to dump it. We decided to take our food home, so maybe Dave could enjoy it later.

We knew the cold intolerance would come eventually, but we didn't think it would happen immediately. At home, we started leaving our pitcher of water at room temperature on the counter. Dave had to use hot pads or gloves to remove foods from the freezer. Even so, he could feel the cold through the gloves—which was a little odd because it was in the middle of summer. Again, we were thankful the side effects were not worse. Dave also appreciated that his hair loss was minimal. He still looked like himself, which gave us both peace of mind, at least for the time being.

Often, Dave's cancer required us to reevaluate and adjust our plans and expectations. For instance, we made the difficult decision to miss my sister's wedding shower on June 30th. Dave had his first round of chemo that week, and we did not know how he would react. In case Dave needed medical attention, we felt it was wise to stay home. We hoped by doing so that we could join Livi and Paul on their special day in August.

We hated to cancel our trip to Illinois, but thankfully, my aunt brought a laptop to the restaurant where the shower was being held. On that Saturday, I dressed Lydia in a little white dress with black polka dots, and we Skyped into the party remotely. It was fun to see family, and they all commented on how much Lydia had grown. I tried to be brave, but I was worried about Dave. He was slept through the wedding shower and barely moved all day.

And so began the year of declining invitations and rescheduling events because of Dave's health. It was unusual for us, but in some ways, it turned out to be a blessing. We were able to rest as a family and do what was best for us. Prioritizing our needs felt challenging at first. Previously, we had often made room in our schedule to help other people and attend various social events. But, we could no longer keep up with it all and were grateful everyone understood.

The following Wednesday was the Fourth of July. Dave felt good after going into the cancer center for IV fluids earlier in the week. He had grown dehydrated from lack of appetite and not drinking enough fluids, but then the IV fluids perked him back up—almost like watering a flower! Dave's mom came to visit that week and seemed relieved that he appeared healthy overall. Since the beginning of May, Dave had lost a significant amount of weight, probably close to twenty pounds.

Dave was not overweight, to begin with, but now near 165 pounds, he looked leaner. Dave always was one to groom himself well; he was never a slob. Yet now, none of his old clothes fit; they hung from his frame. So, Cynda generously took us shopping for Dave. She bought him two pairs of dress pants and three button-down shirts with matching new ties. Dave was pleased he would have something classy to wear to my sister's wedding. He looked sharp!

That summer, I decided to start sharing our health updates online because we knew people would want to know how Dave was doing. We had an extensive network of family and friends around the world; many of them were praying for us as well. I asked Dave how he felt about me posting updates on his health since we didn't usually share many personal details online. He agreed that I should post updates and encouraged me to do what I thought best.

I considered several online platforms but decided to keep it simple and post updates on Facebook. I emailed regular updates to those not connected to social media. Whenever something important happened, I posted an update. For instance, after Dave's port placement, his chemo treatments, or hospital admissions, I reported how it went. Sometimes, updates were close together and sometimes further apart, depending on what might have occurred. The news may have been good or bad.

At the very least, I sent monthly updates to recap how Dave was feeling and how Lydia was growing. Even so, I was cautious about the information provided because I wanted to protect Dave's dignity. I didn't want to share embarrassing colostomy moments or private details of his treatment. Thankfully, Dave was good-natured about it all.

Similarly, I didn't want to highlight the negativity cancer brought or give it any more press than needed. I didn't want my updates to sound like I was complaining, so I chose a different approach. Truthfully, my emotions often sunk when faced with discouraging medical reports or other problems. Yet, instead of immediately posting something, I waited until we had more information.

Sometimes it took a day or two to process the experience, especially when we needed to make tough decisions. However, once we returned to a more hopeful perspective, I summarized what happened and listed some prayer requests. I often shared Bible verses or encouraging quotes that impacted us during each trial. Similarly, I felt it was important to end on a positive note, like, "Thank you for your prayers!" or "God is good!"

As a result, it is possible people didn't understand just how dire our situation was at times. Although we were dealing with life and death, we were determined to set a positive example and look for God in the dark moments. For the family emails, I also included routine updates and pictures of Lydia to show her growth and development. Over time, my updates evolved as I felt more comfortable including additional details and prayer requests.

One possible caveat in sharing our story is that people started offering unsolicited advice. In terms of faith, people told us we just needed to trust God more. But that took a lot of effort amid so many unknown variables. Regarding nutrition advice, some of the suggestions actually could have made Dave's situation worse.

As I sorted through nutrition myths to find kernels of truth, it upset me that people were making assumptions without knowing the full details of Dave's medical problems or treatments. In short, one food or food group, by itself, does not prevent or cure cancer.

Nevertheless, several lifestyle choices may help decrease cancer risks, such as maintaining a healthy weight, exercising regularly, and eating less red meat, processed foods, and alcohol. Choosing more plant foods, such as fruits, vegetables, whole grains, and legumes, can be helpful because they bring so much to the table. In addition to fiber, vitamins, and minerals, plants bring a plethora of antioxidants. Even so, there are no guarantees.

As a dietitian, I knew nutrition was only one factor to consider. But, I didn't want to miss something that really could help Dave. So, I bought a continuing education course from a reputable source to see what the cancer research showed. What I read reaffirmed we were on the right track. There was nothing I felt we should do differently food-wise. Overall, Dave's diet before cancer was nutritionally adequate. If only eating well was enough!

Chapter 5

"When anxiety was great within me, your consolation brought me joy."
Psalm 94:19 NIV

By the middle of August, Dave had completed four rounds of chemo over eight weeks. He seemed to be doing well, and the chemo treatments hadn't been as bad as we expected. Dave was lethargic at times but maintained an optimistic attitude. He had lost weight but felt pretty well overall. Dave's appetite was variable, but I was relieved he seemed like his usual self—happy and upbeat.

My thirtieth birthday was on Sunday, August 12th. I was thankful that, by this point, Dave's appetite had returned. I suggested we go to a funky local restaurant, situated in the Hotel Donaldson, which is in downtown Fargo. Then, we remembered Dave had previously won a gift certificate to stay there overnight. We agreed my birthday would be the perfect opportunity for a romantic getaway. However, because all of our friends were out of town or unavailable, we had to bring Lydia with us!

I was determined to enjoy my first birthday as a mom and our first real celebration since Dave's diagnosis three months earlier. We walked a few blocks window shopping on that warm evening. We took turns pushing Lydia in her stroller and carrying her when she became fussy. Overall, she was a good sport. As long as her needs were met, she was happy. We toured the recently-remodeled hotel before eating dinner in the restaurant.

By the time we returned to our room, it was 8:00 p.m., and Dave was understandably tired. So, we simply watched television and talked. Regarding gifts, Dave was generous as usual. I don't know when he had the time to go shopping! He gave me a beautiful charcoal-grey pearl necklace and a one-hour massage gift certificate.

On August 17th, five days after my birthday, my sister got married in Illinois. Dave and I had previously proposed a break from his treatment so we could attend the wedding. Dr. Lloyd agreed that he was doing well, so we also scheduled a second surgery in late August. This would reverse Dave's colostomy so he could resume normal bowel movements. The little spot found on the June PET scan would be removed from Dave's liver as well.

Chemotherapy can affect the entire body, including its ability to heal, clot blood, and fight off infection. So, the well-timed break gave the side effects from chemo a little time to subside beforehand. It seemed like life was finally returning to normal!

We drove to Illinois a couple of days before the wedding. Lydia was a good traveler, and after ten hours of driving, we stopped at Cynda's house to spend the night. The next morning, we finished our drive to the Chicago suburbs. My parents and two brothers, Patrick and Micah, lived downstate and drove up to meet us. As a family, we made the final preparations before the wedding on Friday. Dave felt well and was his characteristically happy and helpful self.

The mid-afternoon wedding took place in a gazebo on the golf course portion of a country club. It was a beautiful picture-perfect day. Because I was in the wedding, Dave held Lydia on his lap. At almost nine-months-old, she was active and wanted to crawl around and explore. She was adorable in her little black sundress with bright flowers. Dave looked quite handsome in his new lavender button-up shirt with plum purple tie and charcoal pants.

That day was a joyous and memorable occasion for our little family. When I looked at Dave and Lydia together, I could envision special events like daddy-daughter dances and perhaps even Lydia's wedding someday. I hoped we would have more of these experiences together! But with a jolt, I sensed the injustice we faced. I decided not to think that far ahead because I didn't want to spend time managing my emotions and playing the 'what if' game. I needed to stay focused on my sister's special day and didn't allow my mind to wander any further. Instead, I chose to be present and enjoy the day as much as possible.

Friends and family members were eager to catch up with us and hold Lydia during the wedding reception. Since we had skipped the wedding shower, my parents and siblings had not seen us in several months. And, because of the distance, some of my extended family had not seen us since before Lydia was born. We enjoyed celebrating and taking a break from cancer!

Interestingly, everyone commented on how healthy Dave looked. To those who didn't know about the cancer diagnosis, he would have seemed entirely normal. He was well-dressed and looked confident. Also, Dave had his appetite back and ate a variety of food, including Italian wedding cookies, which honored Paul's family heritage.

As the matron of honor, I was supposed to give a speech at the reception. With all that was going on, I hadn't decided what to say beforehand but planned to keep it short and sweet. Then, just before the wedding, I heard an upbeat song, called "Your Love Never Fails," by the Newsboys. I was running last-minute errands in my car, and I was struck by how good God had been to us! Dave's treatment was going well, and I was so grateful we were able to attend Livi's wedding. I felt it was appropriate to share something similar about God's love for my speech.

Of course, weddings often prompt married couples to consider their relationship and vows. Dave and I had also agreed to care for each other in sickness and in health. Now, as my sister's marriage was starting, mine was at risk. Dave and I had dreams and plans for our life together. But would they come to pass? What if Dave didn't make it? As husband and wife, we had always been a team. We were in this fight together, but would that be enough to save him—and our marriage?

By the time I was supposed to speak that evening, I was overcome with emotion and nerves. I also didn't want to bring the mood down on such a happy day, so instead, I tearfully adlibbed, saying something like, "We're so happy for you guys. Welcome to the family, Paul!"

People reacted well and seemed understanding, especially since many of them knew of Dave's condition. Then, my sister graciously surprised me with a special cupcake to celebrate my birthday, and everyone at the reception sang to me. By that point, the pressure was off, and I was able to enjoy the moment!

Our trip to Illinois could not have been better. We had a wonderful time with family and made good memories together. Then, we trekked back to Fargo on Sunday. We drove all day, straight through because Dave had a few appointments before his upcoming scheduled surgery.

On Monday morning, August 20th, Dave had a PET scan to compare to the one from June. Later that day, we met one of the surgeons for the upcoming surgery. Dr. Hyatt was quiet and seemed attuned to what we were feeling. He gave us his full attention.

Dr. Hyatt planned to remove a golf-ball-sized piece of liver noted on the June PET scan. During the surgery, he would inspect the rest of the liver visually and with ultrasound, too. Because Dave's cancer had already metastasized to the liver before his diagnosis, Dr. Hyatt wanted to be thorough. Ironically, Dr. Hyatt mentioned it was good Dave was naturally thin because the surgery would be easier to complete.

Then, on Tuesday, we met with Dr. Callahan, a GI surgeon and colorectal specialist, to finalize a few details before Dave's surgery the following week. He was friendly and had a warm bedside manner. Dr. Callahan planned to 'take down' the colostomy, which meant to reverse the previous surgery and reattach Dave's colon properly. I was relieved he would soon be done with the colostomy as I still felt having a bag was somewhat degrading. Dave didn't deserve that!

Dr. Lloyd, Dave's oncologist, called him to discuss Monday's PET scan results. It was mostly unchanged from the first one in June, as in the chemo had not shrunk the tumor. He was concerned there could be more cancer molecules lurking in Dave's body. Still, we felt confident about the surgery. Before long, we would be facing better days.

The surgery, scheduled for the afternoon of Wednesday, August 29th, would be lengthy, so drop-in daycare was not an option. Once again, our friend, Jackie, came through for us. At 9:00 a.m. that morning, we left Lydia with her and arrived at the hospital twenty minutes later. There were many preparations to do before surgery.

Dave was in good spirits as always and joked with the nursing staff, being a good sport with all that had happened so far on our cancer journey. I thought, "Everything is going according to plan. Soon, the colostomy will be gone, and Dave will be back to his normal self."

I wish it had been that easy!

Then, the pre-op routine began. Dave and I were comfortably chatting with the staff, and the process seemed under control. At 11:30 a.m., however, within a half-hour of his scheduled surgery time, Dave's usually cheerful countenance changed to pain. The color drained out of his face, and he said something was wrong with his stomach. When I touched him, Dave felt clammy. He had not had anything to eat or drink before the surgery, so it seemed odd that he would be in pain.

Dr. Callahan was consulted, but it took some time for him to come. Perhaps this was because he was preparing for the surgery, too. I imagine he was all gowned up and got interrupted by the consult.

"Hi, Dave. Tell me what's going on," he said as soon as he arrived.

"I don't know what's wrong—it just hurts," Dave responded flatly.

"Are you worried about the surgery?" I asked, thinking it was related to stress.

"No, I'm looking forward to it," he answered.

Dr. Callahan said if we delayed the surgery, it could be several weeks before the surgeons and staff schedules could be coordinated again. Together, we decided the best course of action was to proceed with the surgery as planned. Then, Dr. Callahan and his team could see what may be going on inside the gut. Thus, Dave was in surgery by 1:30 p.m., a little behind our previous schedule, but still on track with the overall plan.

After I kissed Dave goodbye, I went to the cafeteria to eat lunch. I knew the operation would take several hours, so I didn't feel rushed. I called my mom and Dave's mom to give them an update and then calmly walked to the surgical waiting room. It was the second time I had been there since May, but this time felt so different. I knew there were many risks, but I didn't feel panicked because everything indicated this planned surgery was under control.

Another difference was that this time I sat alone. Of course, I prayed for Dave, but I also felt relaxed enough to read. Periodically, I checked in via text or phone calls with our families, who were asking how things were going. Jackie sent me cute pictures of Lydia, which also eased any tension I may have felt. I was grateful instead of anxious.

The surgery ended around 5:00 p.m. Dr. Callahan then came to give me an update, while Dr. Hyatt and the rest of the surgical team finished up. Unfortunately, he told me things had not gone as expected. First, the surgeons discovered Dave's small intestine had started to twist on itself.

By the time Dr. Callahan examined it, Dave's small intestine had already begun to turn cyanic (blue) due to a lack of oxygen. He said if they had waited at all, the tissue would have turned necrotic, which means that a portion of the small intestine would have died. It was unclear why this had happened, but I was relieved it hadn't caused more issues.

Second, there was more bad news. Dr. Hyatt's portion of the surgery didn't go as we had hoped either. Instead of just removing one small tumor, he cut out three large, suspicious chunks in the liver and a couple of small spots in the mesentery layer of Dave's abdominal wall. Dr. Hyatt wanted to wait for the pathology report to be sure, but they all appeared cancerous.

As I waited to see Dave, I considered these disconcerting developments. For the time being, I decided not to worry about the cancer prognosis until the pathology report results came back. Instead, I thought about how I could support Dave's recovery. I realized, sadly, life would not be returning to normal anytime soon.

Finally, I was able to see Dave two-and-a-half hours later at about 7:30 p.m. He had spent the time in a recovery unit, like all surgery patients. Walking into his room, I kissed Dave hello and noticed he was hooked up to a variety of monitors.

"Hi, Babe, how are you feeling? Did the doctors tell you about the surgery?" I asked, trying to keep my voice even.

"I'm feeling pretty good," Dave replied, cheerfully. "The nurses have been great, but I haven't talked with Dr. Callahan or Dr. Hyatt yet."

When I gave him a brief update, he, too, was surprised about the additional tumors, but at the time, we just thought the surgery had resolved the issue. Even now, I don't know if Dave's cancer had spread since his initial diagnosis in May, or if the PET scan had just missed those spots. But in all, we were thankful for the colostomy reversal and the removal of the suspicious liver areas. We were concerned, but we knew God could handle it.

An hour later, when I left for the evening, Dave was in good spirits, again joking with the nursing staff. Around 9:00 p.m., I picked up Lydia and drove home. I was exhausted but also relieved the surgery was over. I put Lydia to bed and wondered about all the news we had received. How much more could we take? I sat down at my laptop and wrote a short email update for close friends and family.

The house was so quiet without Dave, and it felt good to make a connection with those who were encouraging us. Writing also helped me gather my thoughts and recapture a sense of order. I was hoping Dave would recover quickly, though I knew it would take some time for his surgical wounds to heal. There was still the pending pathology report to deal with, but I tried to dismiss any fear surrounding it and prepared to go to bed.

The next morning, I wrote a more thorough email update and Facebook post. I mentioned my uncertainty about the pathology report, though I tried to remain hopeful. I requested prayer for my emotions and prayer against infections and blood clots. Of course, Dave was on the standard post-surgical protocol to prevent any complications, but for me, prayer is the first line of defense, not a last resort.

Then, Lydia and I went to visit Dave. He did well overnight, but he hadn't gotten much rest because the staff routinely checked on him and his wounds. Despite his discomfort, Dave didn't use much of his pain medicine, which was self-administered at the push of a button. I don't think it was bravado, but rather he could tolerate the pain and disliked the drowsiness caused by narcotics, like morphine.

Dave preferred to be aware and alert. Indeed, the nurses enjoyed his kindness and sense of humor. Later, on several occasions, he helped his nurses calculate medication doses. As a mechanical engineer, Dave didn't know much about the medications, but he was spot-on with the math! Dave also tracked his water intake and urinary output (I's and O's) for the nurses.

That morning, with Lydia on my lap, I was happy to watch Dave be an active participant in his care. He was a welcome patient, and many of the nurses requested him on their shifts. The staff (mostly ladies) appreciated when he asked good questions. They enjoyed taking care of Dave because he was helpful and listened to their advice. In some ways, it felt like his cancer was on hold as we focused on the recovery process.

Overall, Dave appeared to be doing well, and I was thankful that (so far) he had not been admitted to the oncology floor. It seemed that once patients were admitted there, their prognoses were grim. With the most recent surgery, Dave required a different level of care, but since we weren't doing any cancer treatments, it was like his original diagnosis was in the background. Cancer remained a factor, but I was more than happy to focus on Dave's other needs instead.

I spent as much time at the hospital as possible. I visited Dave early, using drop-in daycare during the morning, and then returned with Lydia after her afternoon nap. Unfortunately, Dave's hospital room was not baby or toddler-friendly. I didn't want her to crawl on the floor, so I often held Lydia on my lap or tried to contain her to the one chair in the room. I also brought the stroller for her to sit or sleep in, but she could only last so long!

When she got antsy, I took Lydia for walks in her stroller. Even though the stroller was lightweight, it was tricky navigating around all the hospital equipment. Thankfully, I could keep all of Lydia's belongings contained in the little basket underneath her seat. Many times, I took her downstairs for a meal or to the family room so she could crawl around while Dave rested or the staff completed their tasks. All the while, Lydia continued to reach developmental milestones, such as pulling herself up to stand and pushing items to help her walk around.

A couple of days after his surgery, Dave started receiving TPN, which provides liquid nutrition through the blood vessels instead of the gut. While Dave wouldn't be able to eat anything by mouth for several days, he still needed adequate nutrients to heal. He had received TPN during his first hospital stay in May, after ten days of not eating anything at all. But this time, it was started right away so his gut could rest. Dave fondly referred to this mixture as his "cheeseburger and fries in a bag."

After the second surgery, we were more realistic about Dave's physical limits. We knew it would take time to heal and didn't want to rush the process. Day by day, Dave grew a little stronger. We were thrilled when he could sit up in a chair for at least four hours in a row. Slowly, he was able to get up and move around more. Dave enjoyed his physical therapy sessions, and he was proud when he could walk down the long hall and back again. Eventually, he could walk two or three full laps around the surgical floor!

On and off during this hospital stay, Dave combatted fevers. His temperature would spike a couple of degrees (around 100°F), indicating a possible infection or internal problem. The fevers were not treated with medication because they were relatively mild, yielded no other symptoms, and didn't last long. Dave did well overall and healed slowly. I tried not to think about the pending pathology report.

A week later, in early September, my mother-in-law came to visit. I am sure it eased Cynda's mind to see Dave after such an extensive surgery. I know Dave was comforted seeing her, too. I was scheduled to work all week at the nursing home, and Cynda was able to help take care of Lydia, Britain, and other household duties.

I was thankful for the extra help because I didn't have to rush back and forth, which saved me a lot of time and stress. Cynda's presence took the pressure off of me to balance everyone else's needs. She and Lydia would do an activity together, like grocery shopping or swimming, and then visit Dave. When I returned home from work, Cynda, Lydia, and I would eat dinner, and then I would go see Dave.

Slowly, Dave was weaned off the TPN and given more solid foods. At first, he was able to choose a full liquid diet (like juice, broth, milk, or gelatin) and later, toast. Then, he was advanced to a regular diet, which meant

Dave could choose whatever he wanted. From a nutrition perspective, fighting cancer required a lot of energy. Yet, Dave still had little appetite and had lost all the weight he had regained during the summer.

As a dietitian, I knew he needed extra calories and protein for wound healing and to increase his overall nutrition status. A "food first" approach is ideal, but Dave was still at risk for being malnourished. At my request, he would occasionally drink high-protein nutrition supplements. He didn't enjoy them much, and for his sake, I didn't push them often!

On September 8th, Dave was discharged from the hospital. He had been there for ten days, which was longer than we expected. When we arrived home, we made it up the stairs to the main living area. Dave rested on the love seat as he did after his first surgery, but this time, he was more alert and engaged. Cynda helped us make the transition home and then left the next morning for Illinois.

Chapter 6

"For God has not given us a spirit of fear,
but of power and of love and of a sound mind."
2 Timothy 1:7 NKJV

While our outlook at this point was hopeful, we still had to make tough decisions. Before the surgery in August, Dave was asked to be a groomsman at a close friend's wedding in September. After thinking it through, we concluded it would not be wise to drive to Illinois after such an extensive surgery. Our friend, Andy, was gracious, but it was just one of the many adjustments we needed to make that year.

Dave spent the rest of September recovering. Once more, I helped him change his surgical dressings and took him to follow-up appointments with his two surgeons. We often took Lydia with us, yet it was becoming more difficult to contain her. Just like Daddy, she wanted to be moving around! Overall, we enjoyed watching the summer turn into fall and were content with a slower pace.

It felt rather cozy inside our warm house as the air outside turned brisk. We relished each moment together as a little family. Dave spent most of his time on the love seat and enjoyed watching Lydia play. She didn't have many words yet, but she was very clear when she wanted her "Da-Da." She sat with Dave on the love seat while he read books to her. When Lydia didn't feel well due to teething, they napped together on the love seat. It was so sweet to watch. I took as many pictures of these moments as I could.

Dave had taken several weeks off work to heal, yet he also wanted to be active! During this time, he was able to complete the deck he had started back in April. He tried to do as much as he could but grew tired quickly. It was taking him a lot longer to regain his energy.

So, one Saturday in late September, Dave asked his coworkers to help finish the steps and attach the railing and balusters. Paul, Dean, Mike, and Deven were all glad to provide the physical labor while Dave directed them. We enjoyed eating pizza and visiting after they finished their work that day.

Dave was proud of the completed deck, though it would need to be stained later. For a brief time, it seemed like we were back on track—a young couple building a life and family together. My fear subsided, and it seemed easier to believe Dave was going to be okay. Perhaps we could dare to make plans for our future, after all.

Then, during the last week of September, Dr. Lloyd reviewed the August PET scan results and the pathology report with us. He stated Dave was essentially 'cancer-free' because of the surgery, which we took as great news. While that may have been what we wanted to hear, it gave us a false sense of security. Specifically, I thought that meant Dave was doing well. But once someone has had cancer, there is always the risk it will return.

Maybe the high rate of recurrence is why, even though Dave's scans showed no cancer, Dr. Lloyd remained the pessimist. As we sat in his office, he again explained, "The FOLFOX combination was supposed to shrink the tumor on Dave's liver, but it didn't." He also confirmed the liver biopsies were indeed cancerous, as were the smaller areas found in the mesentery layer, which covers and holds the intestines in place. So, not only had the cancer cells resisted the chemotherapy, but Dave had even more cancer than we had thought! Thus, Dr. Lloyd wanted us to consider a more aggressive treatment plan.

We were shocked and felt blindsided by his report! For some reason, we hadn't considered the FOLFOX might not work. Dave had regained much of his strength after the two invasive abdominal surgeries. We felt he had made progress. While he did have side effects to the treatment, Dave's overall reaction was better than we had anticipated.

Then again, perhaps our expectations had been unrealistic. Each type of cancer is treated differently, depending on the stage, location of cancer cells, and other factors. Also, there are diverse side effects related to each drug cocktail. For instance, with treatment for breast cancer, it is common for a woman to lose her hair. Dave didn't have hair loss, nor did he appear bloated as seen with other types of cancer. So, I suppose we attributed his weakness, fatigue, decreased appetite, and weight loss more to his two major surgeries than just to cancer or chemo.

Dave had received eight rounds of the FOLFOX regimen, and we had assumed the chemo was working. Overall, he was relatively active. He appeared healthy and had retained a positive attitude, thus far. Since, externally, things looked well, we hadn't questioned the internal progress (or lack thereof). Now, at nearly six months into Dave's treatment plan, this news made us feel like we had to start over.

It wasn't fair! Initially, we were just in for a year of chemo. Dave's original surgeon, Dr. James, had planted that seed in our minds of getting through one year of treatment and then continuing on with our lives. But instead of continuing with the current plan, it seemed we had just gone backward six months—a far cry from being done with cancer!

From the beginning, Dave and I had understood there were no promised outcomes. Yet, we had clung to hope all these months that we were well on our way to finishing chemo and beating cancer. For the first time since his diagnosis, Dave was clearly disappointed. We sat in Dr. Lloyd's cold office, dejected. I was at a loss for words, but Dave muttered bitterly, "What's the point in going through treatment if it isn't working?!"

This was probably the first moment I wondered, "Is Dave going to make it?" I had been struggling with my fears and doubts all along, but Dave's optimism had kept me afloat. So when he began rethinking chemo, I started to understand the gravity of the situation. Previously, he had been so strong mentally and emotionally.

Cancer and chemo were indeed bad enough, but Dave's mindset had strong potential to affect his health, too. It scared me to think of how precarious the balance had become. I knew I couldn't force him to keep fighting, but I worked hard to remind him of all that was at stake.

Until this point, Dave had been willing to go through whatever was needed to beat cancer, including gut-wrenching surgeries and side effects of chemotherapy. While he didn't like being sick, his thinking had always been sensible. But after talking with Dr. Lloyd, it took Dave days to come to terms with the negative report. He hated the forced inactivity cancer and chemo had imposed on him. And now, he questioned if fighting cancer was worth the bother of being sick, weak, and tired. It troubled me.

I had never seen Dave this way before, and it broke my heart. Once more, I feared I was going to lose him. So, one afternoon, I called my Aunt Terry in Illinois before I made dinner. She stopped what she was doing to listen. I told her about Dave's reaction and how I felt. It didn't seem like God was listening to our prayers. "Oh Sweetie, don't forget that God loves you! You don't have to be afraid." Then, she spent at least half an hour reminding me of certain Bible verses about God's love, power, and healing.

As I stood in my kitchen, Aunt Terry quoted Scriptures over me. In particular, I appreciated hearing "no weapon formed against you will prosper..." from Isaiah 54:17 (NKJV). It helped me focus, and soon, I felt my fear leave. Before we hung up, she prayed for me, too. Aunt Terry's prayers reminded me of God's power and presence which brought me peace. That evening, I was so thankful she took the time to listen, to pray for me, and to encourage me.

When Dave contemplated giving up on his treatment, it felt like he was giving up on Lydia and me. Disheartened, I implored him to keep fighting for us. But ultimately, I knew Dave had to decide for himself. If he had chosen to stop treatment, I would have supported him, even if I didn't agree. Thankfully, after one week of rough days, Dave's mindset improved, and he resolved to continue his treatment.

If Dave had decided against further treatment, it might have bought us a little more time, or it could have hastened the outcome. Either way, I chose not to share Dave's internal conflict online because I didn't want to alarm our supporters. I also wanted to protect Dave from what people might think. This decision made it isolating, as we dealt with this struggle alone, though I didn't allow myself time to focus on my own emotions.

Dr. Lloyd's proposed chemo regimen—called FOLFIRI—had two of the same medications as FOLFOX, but the third one was new. Thankfully, the drug which caused extreme cold intolerance would be replaced with something else. However, the possible side effects of FOLFIRI were severe diarrhea and vomiting.

Also, Dr. Lloyd wanted to add an extra chemical agent as an adjuvant therapy. This meant Dave would be receiving treatment in the cancer center every week instead of every other week. It also meant more time away from work, once he was cleared to return to Caterpillar again. There was much to consider.

One of the most severe side effects with the add-on agent (called Avastin) was an increased risk for internal bleeding. Feeling concerned, I spoke up and asked for a second opinion. It was important to learn about all our options.

Dr. Lloyd said we could go to Mayo Clinic about five hours away, in Rochester, Minnesota. He also said he could have his local colleagues review the case and make recommendations. Over the next week, Dave and I prayed about what decision to make.

The time commitment for getting to Rochester and undergoing the weeklong consultation was a concern. Typically, the goal at Mayo is to run all the tests needed to get a full picture and see several physicians during one stay. But, to go there, we would need someone to watch Lydia, so I could be fully present with Dave.

Undoubtedly, our families would have rushed to help with Lydia. However, it felt like a challenge to organize all the details. In the end, Dave and I felt our local hospital was adequately handling his medical case. Our physicians often worked closely with Mayo and routinely implemented their recommendations. The benefits of going to Rochester were slim, and the treatment would not be much different than what we were already experiencing.

Instead, we opted for the second opinion locally. Dave's case was presented to the weekly tumor board for review during the first week of October. We then discussed our concerns with another oncologist, Dr. Muir. His friendliness and warm smile set us at ease. Dr. Muir, was somewhat laid back, yet very caring. He didn't seem surprised by our many questions, patiently answering them one by one. I was relieved to see Dave relax while listening to him.

Dr. Muir calmly gave us a comprehensive medical review. He didn't have a strong opinion on which course of treatment to pursue, but he provided helpful feedback nonetheless. He said it is common for patients to try multiple types of cancer therapies. As such, he implied we might have many changes in the treatment plan over time. Dave and I both felt comforted and satisfied with the answers. Dr. Muir had listened to our concerns, and we were thankful for the time he spent with us.

Overall, the recommendation from Dr. Muir and the tumor board was to switch to FOLFIRI. However, they suggested a different biological agent than Avastin because we were disturbed about its side effects. Therefore, Dave agreed to try Erbitux in addition to the FOLFIRI chemotherapy. The main side effects of this add-on agent included the possibility of a severe rash all over Dave's body. At that point, it seemed the least worrisome of all the options.

October was an important month for other reasons. At the beginning of the month, Dave returned to work. It was a bright spot for both of us emotionally, even though he only worked half days at first. After approximately two weeks of working part-time, Dave was able to return full time and fit his chemo treatments in, too. Everyone at Caterpillar encouraged him to rest when needed. At times, he worked from home while resting on the love seat, as well.

Somehow, we managed to keep a full schedule most weeks. Our friend, Sam, came up to stay for the month and work for a local farmer during the sugar beet harvest. This was his third year doing so. As usual, Sam stayed downstairs in our guest room and helped us around the house instead of paying us rent. We appreciated his help, even more, when Dave was sick.

Like Sam, Dave also joined the harvest. While he had to make some adjustments, he helped out for two weekends in October. Dave found joy driving semi-trucks, and it also provided some additional income. To my great relief, this activity made Dave feel like himself again. The other workers couldn't believe he was sick because he had such a positive attitude.

One Saturday afternoon, Lydia and I went out to visit Dave in the field. The bright blue sky and black dirt were just what we Midwesterners needed! It was very enjoyable, and I made sure to take a few pictures to capture the experience. In years past, Dave and I hadn't taken many pictures beyond dress-up moments, like vacations or weddings. That year, I was diligent in taking pictures of Lydia's growth and development, but in the back of my mind, I also wanted to document our journey.

Given the recent uncertainty of Dave's treatment plan, I felt even more uneasy about his cancer and the unknowns it brought. Losing him seemed like a very real possibility, and I fought against each new wave of fear. If Dave didn't survive, I wanted Lydia to have pictures of her with her daddy, so she could understand how much he loved her. I felt those pictures would help explain our life together with him—who Dave was and why we made certain decisions.

As his strength and energy permitted, Dave continued to be as active as possible. He had a servant's heart and would eagerly help anyone who asked. I didn't make a big deal about it because Dave now spent most of his time on the couch, at the cancer center, or at work. So, I wanted him to enjoy himself when he could. Dave's happiness was just as important as his physical health.

In the fall, our church remodeled a portion of the children's ministry area. Our friend, Pastor David, asked if Dave would help on a Saturday workday in October. They planned to tear down and remove a stage to make more room for other activities. Dave eagerly grabbed his sledgehammer and a few other tools. He was gone all morning and returned full of excitement. After resting on the couch, he told me of all the fun he had there.

Dave also mentioned a new opportunity for us to consider. Pastor David had asked if we would host a new course at the church, called PLACE. It sounded interesting, however, I didn't want to sign up for more activities when Dave needed to rest. But in the end, we decided to help because we felt it was important to serve. Besides, it was held on Sundays when we would already be at church anyway.

Thus, we became facilitators of the PLACE class and taught with several other couples. Each couple took turns rotating through the topics, teaching approximately once during the six-week course. As a class, we watched videos, filled out a workbook, and held group discussions.

I enjoyed helping with the class because we discussed topics like personality, spiritual gifts, skills, heartfelt passions, and life experiences. Dave and I also learned about ourselves during the process. As a result, our marriage grew even stronger because we understood each other better.

It was fulfilling to learn more about my personality and spiritual gifts (simply put: special abilities God gives us to serve others). I loved helping others discover their best qualities. We wanted the participants to focus on their strengths (not weaknesses) and use them to benefit others. With my nutrition background, I already had experience in teaching, coaching, and interviewing people. I started to see how those skills I had been honing for years as a registered dietitian transferred well in the church environment.

When I taught the class, something I was good at and genuinely enjoyed, I was elated. The fact that I was able to serve at church was a bonus. Of course, I had grown up volunteering and serving in my local church and community; my parents instilled that in me as a child. We were taught to give back and did so as a family. We raked leaves, painted, and did other physical tasks. Yet, while I was happy to help, I had often felt like something was missing.

To me, it seemed that serving God should be fulfilling. But since I didn't feel that way, I thought maybe there was something wrong with me. While it's honorable to serve in any area, perhaps I had just needed to find a better fit. Thankfully, leading the PLACE class felt like my calling and brought immense personal satisfaction and reassurance!

Teaching PLACE was healing to me, especially when I heard others verbalize thoughts and feelings similar to mine. Unexpectedly, it brought me great emotional freedom because I always overanalyzed my weaknesses or compared them to others' strengths. In many ways, PLACE gave me more confidence in who God designed me to be. I learned that many of my best traits are abstract. Intuitively, I always knew this, but I never fully understood these as strengths.

For instance, I am good at connecting with people and listening to them process their problems. I enjoy coaching people as they work to mend broken relationships and learn to consider other perspectives. Historically, I might meet with a friend and help her work through a personal relationship issue. I would offer feedback and validation but also explain how the other person may have felt.

Unfortunately, I rarely heard back from people on whether my guidance met its mark. Sometimes, friends would provide updates, but often, there was a lot of time—weeks or months—between check-ins. This happened regularly, which made me question if I made a difference in the lives of those around me. No wonder I often discredited myself!

In contrast, Dave's hands-on skills were tangible. He could change car tires, mow a lawn, or paint a room with ease—and he loved doing so! When Dave completed a task, he had a specific product to show. On the other hand, I only had a coffee receipt. My skills seemed vastly different, so I never felt I did enough. Yet, because of the PLACE class, I realized I didn't need to measure myself against anyone else. God showed me my inherent value, and He helped me understand the gifts and talents He gave me. Thankfully, I soon found my niche!

Remarkably, PLACE gave me words to express myself in new ways. When I learned more about my melancholy-phlegmatic personality, I understood my tendency toward self-doubt. As a perfectionist and high achiever, I often felt frustrated when my effort fell short. Consequently, I sometimes wondered if God was disappointed in me, too.

However, over time, I learned to relax. By God's grace, I finally found peace and joy when I served others. For me, this was a life-changing revelation as I experienced His love and pleasure in a new way. I didn't know it at the time, but those lessons would help me immensely in the coming months.

On October 21st, Lydia turned eleven months. Along the way, she had reached many milestones. Lydia learned to climb up the stairs with help and supervision. She practiced walking by pushing toys around the house. Her personality continued to develop, and we started noticing brief temper tantrums! While Dave was somewhat limited in what he could do, he played with Lydia while I made dinner or walked our dog, Britain.

As October continued, I sought to normalize our lives as best I could. I made seasonal foods, like chili, and some of Dave's favorite foods, like apple crisp. He had little appetite but ate what he could. Dave had lost about thirty pounds overall, but I was pleased his weight was steady.

Dave started the FOLFIRI chemo regimen on October 30th. We were thrilled it didn't affect his appetite as much. He was able to eat a little more, even during treatment. Still, the Erbitux cut into Dave's workday, and he had to stay at the cancer center several hours longer for the additional infusion. The first day back at chemo, Dave arrived at 7:45 a.m. and didn't leave until 2:00 p.m. The timing annoyed him more than the rash that came with the Erbitux. Within a day or so, he had tiny pink spots all over his chest and back.

Chapter 7

"When you pass through the waters, I will be with you; and when you pass through the rivers, they will not sweep over you. When you walk through the fire, you will not be burned; the flames will not set you ablaze."
Isaiah 43:2 NIV

As we moved into November, Dave's high spirits returned. Overall, the new treatment was going well. I watched Dave closely for signs of decreased morale, but he seemed to be back to his usual self. He didn't complain about his new chemo regimen and used his time in treatment to rest or catch up on emails. Sometimes, Dave would borrow an iPad at the cancer center to help pass the time. His optimism brought me comfort.

While the new chemo side effects now included a rash and hiccups, his nausea was less than before. But, Dave's appetite remained poor. His abdominal wounds from his August surgery were healing, but progress was slow. Therefore, I suspected he was not getting all the nutrients he needed for regaining his health and healing his wounds.

For several days in a row, Dave had mentioned that his backside hurt when he sat or lay down. Since he rested more than he was active, his pain was almost constant. He tried lying in different positions on the love seat, but could not find comfort. Finally, one day, Dave seemed to have enough.

"Natty, can you come into the bedroom for a minute?" he asked.

I was shocked when Dave showed me a half-inch deep open wound about the size of a quarter on his coccyx (tailbone area). Though I am not an expert on wound care, it looked like a pressure injury based on my work experiences. Most of the time, skin breakdown indicates decreased nutrition status. Pressure injuries can also imply one needs to move around more to relieve the stress from that area.

We mentioned it to Dr. Lloyd at Dave's next appointment, and a wound nurse added a special dressing to protect the area. Otherwise, I worked to feed Dave extra calories and protein, which was already tough. At home, he also sat on a fluffy pillow to help the irritation.

When updating social media, I mentioned Dave needed to gain weight or at least remain steady. To our surprise, people started sending food gift cards and homemade goodies. We also received a frozen mail order of Portillos' Italian beef, a Chicago area specialty, and a huge order of various meats and sides from Omaha Steaks. We were encouraged by these generous gifts. Dave did his best to consume what he could, however, he rarely finished his food in one sitting.

Around this time, Dave also discussed a second concern with his GI surgeon. Regarding pain near the top of his incision line, Dr. Callahan concluded Dave's sternum must have cracked during surgery when his abdomen was pried open. Other than healing crooked, it would likely be fine in the long-term. Dave accepted there was nothing to be done. I was upset, however, and thought to myself, "Of all things, how much more pain does he have to endure?!"

Our cancer journey often felt like a nightmare, and we yearned to one day wake up from the chaos and return to our normal lives. I now understand our lives would have been markedly different post-cancer, had Dave survived. There is no way anyone could go through something like this and remain unchanged. If anything, we would have lived with the knowledge that cancer could return. The risk and uncertainty would have always been lurking in our minds.

Dave had always been eager to help people, and he volunteered whenever he could. He had a variety of skills, so people often came to Dave for help. However, with cancer, it seemed we were the ones who needed all the help. Through it all, our church family continued to support us in practical ways. These friends became the 'hands and feet' of Jesus in ways we had never experienced. We relied on their help and encouragement to get through our trauma.

In 1 Corinthians 12, the Church is referred to as the Body of Christ. As we learned to ask for help, various friends, neighbors, and coworkers also pitched in. Through this, we gained perspective on what Christians can accomplish when we pull together, instead of arguing about doctrinal differences. Similarly, it was gratifying to be a part of something that felt bigger than us and to see people reaching out from various parts of the world. As Dave and I shared our struggles and successes, there was collective excitement to see what God was going to do.

Dave and I had grown up in different church denominations, but we had learned similar fundamental truths about God. As children, we both had attended Sunday school and learned Bible stories. This solid foundation filled us with hope when things were bad or when we received upsetting medical reports. In our turmoil, we clung to our faith as the only sure thing we knew. We reminded ourselves that God is good, even when we could not see the goodness in our circumstances. Though, at times, it was difficult to feel God's love when daily life was so full of stress.

We were operating at max capacity and could not handle anything beyond what we needed to know or do for cancer. So, we relied on the basic tenets of our faith to get us through. On the toughest days, sometimes all we could do was sing. Simple songs like, "Jesus Loves Me," brought us great comfort like never before. The familiar chorus cheered us up and helped us be more God-focused instead of crisis-focused. As we sang, "Yes, Jesus loves me," on repeat, our hearts would be filled with peace again.

That November, I stumbled upon *Jesus Calling*, by Sarah Young. This devotional book is written as if Jesus Himself were talking to you. I started reading it to glean any hope I could. The book was written as if Jesus Himself were talking to you. Soon, I discovered short, encouraging messages on the importance of cultivating gratitude. With all the tasks I had to do, those few minutes in the morning were sometimes my only quiet time with the Lord. I prayed throughout the day, but I was always on the run. It felt reassuring to remember the day's reading and to refocus myself as my composure frayed.

The third week of November brought Lydia's first birthday. We had a simple party with the couples in our small group from church. We didn't buy a special cake because Dave wasn't feeling well that week and had no appetite. We were just content to be together, and having a large cake seemed unnecessary. Instead, we settled for some random white cupcakes with Kelly-green frosting, knowing Lydia wouldn't remember anyway. She had fun and enjoyed all the attention!

As we helped Lydia open the gifts from our friends, I was grateful Dave was still with us. We took pictures together and tried to stay in the moment. However, I was subtly aware Dave might not be at Lydia's second birthday. As I considered this, I reflected on all that happened in her first year. Not only had Lydia grown before our eyes, but Dave had been battling cancer for six of those twelve months!

Later in the week, Dave and I took Lydia to a portrait studio. Previously, we had done family pictures with her as a newborn. Now, we wanted to commemorate her birthday. On a whim, Dave and I jumped in the frame for a few photos, too. We bought several pictures of Lydia and just one copy of our favorite family photo. I am so glad we did; it was one of the last family photos of the three of us.

In the back of my mind, I was aware Lydia might be interested in knowing what had happened when she was so little, regardless of the outcome. I perceived our choices would matter to her. I wanted Lydia to understand that, despite difficult circumstances, we can thrive. The choices Dave and I made always considered her well-being, too. We did the best we could!

For example, I kept nursing Lydia through her first year, despite the time and effort it took. It was a demanding task, but I felt it was worth the sacrifice. I never considered switching her to formula, probably because, in my go-go-go state of mind, I couldn't think about other options. Often, nursing Lydia was the only time I took to sit down! However, in hindsight, perhaps offering her formula would have been a sanity saver for me! Ultimately, no matter what loving choice a mom makes, the child will adjust.

It was a balancing act, as I tried to honor both Dave and Lydia. I tried to document each of Lydia's milestones, such as eating certain foods, holidays, sitting up, crawling, walking, and talking. I made sure to keep up with Lydia's 'well-child' appointments and vaccines, with one exception. At the doctor's recommendation, I chose to delay the chickenpox vaccine because Dave could have developed shingles from it.

After Lydia's birthday, we also celebrated Thanksgiving with our church friends. Once again, instead of traveling to Illinois, we stayed close to home. Chemo was postponed because of the holiday, so it felt like a blessing to have another week off. Dave felt well that day and had a good appetite. He ate his meal, along with a few snacks and desserts, while we all watched television. Seeing Dave eat so much food seemed like a good sign.

Then, for the first weekend in December, we invited Dave's family and my family together for another birthday celebration for Lydia. We met in Lake City, Minnesota, on the shores of Lake Pepin, which borders Wisconsin. That way, most people would have an eight-hour drive or less instead of the lengthy trip to Fargo.

Despite cancer depleting his energy, Dave was eager to organize the trip for us. He had plenty of time on the couch to make plans and rent a block of condos. We were so thankful everyone made it. Dave's sister also decided to come with her family. Brooke, her husband Dale, and their four kids drove from Florida by minivan to see us!

For early December, the weather was surprisingly good. We went shopping, ate pizza, and visited The National Eagle Center in nearby Wabasha, Minnesota. Then, we all piled into the living room of one of the condos to celebrate Lydia's birthday and four December birthdays, including Dave's upcoming thirty-fourth. It was such a joyful time together.

We didn't know it then, but it was Dave's last birthday celebration, and the last time we were all together when he was feeling well. The trip went smoothly, and everyone had a chance to create good memories with Dave and each other. But soon after this, his health slowly began to decline.

After we returned home, we resumed our somewhat crazy schedule. One evening, we took Lydia to get groceries. Dave wasn't hungry for many foods, but he enjoyed adding up the subtotal as we put items into the cart. I appreciated his diligence to keep us on track financially each month because, as a foodie, I often added extra items to the cart! As we left the store, the weather had started to spit ice and snow. We wanted to get home for the evening and stay put.

When we pulled up to a stoplight, we were about the fourth car back. Dave was driving, as he usually did, while I was in the passenger seat. Lydia was content, sitting in her car seat in the back. We talked about making dinner and putting Lydia to bed afterward. The light turned green, and Dave started to creep forward. Then, BAM!! With no warning, a car hit us from behind! My head hit the seat with a loud thud. It was jarring, but at the moment, I was more concerned with Dave and Lydia.

The speed limit there was thirty-five mph, and the impact propelled us forward into the car ahead of us, damaging both ends of our small Santa Fe. Dave took his cell phone out to call the police. I jumped out to check on Lydia, not knowing what I would find. When I got to the backseat, she appeared safe and sound even though she was screaming at the top of her lungs.

After half an hour, the police officer arrived. There had been a couple of emergency calls, which put our traffic situation on hold. After questioning all of us, the officer cited the driver who hit us. Dave usually kept his emotions under control, yet that night he was visibly upset after the car accident. We were safe, but having our car in the shop for several days would be an inconvenience. The accident was one more thing to add to our never-ending list of challenges.

Both fenders on my Santa Fe were damaged, and several components in the engine area needed to be fixed. We also had to go shopping for a new car seat per insurance regulations. As if we didn't already have enough going on! After a lot of paperwork and phone calls, the other person's insurance company paid for our repairs.

Subsequently, I had a headache and pain in my neck and shoulders. Dave wanted me to get checked out by my primary care physician. However, I told him, "I really can't take the time to go to the doctor. There's so much to do!" My headache lasted two weeks, and I continued to have back and neck problems for a long time afterward. I should have gone as Dave suggested, but I had difficulty taking time for myself.

I continued to manage the house, our dog, Lydia, and Dave's treatment plan. Additionally, I worked at one or both of my jobs every week. I rarely had any downtime. I wasn't sleeping well due to stress and the pain in my back, shoulders, and arms. I also attributed this to shoveling snow, carrying Lydia and all her gear, etc. I tried basic stretches, bought new pillows, and scheduled periodic massages. Nothing seemed to help me long-term. Looking back, perhaps I would have benefited from a calming exercise like yoga!

Dave's birthday was on Monday, Dec 17th, and thankfully, it was not a chemo week. We enjoyed a quiet day together. Dave received another mail-order of food from Omaha Steaks, which encouraged him to eat. Our old neighbors from Decatur, Illinois, also ordered an ice-cream cake from our local Cold Stone Creamery as a surprise. Later, Dave and I went out for a celebratory dinner. He ate a good amount of food and felt well.

The next day, Dave called me into the bedroom, where he was resting. "Hey Natty, can you take a look at this?" He showed me a small, hard spot on his lower abdomen along his incision line (from August) that had yet to heal. Like the pressure injury on his coccyx, it was quarter-sized. For days, Dave had been walking hunched over because of the pain.

We talked about showing Dr. Lloyd, but the timing wasn't right. Dave was not scheduled to see him again until just before the next round of chemo. Plus, Christmas was quickly approaching, so our options for impromptu appointments were limited. After a little discussion, we agreed to wait it out. We assumed it was just a minor wound that would heal with better nutrition and time. The thought that it might be more cancer never occurred to us.

Part II

Standing in Faith

Chapter 8

"The Lord is my rock, my fortress, and my savior;
my God is my rock, in whom I find protection. He is my shield,
the power that saves me, and my place of safety."
Psalm 18:2 NLT

When Dave was sick, we opted to stay home and rest when possible to conserve what little energy he had. This preference affected both our daily plans and travel plans. Because we saw family in early December, we chose to spend a quiet Christmas on our own. While it was a chemo week, due to the holiday, we again decided to postpone Dave's treatment.

Back when we lived in Decatur, Illinois, someone gave us an artificial Christmas tree. We brought the Christmas tree with us when we moved, and we enjoyed decorating it with old-fashioned ornaments. We loved the log cabin feel it brought to our home. However, when Dave was sick, we didn't put up the tree because it was too much work; we decided not to waste all that precious time and effort. Instead, we found joy in watching Lydia open her gifts.

Of note, Caterpillar typically shuts down for general maintenance between Christmas and New Year's Day. Dave and I were grateful for the timing, which seemed like a gift in itself. We chose to stay home and enjoy the much-needed break from work and chemo. Dave and Lydia relaxed on the love seat together, and we reflected on all that had happened that year. We didn't know then, but our circumstances would gradually turn worse in the coming months.

Starting around New Year's Eve, Dave began getting a cold. He didn't have chemo the first week of the year due to more holiday scheduling. But even with three weeks off of chemo, Dave felt miserable. His cold and the spot on his abdomen concerned me, but still, I tried to remain positive. His condition had been relatively stable, and I longed for that to continue.

My email update at the end of 2012 gave a recap of the weather, the holiday season, and some pictures of Lydia now at thirteen months. To end my note, I wrote: "Well, this was a wild year, but God has been so good to us. We would never have wished for cancer, but He took something evil and turned it around for our good. We are floored by the huge outpouring of love we have received. Thank you!!" At the time, we had no clue how much more chaotic life would become.

That first weekend in 2013, we drove two hours to meet Dave's dad, Denny, who was passing through Alexandria, Minnesota, for a short visit. At first, we went out to eat and did a little exploring. However, Dave's cold quickly sapped his energy, and then he preferred to stay in our hotel room and sleep. He felt so awful that I could not convince him to get up. It worried me, but I decided just to let him rest. Then, I took Lydia to the hotel room next door to see Denny. We didn't see him often, and I wanted to make the most of the opportunity.

The following week, on Monday, January 7th, we celebrated our 5th wedding anniversary. We were married on a cruise ship in the Port of Miami, Florida. It had been a warm, beautiful day as we had celebrated with forty of our closest friends and family. Now, it was cold and dreary as we lived out our vows with dramatically different circumstances. Thankfully, by this time, Dave felt somewhat better. His cold had mostly resolved, so we took Lydia with us to celebrate at a local steakhouse.

I appreciated Dave's effort to make the evening enjoyable despite his fatigue. While we waited for our food, he reached across the table to hold my hand. We talked about all that had happened in those five years, and we were grateful for our time together. God had been so good to us. We knew we faced many unknowns, yet we chose to stay in the moment. Dave ate what he could at dinner and went to bed shortly after we returned home.

The next day, Dave received another round of chemo, though he didn't get a chance to meet with Dr. Lloyd. This was probably the worst session he experienced, and it completely exhausted him. That week, Dave went to work when he could, but otherwise stayed on the couch at home. I worked a couple of days and took Lydia to daycare so he could rest. When we were home, I tried to keep her quiet.

Thankfully, the following work-week, January 14th-18th, Dave was scheduled to take a 'layoff week.' Instead of eliminating jobs after the 2008 economic recession, Caterpillar opted to save jobs with this creative solution. Each employee rotated through a series of unpaid breaks. This affected everyone in all levels and departments. Dave went through three layoff weeks while he fought cancer. Each one turned out to be well-timed.

During Dave's January layoff week, he felt ill. But, I was grateful he didn't have to take time off because I worried it might jeopardize his job. We didn't want his employer to think he was unable to fulfill his job duties. Caterpillar was quite generous with us, and we didn't want to take their kindness for granted.

That week, Dave again dealt with some rough emotions. He asked, "If this is how it's going to be, why would I want to live like this?" I understood he was speaking from his pain because Dave wasn't one to pity himself. I knew he needed to work through his emotions on his own terms, but it was an awful day for me as I considered the alternative! So, I turned on the local Christian radio station, hoping to hear something that would improve his mood—and mine.

I took care of Lydia and washed dishes while Dave mulled things over on the couch. I prayed while I kept an eye on him. I didn't know what else to do. Thankfully, after about five hours of contemplation, prayer, singing, and listening to music, Dave snapped out of his funk and was more cheerful. Finally, he seemed at peace, back to his normal self, even though he didn't feel well physically.

In my online updates, I purposely didn't mention any of the misery of that week. I merely implied that round of chemo had been tough. There were several reasons for my lack of direct communication. First, I wanted to protect Dave's dignity. People had already given us advice on topics like faith and nutrition. I didn't want their opinions on Dave's mental health or emotional state! Also, I respected his right to choose how to live out his life, though I did what I could to buoy him.

Most of the time, I intentionally kept my email and Facebook updates uplifting. I didn't want to drag everyone down with us as Dave always seemed to bounce back. Even when I did share our doubts or other negative aspects of our journey, I always brought it back to the positive. Generally, this might be something we learned or a Bible verse that helped us get through the problem. I did tell our families and close friends more of the details. But, I wanted to spare them the emotional roller coaster we were on.

It's also possible I didn't want to admit how bad it was, seeing Dave's health gradually decline. In hindsight, we might have had an easier time if we had shared a little more of our burdens with those closest to us. But, we rarely had time to process it all ourselves. Dave and I were focused on daily life, not how we felt physically or emotionally. We were in survival mode!

By Sunday, January 20th, Dave finally felt a little better, which was good because, that day, my Uncle Charlie and Aunt Mamie flew in to visit. I had mentioned how relentless the last few weeks had been, and they sprang into action. My parents couldn't come on short notice, but Charlie and Mamie could. It was 50°F when they boarded in Ohio, and it was -30°F when they landed in Fargo! You know someone loves you when they volunteer to go through an eighty-degree temperature drop on your behalf!

Monday, January 21st, was Martin Luther King, Jr. Day, and Dave had the holiday off work. That night, we took Charlie and Mamie to an Italian restaurant for dinner. Happily, we all took leftovers home! The next day, I took Dave for a routine CT scan and chemo. It snowed two inches overnight, and Uncle Charlie graciously shoveled the driveway for us. He and Mamie stayed home with Lydia.

After the CT scan, we saw Dave's oncologist. We hadn't seen him in weeks because of the holidays. Dr. Lloyd decided to postpone chemo for yet another week because Dave had felt so weak and nauseous after the last round. The lab report showed Dave's platelets had not fully recovered, though he felt better than he had all month. With chemo and its effects delayed, Dave eagerly took Uncle Charlie to tour the local air museum.

Later that week, Dave and I went to another appointment with Dr. Lloyd to review his CT scan results. His scan showed a couple of areas to watch, but no evidence of cancer. However, to our surprise, we learned Dave had pneumonia! We were relieved to know his coughing was due to pneumonia and not more cancer. It also made a lot more sense why Dave had felt so bad for three weeks!

Dave also (finally) showed the quarter-sized wound on his abdomen to Dr. Lloyd. He thought it was infected and gave us a prescription. We agreed to continue monitoring it. Then, we celebrated the excellent CT scan results with Charlie and Mamie. It seemed like we might get a reprieve from cancer, after all. We bought Dave a cake, though he was not hungry for it.

We thoroughly enjoyed our visit with Charlie and Mamie. In addition to praying for us and encouraging us, they helped me by watching Lydia when I worked. At night, Charlie, Mamie, and I watched movies or played cards while Dave rested a few feet away on the love seat. Our weather was much more frigid compared to Ohio, though neither of them complained. Their visit was a bright spot after so many troublesome weeks.

Quite often, Dave and I found comfort in praying together. At the start of this cancer journey, perhaps our prayers were more lighthearted. "God, thanks for helping us get through this." But as time went on, our prayers became more urgent. Sometimes, in our exhaustion and emotional trauma, we couldn't think of anything new to pray. Our desperate pleas were usually nothing fancy: "God, please, please heal Dave." As we repeated the same prayers, it sometimes felt like God wasn't listening.

But thankfully, we learned a more effective way to pray using Scripture. This helped with the emotional ups and downs because we learned to pray using terminology from the Bible, which is called the "Sword of the Spirit" (Ephesians 6:17). As Christians, we believe the Bible is the inspired Word of God. Using His own words is essentially speaking the Truth back to Him, agreeing with what He has already said He would do for us.

For instance, Psalm 23 is probably one of the most famous passages in the Bible. Psalm 23:1-2 (NLT) says, "The LORD is my shepherd; I have all that I need. He lets me rest in green meadows; he leads me beside peaceful streams." We would use some or all of those words and personalize them in our prayers. "Jesus, You are our shepherd. In You, we have everything we need. Thanks for letting us rest; help us feel Your peace." The imagery of a peaceful meadow with a small brook nearby was also calming.

Additionally, my sister and I chose to read one chapter of a book and discuss it over the phone for a few minutes each week. I didn't have much personal time, but our mini book club was encouraging and helped us feel even closer. Together we read *Battlefield of the Mind*, by Joyce Meyer. We started it after Dave's second surgery and continued it through the winter. The book was compelling and challenged the way we thought about our circumstances.

As I read, I grew more aware of how much I had let fear control me. I recognized my patterns of worry, doubt, and discouragement. I knew I needed to change my default from fear to faith unless I wanted to stay stuck in the wilderness like the stubborn Israelites after they were freed from Egyptian slavery. It also made me aware of when I wanted to complain and how detrimental it truly was.

On my own, I also read through *The Secret Power of Speaking God's Word*, also by Joyce Meyer. This small book lists topics, such as courage, fear, anxiety, disappointment, stress, trust, wisdom, and the goodness of God. It matches Bible verses with each topic, which makes it easier to pray. It was a helpful resource in times of need.

Joyce Meyer uses the example of David and Goliath found in 1 Samuel 17. Goliath taunted the Israelites and made fun of David (who bravely volunteered to fight the giant). David's reply to Goliath starts in verse 45. "David said to the Philistine, 'You come against me with sword and spear and javelin, but I come against you in the name of the LORD Almighty, the God of the armies of Israel, whom you have defied.'"

I love that verse because I was able to say something similar, like, "Satan, you come at me with x, y, and z, but I come at you with the Word of God." The variables could change depending on the day, but I often looked up the verses for fear and stress. It was quite empowering because it gave me something to focus on instead of staying stuck on the problem.

I'm grateful I found all these tools. Before I did, I was a mess. I would be confident one moment, walking in joy, peace, and thankfulness, and then we would get more bad news, and I would have to deal with that. I didn't always feel capable of expressing my emotions, but I slowly learned how to process them. Our daily experiences were often full of turmoil, making me wonder if my husband would survive. I questioned God's plan for us and hoped He would come through for us and heal Dave.

Then, in early February, we again facilitated the PLACE class on Sundays. The participants were amazed that we were still helping, despite the fact Dave was sick. But we just felt it was the right thing to do—to serve and do our part. Dave and I were only scheduled to teach one week out of six, so we didn't feel the commitment was too much. I found great personal fulfillment in the class, and it didn't feel like a burden. We both looked forward to it!

Nonetheless, as I look back, I can see how much activity I was doing each week. My schedule was full as I bounced between two jobs, but I enjoyed helping others and using my skills. Besides, Dave and I had always set big goals together. My choice to work helped us achieve specific priorities, such as saving for retirement or donating money to our favorite charities. Despite Dave's cancer and the resulting stress, we remained committed to those goals.

For my on-call position at the nursing home, I worked several times a month, usually two or three days in a row, but sometimes a full week. At my clinic job, each week, I was putting on presentations and seeing several patients on the days I worked. Of course, I was still running our household and visiting Dave at the hospital. I also worked on other goals, like my continuing education to retain my licensure as a dietitian.

Professionally, I don't share much about my private life with my patients. But sometimes, a patient asks a relevant question and it is appropriate to answer with personal experience. When Dave was sick, some of my patients were facing similar circumstances and asked me for updates at their appointments. Occasionally, I became teary-eyed and needed to apologize or explain why I was crying. In those cases, the patients would encourage me while I dried my tears and did my best to finish the appointment.

As time went on, Dave slowly grew weaker. His February layoff week included Valentine's Day, so I surprised him with chocolate-covered strawberries. He didn't have much appetite but made room for one of his favorite treats. Otherwise, I kept the house and Lydia quiet so he could rest. When

Dave slept, I found myself memorizing his facial features, his profile, his hands, and his overall form.

I felt compelled to take it all in, as if I might not get another chance. I was growing used to seeing him there on the couch, though it was far from his usual preference. Before cancer, Dave had been very active and hardly sat down at all. Now, he was in discomfort or pain much of the time, and the couch and love seat were the only comfortable places he could rest. Dave disliked being so exhausted. But, there wasn't much either of us could do about it.

One afternoon, Dave was on the couch when I arrived home with Lydia. He was talking excitedly with his supervisor, Paul. I heard Dave say, "Oh, that's amazing. That's wonderful news!" A few minutes later, Dave sighed, and speaking to Paul, said with a smile, "Wow...that makes my whole day better." After he hung up, he told me the good news.

"Paul called because I just received a US patent for one of my designs in Decatur!" I remembered Dave telling me about it years before, but I didn't understand all the engineering terms! He had designed a new way to build the planetary gears in the rear axles of Caterpillar's largest mining trucks. This was projected to save the company millions of dollars and avoided 'failure' in the field (which resulted in better profits, less down time, and increased customer satisfaction).

Dave called my dad right away to share the good news. Dad was very excited and impressed, too, saying, "I'm so proud of you, Son." Indeed, the psychological effect of Dave's accomplishment lasted for many days. All week, he was happy and quietly relished the fantastic news. Getting the patent was the crowning achievement for all his hard work, both in Decatur and West Fargo. If only Dave had lived to receive the award in person!

Chapter 9

"See, God has come to save me. I will trust in him and not be afraid. The Lord God is my strength and my song; he has given me victory."
Isaiah 12:2 NLT

I continued to go to as many doctor appointments with Dave as I could. He was readmitted periodically for IV fluids and pain medication, but I was grateful when he was home.

During the third week of February, we took Lydia with us to see Dr. Callahan, the GI surgeon. The spot on Dave's abdominal incision scar still had not healed, so he biopsied the area. A few days later, we returned to discuss the results. Unfortunately, Dr. Callahan told us that the biopsy revealed more cancer.

"What?! How could there be more cancer?!" I asked. Only three weeks before, we had received a clean PET scan report. We had thought that meant Dave was in the clear!

Dr. Callahan explained, "It might not have shown up on the CT scan in January because it looked like scar tissue."

Dave looked shocked and disappointed but didn't say much.

A few days later, on Friday, February 22nd, Dave was resting on the couch after work when he sat up and abruptly told me, "Natty, I need to get to the hospital right away."

Surprised, I asked from the kitchen, "Okay, but what do you mean?!"

"My stomach doesn't feel right, and I want to be seen. My gut feels like it's twisting on itself again." It felt similar to what had happened before his second surgery in August.

Not wanting to waste time, I called ahead to talk with a nurse. She said to come as soon as possible to the cancer center. Of course, since we were at home, Lydia was with us. We grabbed her and the diaper bag, buckled up, and left the house. I didn't think we had time to stop at daycare, so I called our neighbor, Elissa, to see if she could watch Lydia.

It was already late afternoon, and given Dave's level of discomfort, I thought we might be at the hospital for a while. I was conflicted because Dave wanted relief, but Lydia also had ongoing demands. Elissa didn't answer the phone.

"Let's just take her with us," Dave said. But, I started driving around the block toward Elissa's house. "What are you doing?" Dave asked.

"Let's just run by Elissa's house. If she is home, I know she will take Lydia for me. Then, I can focus on you and not have to hurry back."

A minute later, I rushed up to the door and rang the bell. Elissa greeted me with a big smile, "Hi, Natalie, how are you?!"

Grateful she was home, I said, "I can't stay long; Dave's in the car. I'm taking him to the hospital." I paused. "Could you please watch Lydia for me? I know it is last minute, but I tried to call. I don't want to take her with us because I don't know how long we will be gone."

"Sure! Bring her in! I was doing laundry and didn't hear my phone. My boys are just getting up from their naps, and they will be glad to see her." Relieved, I ran to the car to grab Lydia and her diaper bag.

At the door, Elissa happily took Lydia for me. I started to get emotional, and said, "Thank you. I'm not sure when I will be back, but I will keep you posted."

Elissa gave me an encouraging hug. "No problem! You take care of Dave. We will be fine. And, if needed, Lydia can sleep over here."

Over my shoulder, I called out, "Thanks again, Elissa! You're the best!" Then I ran back to the car and raced across town toward the hospital.

When we arrived at the cancer center, Dave was restless and quite uncomfortable. After some IV fluids, he perked up a bit as usual. But, the on-call doctor decided to admit him for observation, in case he needed something more.

When Dave felt his worst, he understandably didn't want to talk much. He often preferred to lie in his hospital bed and pray the moment would pass. He didn't feel like processing it with me—he just wanted relief! I prayed for him, held his hand, or did whatever he needed at the time. But when I needed more support or encouragement, I called someone in my family or a close friend.

I might call my mom, dad, or sister. If they were unavailable, I would call someone else like Aunt Terry, Aunt Mamie, or Aunt Deb, for encouragement. They prayed for me and helped me see the issue in a new light. Often, they reminded me to keep my focus on Jesus instead of the problem. I was grateful to have such a strong support system!

By this point, it seemed Dave was in and out of the hospital regularly. I was exasperated. Sometimes, I also resented that he was unable to help around the house. It was not Dave's fault, though, and I didn't want to upset him. He certainly would have helped more if he could!

So, that day in the hospital, I went to the waiting room to make a few phone calls and gain some perspective. After I had vented over the phone, I sent an email update to those in our inner circle and posted prayer requests on Facebook. Online, I asked for prayer that Dave's gut would calm down and mentioned the biopsy results were cancerous.

The next day, Dave's gut did settle down. We were both relieved to avoid surgery. Then, I told him how stressed I was, running all over town and trying to do so much. I had shared this with my aunts on the phone the day before, but I hadn't told him since he hadn't felt well then. I had spent several months juggling everything but couldn't do it anymore. We agreed that something needed to change in my schedule.

Dave suggested that I quit one of my jobs. "Are you sure?" I asked, surprised. I had considered resigning months earlier but didn't. Dave had always valued my contribution, so I thought he would want me to keep working.

"Well, yeah," Dave said. "Seeing you all stressed out is stressing me, too! I think it would be easier for both of us if you didn't work so much."

We continued our discussion, and my burden lifted a little. If I had known my stress levels were affecting Dave, I would have quit sooner. I had been trying to maintain so many different areas of life but was quickly burning out. After some thought, I made a decision. I hated to have to choose between two good jobs, but the clinic position was more flexible.

Later, when I resigned at the nursing home, my supervisor, Lisa, was somewhat disappointed to lose a reliable worker, but she was also supportive. I felt terrible about quitting suddenly, knowing it would be challenging to hire and train someone before Lisa's next day off. Thus, I agreed to fulfill my commitment through my scheduled days in March.

My part-time job at the clinic was easier to coordinate because I made my own schedule each week. My goal was to go in two days per week for a few hours each time, but even that became difficult. Yet, it was a blessing to have favor with that company. They paid me even if I was unable to come in on a given week! Essentially, they paid me a 'retainer-fee,' so I was always available but didn't have to go in if I didn't have patients that week.

I was thankful for their generosity and God's provision. I was able to spend more time with Dave, and God still met our financial needs. Looking back, I could not have handled all the stress without His help!

While cancer took much of our attention, Dave and I had to consider other big topics as well. We had met with an attorney in the fall to discuss making a will, in case we were not around to raise Lydia. The uncertainty of cancer prompted us to plan for her future. Once the papers were ready, however, Dave didn't feel up to signing them. For several months, I gently reminded him we needed to make an appointment to sign everything. But, he was always resistant, though it had been his idea to start the process.

Maybe signing the paperwork sounded like a lot of effort when Dave was already exhausted. Or, perhaps it had to do with acknowledging he could die. I'm sure it was a painful realization for him. I tried not to press him, but I wanted the peace of mind having those documents would provide. By the end of February, Dave was spending more time at the hospital and couldn't sign the will, even if he wanted to do so.

Indeed, the winter of 2012-2013 seemed never-ending for many reasons. Fargo is well-known for its brutal winter weather, but we had grown accustomed to the frigid temperatures. We knew to dress warmly and be prepared—for us, winter generally wasn't a big deal. Yet, that year, the temperatures seemed even more extreme. It seemed the snow came more frequently and piled up faster than usual. It might have just been our perception, but everything felt more drastic!

Generally, Dave enjoyed taking charge of all the outside work. He would mow in the summer and clear snow in the winter, and I appreciated everything he did. Dave often went out of his way to help our neighbors, too. But with cancer, he needed some help. Our friends had graciously mowed for us over the summer, which was much appreciated. Then, when winter weather came (in early December), I took on shoveling the snow to let Dave conserve his energy.

We had a snow blower, but it was too big and bulky for me to push effectively. So, whenever it snowed, it took me about forty-five minutes to shovel the entryway, driveway, and sidewalks. When combined with other daily stressors, and even the strain from our fender bender in early December, my upper body was in pain much of the time. The mounting tension in my arms, neck, shoulders, and back paralleled the internal emotional battle I was facing.

I already had my hands full, and now I had more to do! Occasionally, a neighbor would help out with the major drifts, but most of the time, I cleared the snow on my own. In hindsight, we could have hired a snow removal company, but at the time, we were too busy thinking about other things! Besides, our schedule was somewhat erratic, and it would have been tough to wait for someone to dig us out in an emergency.

Also, we were still adjusting to parenthood, which probably looked different with cancer. Our families were undeniably supportive, but they could not come help as much as they would have liked. Sometimes, I envied my friends who had the convenience of family, as they had built-in help with childcare. Though, in reality, living close to relatives does not mean automatic support. Our local friends were quite helpful, but we still did many things on our own.

I had always seen myself as rather stoic, but as life with cancer pressed in, my true nature squeezed out. God used the extreme weather, stress, pain, and the lack of family nearby to refine my character in ways only He could. It seemed God had gone to war against my fear—and I was caught in the middle. The stage was set for a dramatic intervention.

Before cancer, Dave always went above and beyond to help with housework and family life. But now, I struggled with not getting his help.

I felt overwhelmed with all the added responsibilities. In some ways, the increased mental load only added to my emotional burdens. On an average day, after work, getting groceries, and picking up Lydia from daycare, I would make a plan for what to do when we arrived home.

"Alright, I have to get Lydia inside, unload the groceries from the car, and at least put away the frozen items. I'll put Lydia down for a nap in her crib, so she is contained while I quickly walk the dog and get the mail. But first, I'll put on all my outdoor gear (which included a face mask, gloves, different layers, and boots). Then, I should clean up the driveway with the shovel. Next, I'll need to get back inside to check on Lydia and start supper before Dave gets home. Oh! I should throw in a load of laundry, too!"

Some of this scenario is normal for parenthood and marriage. But even with getting up at 4:00 a.m. regularly, I rarely felt like I was able to take a moment and rest. I wish I could say I had a good attitude. However, shoveling snow brought out my worst traits! I was already trying to manage my fear and sadness. Now, I had to deal with anger, bitterness, and resentment, too! I had never been in such an extreme situation, and my negative energy shocked me.

Before cancer, I thought I was good at diffusing adverse emotions. Dave and I usually had minimal conflict in our marriage, and I've always gotten along well with most people. But those quiet early mornings outside gave me time to reflect on our situation. As I considered my ugly emotions, I gained self-understanding. I began to see how much I needed God's grace.

While I naturally tend to avoid confrontation, I realized how often I minimized my feelings. For instance, I brushed off offenses like they didn't hurt. I seldom shared my opinions or spoke up to defend myself. Perhaps I thought it was the Christian thing to do, to not get upset and let things go. But, by not dealing with my emotions, I unknowingly let those wounds fester. And, by consistently ignoring how I felt, I was doing myself a disservice.

Fear had become a subtle stronghold over many years, but everything exploded after Dave grew sick! Cancer threw chaos at me faster than I could deal with it. As this disease unraveled our lives externally, fear and stress undid me from the inside. It was critical to address my ugly emotions before they got the best of me. Life had turned sour, and it was easy to get sucked into the negativity. But I was at risk of poisoning others, too. So, I laid down my self-reliance and let God show me how to make lemonade on His terms.

I didn't understand it fully at the time because I was in so deep. But, by letting God help me, He exposed the root of my fear and doubts. Gradually, I saw that my doubts stemmed from questioning His character and love for me. There was a disconnect between who I believed God was and who He actually is. This misconception was based on my own faulty character.

As I worked through these issues, I could see the magnitude of God's mercy and forgiveness. In time, I discovered His grace is not a matching program, as in equal amounts of grace to cover our sins. No, His mercy and grace are abundant—far more than any of us deserve! Indeed, we can grow through conflicts if we let God use them to change us.

However, on Monday, February 25th, I still had a long way to go in processing all that. Dave was still in the hospital, and I had a million things to do before going to visit him that evening. I wrestled with my attitude as I walked with Britain in the bitter cold. Instead of letting her play in the snow, I forced her to walk faster to the community mailbox, about five houses down the block.

At that moment, my outlook was about as foul as the weather. For many weeks, Dave and I had both sensed God was going to do 'something' in the spring. The feeling was mutual, though hard to define. We frequently asked each other, "What do you think that means?" We had been filled with anticipation as we discussed the possibilities and hoped for a miracle.

Winter, of course, is the dormant season, where life is put on hold. Some things even die. It seemed spring should have been around the corner, but compounding snow storms made it feel like the longest winter of my life. I craved the regeneration of spring.

Yet on that blustery afternoon, I was bundled up in many layers, while Britain and I walked past snow piles higher than my waist. I grumbled under my face mask. The freezing wind howled around me, mockingly. This season seemed so cruel and unfair. Would it never end?! "Grr...I hate this weather!" I blurted out, "I don't think spring is ever going to get here!" Then, I hurriedly finished walking the dog and stomped back inside.

While my angry outburst had not been aimed at God directly, I had, in effect, accused Him of having limited power that day. I thought to myself, "Isn't God aware that we were facing the biggest challenge of our lives? Doesn't He care?!" Yet, I realized later how He was wise and merciful when He offered no defense that day.

Instead, He waited until a few days later when I was calm! Then, God spoke to my heart in a way only He could. I hadn't told anyone about my outburst earlier that week when walking Britain. As I drove along 42nd Avenue, on my way to drop Lydia off at daycare, I was in my thoughts. Suddenly, in my heart, I sensed the voice of the Holy Spirit speak softly to my soul. The tone of His voice was wounded and caught my attention.

He said, "I always bring the spring, and I bring the summer too." Immediately, I was ashamed. In my mind's eye, I could see the pain and sadness I had caused, similar to if I had said something hurtful to Dave. Tears rolled down my face as I drove over a bridge. I recalled the rashness of my anger a few days prior and was upset with myself because I had been reckless with my words.

Still, this moment with God impacted me deeply because I needed to hear from Him in a personal way. I apologized, "Lord, I'm so sorry. Please forgive me. Thank You for being so gracious." I had needed the reminder that not only was He in control of our circumstances, but He was faithful to His Word. Not only did He promise to bring the spring, which was one thing we were hoping and waiting for, but He also had good plans for the summer. (This metaphor brings me hope and comfort even today.)

Dave came home that week, but less than twenty-four hours later, he was back in the hospital. His stays there were growing more prolonged and more frequent. Each week he went in for nausea, dehydration, pain management, and general discomfort. Then, upon each discharge, we were loaded up with a ton of prescriptions. Of course, I was the one who would go to the drugstore, carry Lydia in, and wait for the order to be filled as I thought of all I needed to do when I returned home.

On Friday, March 1st, Dave's oncologist, Dr. Lloyd, stopped by to see him during morning rounds. I was at work and didn't know this conversation was happening. After reviewing his medical information, Dr. Lloyd told Dave his condition was poor. "At best, I give you six months. If you want to try Mayo now, you could. But, it would likely only be experimental drugs at this point. I could help get the process started."

Dr. Lloyd went on to say, "If you were my brother, I would recommend hospice." I imagine this was the most empathy he could offer. To compare Dave to a family member probably meant that Dr. Lloyd cared for him. Yet, he wouldn't allow himself to show emotion.

When I arrived that afternoon, Dave told me what had transpired. "What?!" I cried in disbelief. "How could he have had such an important conversation with you when you were alone?!" I was devastated to think we were now at the point of hospice—no one had ever alluded to that. But, my anger toward Dr. Lloyd brought out a fierceness I can't quite describe.

Perhaps, in my heightened emotional state, I was blowing things a little out of proportion. Dr. Lloyd needed to do his job, which often meant being realistic and bringing bad news. Still, I felt it should have been handled differently. In my opinion, he should have scheduled an appointment with both of us instead of cornering Dave. I was also upset with myself because I had gone to work first instead of the hospital. I needed to fulfill my work obligations, of course, but I was frustrated nonetheless.

Dave seemed fine on the surface, though he was a little quiet. Sitting on the edge of his bed, I grabbed his hand and said gently, "I'm so sorry I wasn't here, Hon. I hate that you had to be alone." I paused, then asked, "How did that news make you feel?"

Dave shrugged his shoulders. "I don't know. I guess I'm just taking it all in." A few moments passed before either of us said anything else.

"Well, what should we do?" I asked quietly. It was not at all the news I had expected to hear that day.

Dave looked me directly in the eyes and said, "I think it would be wise if you learned how to take care of the budget on your own."

I knew it was severe when Dave said I should start taking over the finances. We talked a little longer, at the time choosing not to make any decision about Mayo until we had more information. Then, I needed to say goodbye and head home.

Outside, on my way to the hospital parking lot, I ran into our friends, Pastors David and Ischee, who were coming to visit Dave. I quickly explained to them what Dr. Lloyd had said. They were both as shocked as I was. Ischee hugged me, and then they prayed for me in front of the hospital. We parted ways, and I tried to dry my eyes before picking up Lydia.

Later that week, Dave was still hospitalized when I sat down with the checkbook. Before we were married, I had always been a good steward financially. But, because Dave enjoyed tracking our money habits more than I did, I happily let him! I appreciated that he took care of the budget each month because it was one less task for me. Even so, I was always financially aware month-to-month as we regularly made money decisions together.

A few years before, we had attended a class called Financial Peace University, by Dave Ramsey. Not only did this put us on the same page in our marriage, but it also gave me an understanding of our financial situation. Thanks to Dave White and Dave Ramsey, I knew what to do!

While I had to make some choices on my own, I often took our laptop to the hospital to review the budget with Dave. I asked questions, and he taught me how to use his Excel spreadsheet, where he always tracked our financial information. I'm grateful that Dave empowered me so I could manage our finances on my own. Little did we know how these experiences would pay off.

Chapter 10

"May the God of hope fill you with all joy and peace as you trust in him, so that you may overflow with hope by the power of the Holy Spirit."
Romans 15:13 NIV

On Wednesday, March 6th, Dave was discharged from the hospital once again. Lydia and I picked him up around lunchtime. Before we left, the nurse went over Dave's medication list and various instructions. A few minutes later, a volunteer brought a wheelchair for him. After loading Lydia back into the car, I drove around to the hospital entrance to gather Dave, who waited with the volunteer.

I was hungry, and I was desperate for our situation to feel normal again. Generally, Dave loved to eat out, so I suggested we try out a new car-themed restaurant our friends had mentioned. I hoped the familiar car memorabilia would make Dave happy and perk him up. As we sat down, the chipper waitress told us all about the daily specials, not perceiving anything of our situation. We listened as she talked and then reviewed the menu.

Dave said he wasn't really hungry, but that I could order something if I wanted. He sat there, trying not to look miserable.

"What do you mean, Babe? Aren't you hungry?" I asked.

"No. My stomach still feels full."

I was concerned but didn't fully understand what he was saying. When the waitress returned, I ordered a chicken sandwich and an appetizer in case Dave wanted to try something small. Soon, the food came, but he didn't eat.

"Do you want a cheese stick, Dave?" I hoped something would sound appealing and increase his strength. (If only it were that easy!)

"Natty, I'm sorry I'm not more energetic today. I know you have wanted to try out this place, so I just agreed to come." He paused, "But, I'm not feeling well."

Suddenly, I knew we needed to go home. The food was greasy, and my stomach was starting to feel ill, too. Lydia was getting cranky and needed a nap. What terrible timing!

"That's okay, Dave. I didn't know you felt so bad. I thought this would cheer you up." Then, I quickly found the waitress and paid our bill. She gave us a take-home container, and we went home. I felt let down, but I didn't know how to communicate this to Dave when he already felt so bad. He was exhausted, and I didn't want to burden him further.

Dave and Lydia both fell asleep at home, so I went to Walgreens to fill Dave's anti-nausea prescription. I asked the pharmacist, "Can you please give my husband more than just six pills of Zofran? Otherwise, I have to keep coming back every other day."

She was sympathetic and gently said, "I'm so sorry. But, I can't give you more than your insurance will allow."

I was frustrated but tried to be understanding. It was hard to remember a time before cancer when Dave took no medications. Nonetheless, I wandered around the store while I waited for the prescription. I loaded up the cart with anything which might prove useful in caring for Dave, like small containers to organize his many medications. I threw in other random items, too, such as a small blanket, crossword puzzles, and magazines. When I returned home, he and Lydia were both still asleep.

Later that day, a friend called to ask for help getting his car out of a ditch. Dave always carried tools in his truck, a three-quarter-ton Chevrolet, including a set of chains for inclement weather. I thought it was odd timing, but perhaps he didn't know Dave had just gotten out of the hospital. I would have encouraged my husband to stay home and rest, but he felt compelled to help any way he could. Dave returned home an hour or so later, tired but happy. The fact that he was needed energized him.

Then, after being home only a couple of days, Dave grew even more uncomfortable. He was readmitted to the hospital on Saturday, March 9th, for IV fluids and pain medication. I was running out of ideas to help Dave at home—it unsettled me that nothing seemed to bring him relief. I began wondering, "How am I going to get Dave into the car in an emergency? What would I do with Lydia if Dave became extremely sick in the middle of the night?" Both of them depended on me for help.

Also, I was a little disappointed because we were supposed to teach the

PLACE class at church the following day. We had looked forward to teaching as a couple because it was a way for us to serve together. Instead, we explained we couldn't be there because of Dave's hospitalization. Of course, our friends understood. We later learned that the entire class of about twenty-five people spent a portion of their time praying for us in our absence.

The following work-week—March 11th to 15th—was Dave's third layoff week from Caterpillar. Once again, we were grateful for the timing. Up until this point, Dave had done his best to work as many days as possible each week. Sometimes he was in-and-out, and back again, for chemo or other doctor appointments. While Caterpillar had been understanding so far, Dave and I both felt the options were limited if he could no longer work at the same level.

No one at Caterpillar had said anything about Dave's attendance. His supervisor and the Human Resources (HR) department had been generous with giving him the time off, and we were grateful for their kindness. But, we also knew Dave was paid to work, not to be sick! Reflecting upon this work situation, we thanked God for the layoff week. Simultaneously, I worried Dave might lose his job, which would result in the loss of our health insurance.

Silently, I prayed, "Thank You, Lord, for your provision. Please protect Dave's job." I felt if cancer didn't kill Dave, losing his job might. He loved being an engineer for Caterpillar!!

(NOTE: When I was writing this book, I requested permission to use the Caterpillar name. It was granted on the condition that I added this clarification: "From an HR and company policy standpoint, Dave's position was never at risk. Our intent is not to influence your recollection, but to ensure that the statements on Caterpillar's benefits are factually-based and are the benefits that we continue to offer employees who unfortunately are in the same situation.")

By God's grace, we had not suffered financially because of cancer. We had met our health insurance deductible almost immediately, and the majority of our medical expenses were fully covered. Physician visits, chemotherapy, and medications are quite expensive. From my work experience,

I also know feeding someone through the veins via TPN is costly. Without such comprehensive health insurance, we would have been ruined! We were amazed to see God behind the scenes working it out in our favor.

To not have exorbitant medical bills is mostly unheard of with cancer and other significant illnesses. In fact, when I turned in my resignation at the nursing home, my supervisor, Lisa, had been worried. With compassion, she said, "Natalie, some of us were talking, and we want to throw you a benefit to help with all your medical costs. Would that be okay?"

Shocked, I replied, "Wow, Lisa, that's extremely kind of you. But let me talk with Dave first. I'm not sure what we need." At that moment, I realized how much God had provided for us. I didn't think we needed the money, but I wanted to be sure I wasn't overlooking something.

Besides Dr. Lloyd's initial comment to Dave regarding hospice, no one had brought it up again. At the time, I wasn't thinking about the loss of income or resources that would inevitably occur if Dave died. I could only focus on one day at a time. Later at the hospital, I told Dave what Lisa had suggested. He agreed we were covered financially. I asked for his further input. "So, how should I tell Lisa we don't need a benefit? I don't want to seem ungrateful."

Dave suggested, "Just explain we are doing well, and we don't need a benefit." Lisa was surprised, but also very glad to know we were covered. Yet, being financially stable didn't automatically reduce my stress.

While I had agreed to continue working for Lisa through my previously-scheduled dates in March, she was able to find a replacement for me sooner than expected. She hired a recent graduate, which meant I didn't have to complete my last commitment there (one final week in March). It was just one more example of how we felt God's perfect timing had orchestrated our steps. As Dave grew weaker and was in the hospital more often, I was glad to be able to sit with him and not miss anything.

Nonetheless, by March 14th, I had reached a breaking point. With Lydia at daycare, I went to Barnes & Noble to clear my head and write down my thoughts. Generally, I liked getting work done there because I could focus. I didn't feel the need to do laundry, dishes, or clean the house. Usually, I would sit in the café working on continuing education or other small projects. However, that day, I went to the bookstore to have a little 'come-to-Jesus' meeting. Everything was going downhill fast, and I needed some serious answers.

Dave was in the hospital yet again, and I feared his job might be at risk (though I understand now that it was not). To make matters worse, I was also conflicted about not being involved with PLACE. I had a strong sense I should be involved with the class, but needed to take a step back due to Dave's declining health. It felt like God was asking me to walk away from something when I was so passionate about it.

At the bookstore, I bought a cup of coffee and wrote all my thoughts down on paper to see if I could gain perspective. Spiritually, I felt this was a make-or-break moment. For most of my life, I had consistently prayed and relied on God to help me make wise decisions. But that day was different—I was questioning the concept of God Himself! Was He really as faithful as I had always thought? Or, was it time to go our separate ways? My very foundation felt shaky as I began to weigh all the 'evidence.'

I took a sheet of paper and listed every painful memory or difficult decision I could recall. I have plenty of good memories, but my goal was to see if God had come through for me when I faced other problems. For example, I wrote down how He helped me through a close friend's death years before. I also wrote about how God helped me discern where to attend college; how to pay for school; and whether I should marry Dave. I wrote down every moment or decision, from my earliest memories until Dave and I came to North Dakota. As I reviewed the list, I was in awe.

It was humbling to see God's faithfulness on paper! Surprisingly, I had fully covered one side of the paper with nearly thirty years of memories. I listed examples like how God had provided finances for school through various scholarships, grants, student loans, work-study, *and* another part-time job! I was grateful to see how He had given me close friendships and family, too. As I sipped my coffee, I admitted, "Okay, God. That's pretty good. You have been faithful all these years."

Then, suddenly I sensed the Holy Spirit's command, "Now, write down how I've been faithful to you this year." I hadn't expected His quick response or His direction. It seemed the tables had turned—now it was God's turn to defend Himself! Compelled, I turned the paper over and started listing things chronologically. I wrote for several minutes, wiping away tears as they rolled down my face.

When I finished, I was stunned to see the paper filled with answers to prayer. I could see firsthand how God had been working on my behalf. The first side of the paper covered events from throughout my life, and the other was packed with just those ten months. Wow. Even now, I get goosebumps when I review the paper showing God's lovingkindness to me.

That afternoon, I could feel my faith shift forward as I went to pick up Lydia from daycare. I was exhausted and still didn't have all the answers regarding our cancer journey. However, God had made clear to me His faithfulness, even when I was unsure about my faith in Him. What mercy and grace! I wish I could say that everything was smooth sailing after that. But, at least, it felt like a start spiritually.

A few days later, on Sunday, March 17th, all my emotions came to a head. Dave remained in the hospital, and I was barely holding on from one day to the next. Despite my earlier bookstore experience, I still had considerable doubts. Even though God promises in Hebrews 13:5 to never leave us nor forsake us, we don't always feel His presence. This is normal, but in those moments, our feelings can make it seem like He has abandoned us. And when God is silent, it often feels like He doesn't care.

That morning, I was at home before church trying to gather my thoughts. Dave's health kept getting worse, and it didn't seem like God was listening at all. My prayers seemed to produce the opposite result. Was God even there?

Generally, there are many good reasons why it is important to attend church. Most of all, it is a way to connect with God through worship and hearing His Word. I also enjoy seeing friends, being encouraged, and serving others. However, that morning, I thought about skipping church altogether. If I couldn't find God, why bother?

Walking around my basement, I battled confusion and a bad attitude.

Half-heartedly, I muttered, "Where are You, God?" Then with more emphasis, I blurted out, "Where the Hell are You, God?!" Mercifully, He didn't speak to me in my anger. Yet, immediately, this thought occurred to me: "I don't know where God is—but, I do know where His people are." I repeated that out loud several times, slowly mulling it over.

Suddenly, in that rock-bottom moment, I knew I needed to be at church that day. Even if I had trouble connecting with God, I was confident the people at church could point me to Him. I knew others were getting their prayers answered and thought, "Maybe they can intercede for me or reach Him on my behalf!" Of course, we all have direct access to God through His Son, Jesus Christ, but on that day, I was just happy to be near His people.

That Sunday was a defining point in my life because when I was at my lowest, God showed up, without a doubt, through the people at church. It felt surreal. During each portion of the service, God provided people to minister to me. About every ten feet, people stopped, hugged me, and prayed for me!

Our church has a large sanctuary, and we started the service with worship songs first. On both sides of the altar or stage area, trained volunteers are willing to pray for peoples' needs while everyone else is singing. My heart was heavy, and I couldn't focus on the music. So, I left my pew and walked to the designated area to request prayer. I introduced myself to a married couple, and I gave them a brief recap of Dave's cancer, chemo, and his current status.

"I don't even know what to pray for right now," I said. "I am completely worn out. We need healing and answers. Also, we want to avoid a third surgery, which could be even more damaging." To my surprise, the couple who prayed for me both were cancer survivors. They understood my concerns, and I felt God had put them in my path on purpose. After each laying a hand on my shoulder, they prayed for Dave, and for God to encourage me and strengthen me. I was sad and tearful, but also strangely in awe.

The worship time ended, and then we had a few moments to greet those around us. During this time, I said hello to a group of friends I had met through the PLACE class. "Natalie! How are you doing?" they asked. I burst into tears again but had no words. Immediately, five people laid hands on me and surrounded me with prayer. I barely knew them, yet I was honored they would minister to me in this way.

As the service resumed, I slowly made my way back to my seat. But as the lights went low, I couldn't find where I had been sitting. I walked right passed my row before I realized my mistake. I was confused but quickly became glad when I saw my friends, Ischee and Janet, sitting where I had left my coat and purse. "We just wanted to encourage you, Natalie!"

The fact that I didn't have to sit alone was particularly impactful. Dave had been in the hospital so frequently that I had begun taking Lydia to church on my own. It was a relatively large church, so I didn't recognize everyone sitting around me each week. Therefore, it often felt like I was sitting by myself. God used these dear ladies to combat another emotional experience I had a few Sundays before this one.

On that specific day, I had sat alone in a pew. I tried to concentrate on the songs, but a little voice in my head kept mocking me. It said, "This is just how it's going to be. Yes, this is how it's going to feel when Dave's gone. You're going to be all alone, with no one sitting next to you. You might as well get used to it."

I don't know if this was a spiritual attack from Satan or just my own doubts and fears swirling around. Either way, it upset me so much, though I didn't tell anyone about it when it happened. So when Ischee and Janet sat with me, I felt comforted and relieved. I knew God had spoken directly to my heartache and distress.

At that moment, I started to see a pattern and give God credit whenever something good happened. I was on autopilot, just taking it one minute at a time. But, the credits kept stacking up in God's favor. Interestingly, the sermon series for several weeks had been about being steadfast in our faith and moving forward despite trials. These messages resonated with me, and it seemed God had planned the timing of those words to match what we were going through.

Toward the end of the sermon, my phone rang unexpectedly. It was my dad! My parents would have usually been at their church during this time, so I rushed out thinking it was an emergency. I returned the call, but Dad didn't pick up. (I later learned he didn't mean to call me.) I left a message, and as I put my phone away, I ran into more friends in the hallway.

Dean and Jackie were waiting for the first service to end, so they could go into the sanctuary and attend the second service. They hugged me, saying, "How are you, Nat?" I just started weeping. Just then, Pastor Bob, who had finished preaching, saw me and came over. They all prayed for me on the spot.

As I was picking up Lydia from the Children's Ministry, Ischee stopped to hug me again before we left. The whole morning was incredible, and I felt more connected to God. He had lovingly reached out to me because I hadn't told anyone how I was feeling earlier that morning.

After a quick lunch, I put Lydia down for a nap in her crib and went back downstairs. There, I laid on the floor, face-up, crying, and thinking about all that had happened that day.

"God, I am so sorry for doubting You," I prayed. "Please forgive me and help me trust You more." Soon, I moved to the couch and took a short nap before calling Dave.

Before I fell asleep, I thought, "Wow. Church was awesome. The only thing to add would be if Owen and Krystal came to the hospital to visit and pray for us today. Seeing them would be such an encouragement!"

Later that afternoon, Lydia and I visited Dave. He was weak but happy to see us. Lydia sat next to Dave on the bed while I told him about church. We weren't there long when we heard a knock on the door and in walked Owen and Krystal! It was so refreshing to see them, and I smiled to myself when they said they wanted to pray for us. As our church rallied around us, it took my faith in God to a whole new level.

Earlier in the week, God had proven His faithfulness (on paper). Then, at church, He had confirmed His presence, even if I had not always felt it. That was the final proof that I needed. I decided to let go of my agenda—praying for Dave to be healed—and humbly trust God. I still believed He could heal Dave, but, I didn't attach my faith to the outcome. I was tired of being afraid. Instead, "I trust You, Jesus" became my simple prayer.

Ultimately, I understood God would be faithful to me regardless of whether Dave survived or not. I knew He was with Dave and was helping him, too. I also felt assured He would take care of us—Dave, me, and Lydia—no matter what happened. From that moment forward, I just sought to stay present with God, not try to get ahead of Him, whatever life brought.

Despite my sometimes negative attitude, my fear dissipated as I saw God show up more and more. The worse our outward circumstances became, the more internal peace He brought. It had to be the "peace that passes all understanding" because it certainly didn't make natural sense to have this serenity amid such chaos (Philippians 4:7). Indeed, our situation grew so crazy and so far out of hand that trusting God was the only option we had left!

For many months, I had felt somewhat passive about asking people for even more help. The distance was challenging for our families, so we hadn't depended on that as an option. It seemed God had us in a holding pattern because Dave had done so well for so long. Then, after that momentous morning at church, I felt the time had come to request more help.

I quickly realized I could no longer do everything on my own. So, I started calling people to help with more significant favors. Our friends, Pastors David and Ischee volunteered to keep our dog, Britain, until we could take her back. Some of our other friends volunteered more frequently to watch Lydia while I sat with Dave in the hospital.

Within days, our situation would change for the worse yet again, prompting my parents to come for an extended stay. They were a welcome answer to prayer.

Chapter 11

"God is our refuge and strength, an ever-present help in trouble."
Psalm 46:1 NIV

The next morning, March 18th, Lydia and I went to see Dave in the hospital. On the way there, I heard a song, "God of this City," by the Irish band, Bluetree (sung by Chris Tomlin). The lyrics spoke to my heart, and I began praising God for all He had done. The song filled me with hope that He had better things ahead for us.

Feeling a mixture of emotions, I applied the lyrics to our brief time in Fargo, praying God was not done with us yet. Sobbing in my car, I clung to the truth that He still had a good plan, even when we could not see it. At the time, my heart's cry was to interpret the song in terms of wanting Dave's healing and for him to live, but I have since seen it also as a song about God's faithfulness.

When we arrived at Dave's room, he greeted us cheerfully. I briefly mentioned the song to him, though he had not heard it yet. As we talked, Lydia scouted out his room, happy that she could explore on her own. I kept an eye on her so she wouldn't get close to Dave's medical equipment.

Soon, I noticed a small container of red gelatin from his bedside table. Holding it up, I asked, "Oh, Dave, did you eat some food?"

He hadn't been eating much over the last few weeks.

"Well, I drank a little water, which filled me up, so I saved that for Lydia," he said, nodding toward the gelatin. Dave was proud of himself for drinking the water, and I loved that he had thought of Lydia.

She came over when she heard her name. When I picked her up, she saw the gelatin. At almost sixteen months old, Lydia had never tried it before. She reached for the curious red object, which prompted Dave to sit up and grab it for her.

"Hey, why don't you let her sit with me?" Dave suggested. "She can sit on my lap, and I'll help her with it."

This was a special moment, because Dave was usually too exhausted or

Lydia was too squirmy for them to sit together in his hospital bed. So, I put her in his lap and he fed her. Lydia snuggled right in and ate every last bite.

Of course, Lydia was thrilled at the opportunity to sit with Daddy. We snapped a picture, and it is still one of my favorites of them. I never would have guessed it at the time, but this was the last photo of Dave and Lydia together. I'm grateful we were able to capture such a sweet experience.

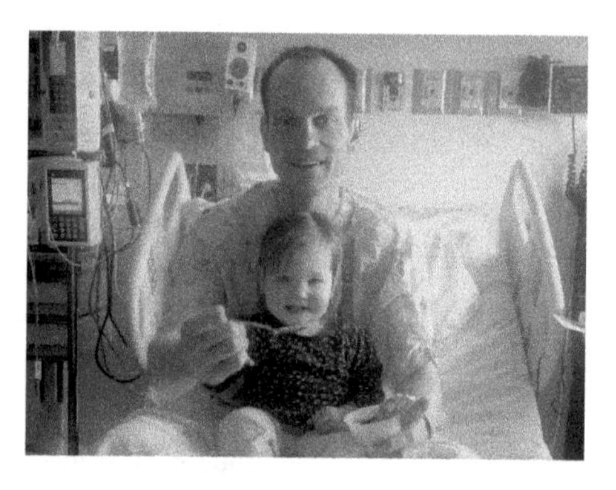

The next day, the nursing staff proposed we begin parenteral nutrition at home since Dave seemed to be stable. He had already been receiving it in the hospital, but going home with it was new. We received thorough training on the home TPN system, however, it was difficult to concentrate because neither of us felt well. Dave was exhausted from another round of chemo, and I was coming down with a cold. After some discussion, we decided to postpone the discharge until the next day.

That afternoon, a pastor from church came to visit, and he told us about some similar experiences in his family. He was also familiar with Mayo Clinic and gave us some tips to consider if we decided to go. It was comforting to meet someone else who understood the ups and downs of our in-and-out-of-the-hospital struggle. After spending several more hours at the hospital, I kissed Dave goodnight and went to pick up Lydia.

That night, Dave's nurse requested stronger pain medication that finally allowed him to rest comfortably. We soon discovered this nurse also went to our church, and Dave was convinced she had prayed for him all through the night. He slept so well and was grateful for the pain relief. Wednesday was a much better day overall, and we were able to complete the home TPN training successfully.

Before Dave was discharged, we started the paperwork to go to Mayo Clinic in Rochester, Minnesota. After Dr. Lloyd's suggestion a few weeks before, we decided to go after all. A new physician working on Dave's case pulled some strings to get us an appointment on April 23rd. It was a month away, and we knew there were no guarantees. At this point, Dave's prognosis was grim, but we hoped he would qualify for an experimental therapy.

When we arrived home from the hospital, I quickly went about setting up the TPN system, trying to remember all I had just learned. My clinical skills served me well, though Dave also coached me through the process from the couch.

"Natty, don't forget the new batteries. That tube goes over here. These bags of solution need to go in the fridge. Oh, get Lydia! She's going for the backpack." It was a lot to manage, but somehow we both caught on pretty quick. The worst part was that Dave had the rest of his chemo treatment and TPN running concurrently.

In the hospital, Dave's TPN pump was set to run over twenty-four hours, but at home, we set the pump for twelve hours at a higher rate so he could be more mobile during the day. At bedtime, it was tricky organizing all of the equipment, bags, and various tubes! Also, the extra fluids meant Dave had to use the bathroom more frequently, so I set my alarm to sound every two hours to be proactive. Soon we got into a rhythm.

At this point, Dave often walked hunched over because his abdomen felt better that way. He wore his chemo bag with its pump and tubing hanging from one shoulder, attached to his port. His TPN backpack and its pump hung on his other side, with the tubing attached to the PICC line in his left arm. It was a challenge to not get everything all tangled up!

Dave was fairly weak and nauseous, so I went ahead of him with a puke bucket. I also helped carry all of his gear, silently praying he wouldn't lose his balance or fall. Coordinating our steps, I moved backward around the side of the bed, out of our bedroom, and across the hall while Dave inched forward.

Thankfully, Lydia was a good sleeper, though, on occasion, she needed me in the middle of the night, too. Dave did the best he could and didn't complain. He seemed surprised I woke up with him each time during the night. Later, he kissed me, and said, "Thank you for your help, Natty. You didn't have to do that, but I really appreciate it."

To me, it was a small thing. I couldn't imagine not helping my husband. He was so brave and had such a positive attitude. "Well, we're a team, and it's no problem at all," I said. "We got the system down pretty well, after about the third time, didn't we?!"

Dave did well with TPN at home. The fluids and nutrition kept him hydrated, which also gave him more energy. He was able to catch up with some work-related duties but didn't go into the office much. Mainly, he checked in with his team and answered questions from the love seat in our living room.

The HR manager, Joe, discussed some options with us. He was kind but understandably needed to do his job. In the end, he suggested that Dave consider going on short-term disability. It would last up to six weeks and provide Dave with his full pay through that time. The offer was generous and allowed him to stay home and rest without penalty. We were grateful. Dave made plans to meet with Joe the next time he was in the office.

My mother-in-law, Cynda, came up to visit the following weekend. Her visit had been planned far in advance, but the timing turned out to be an extra blessing. Dave felt as well as he possibly could. He was in good spirits and glad to be home. It felt like a reprieve. This time was as close to normal as we could expect.

With Cynda there, it was great to have help with Lydia and with household duties again. During that week, Dave caught up on a few small projects. One day, he was downstairs working on the computer. Cynda and I were upstairs with Lydia. He called to me and said, "Natty, can you come down here for a minute?"

Lydia was content to stay with Cynda. As I walked downstairs and into the office, Dave finished working on a document. I noticed the office was messy, in need of cleaning. Dave was usually well-organized and worked hard to keep everything tidy. But now, everything piled up. "Hey, Babe, what are you doing?" I asked.

"I wanted to show this to you," Dave explained. "I put together a password list of all our various accounts. It has our financial information, email addresses, travel (reward) programs, work accounts—pretty much everything I could think of."

Dave had previously mentioned he was making a list and had asked for some of my account information. Yet, I didn't expect it to be so comprehensive! Dave had created a password for the four-page list, so only the two of us could access it. He had included information about each account, websites, and telephone numbers for reference.

"Wow, this is great! Thanks so much for doing this, Hon!" I said, in awe. "I didn't realize we had so many different things that need passwords!"

Dave also had me review how to open the safe and showed me where he had stored some emergency cash and a small amount of money which he had planned to use to restore his red 1965 Chevelle. Dave told me, "I want you to know this is here if you need it."

When he wasn't getting caught up around the house, Dave slept on the love seat or in our bedroom. While he rested, Cynda and I talked about him, our cancer journey, and our faith. We both found it comforting to encourage each other. Because Dave was her firstborn, they shared a special bond. Understandably, Cynda had taken his diagnosis especially hard.

We had an enjoyable week-long visit together, and Dave felt pretty well. Then, on Saturday, March 30th, he started feeling ill again just as Cynda was preparing to return home to Illinois. We discussed our options, and Cynda offered to take Dave to the hospital. It was out of her way, but I'm sure she was glad for extra time with her son.

Given his recent history, we weren't sure what to expect. Dave had been in the hospital for most of March. I knew it didn't bode well for a good outcome. In fact, with this next hospital admission, I had an odd feeling he might not return home, but I tried to shake it off. Of course, I didn't tell anyone else about this because I didn't want to believe it myself! Yet, when Monday, April 1st came, it felt like a cruel joke that Dave was still there.

At this point, the physicians, nurses, and other medical staff were constantly in and out of Dave's hospital room. We hardly had any time to ourselves. We tried to make the best of it, but once again, there was a buildup of gas and waste in Dave's system. He was very uncomfortable and had trouble getting settled in any position.

During this time, Dave responded when someone asked him a question, but he didn't offer much in the way of conversation. When I visited, I told him a little about my work or Lydia, though I didn't want to tax him too much. He preferred the television off in his room, so I quietly read or played games on a small tablet. Occasionally, I would get him a glass of ice chips from the waiting room.

As I sat with Dave during those first days of April, I observed several subtle changes. I noticed he wore his glasses full-time now instead of his contacts. Also, Dave was partially deaf from birth and wore a hearing aid, yet I saw he wasn't wearing it regularly. I noticed when the magazines I had brought didn't get read because they were in the same place I had left them the day before. I also noticed Dave wasn't using his phone as much.

One afternoon, he mentioned that he had read an encouraging email. He hadn't forwarded it to me, so instead of making him explain it to me, I asked to read it on his phone. That's when I saw several unread emails in both his personal and work accounts. Dave was generally very prompt, so this surprised me. It seemed he wasn't getting back to everyone as quickly now.

"Hey, Babe, did you know you have quite a few unread emails? Also, it looks like you missed a call from my dad and some texts."

"Yeah," Dave said softly, with his eyes closed. "I just haven't gotten to them yet."

With a nervous feeling, I recognized similarities between how Dave was before his first, emergency surgery, and now. I saw that he was slowly disconnecting from daily life. At this point, I realized the odds were slim Dave would survive. However, he and I kept talking about healing because we believed anything was possible for God.

Sometimes, I read to Dave from a small book, *Healing Promises*, by Pastor Joseph Prince. Each page contained a brief example where someone in the Bible was healed, with a short devotional afterward. In his book, Joseph Prince points out grace as God's unmerited favor. We can't earn God's favor or healing because His grace is freely offered (Ephesians 2:8-9).

The book was encouraging; however, we didn't see healing, or really, any improvement at all. While I tried to rest in God's grace, I wrestled with feeling like I needed to fast more, pray more, read my Bible more, or do more in general. These are worthwhile spiritual disciplines when done with the right attitude. Yet, I was at a loss because nothing seemed to produce the result we yearned for—Dave's healing. I couldn't figure out how to get it 'right.' Of course, God's grace is not a magical formula, and I could not force Him to do what I wanted!

During those first days of April, I also asked lots of questions of the medical staff, trying to find answers to what was happening to Dave's body. He was not talking much, so I spoke up for him. I asked the nurses and physicians why he was not getting any real relief, why he had not had any bowel movements, and what was being done about it. Often, they just added another medication to combat his symptoms.

For over a month, we had been waiting. Our days at the hospital consisted of checking labs, monitoring pain levels, and adjusting medications. But no real solution or explanation was offered. Online search engines have a place, but I felt it was better to get the majority of our information directly. Unfortunately, we were often left to make our own conclusions.

Finally, on Thursday, April 4th, after I had unsuccessfully tried to find answers to my questions, one of the physicians, another surgeon, decided to send Dave for a CT scan. Dave had been having slight fevers on and off. He was receiving an antibiotic, but no one knew why his temperature kept spiking. The surgeon was concerned Dave was in danger of a perforated bowel. If a rupture occurred, all the toxins that had built up would leak out into his bloodstream and likely cause sepsis (an extreme, often fatal infection).

Shortly before the CT scan, my Uncle Gary called. Earlier that morning, I had called my aunt and uncle to give them an update and ask for prayer. That morning, after speaking with me for a couple of minutes, Aunt Terry said Uncle Gary would want to catch up with us when he got home. When he returned my call that afternoon, I happened to be at the hospital with Dave. Because he would be going down for the CT scan, I let him talk with Uncle Gary first.

I sat gingerly next to Dave on the edge of the bed, listening. As they spoke, I saw his face light up. I couldn't quite hear what Uncle Gary was saying, but it resonated with Dave.

"Yeah...yeah," Dave kept saying, in an excited tone. "Oh, wow. Thank you so much, Uncle Gary. That's just what I needed to hear." He sighed with relief.

In just a few short minutes, I saw joy and peace on Dave's face, where pain and discomfort had been only moments before. I heard him say as if he were repeating Uncle Gary's words, "There's nothing I can do to earn God's grace...that's so great...it's a gift." In awe, I waited. Uncle Gary had to leave but promised he would call back soon. We told him about the CT scan, and he said he'd be praying.

As soon as Dave hung up the phone, I asked what happened because I had never seen him like this before. Dave relayed the conversation. "Uncle Gary just explained that it's not what I do for other people that gives me favor with God. He loves me just because I am Dave, not because I do good things. There's nothing I can do to make God love me more—or less."

Suddenly, I understood a portion of Dave's self-worth had been based on how much he served people. He loved helping people, and people noticed. They often said thanks, but even when they didn't, Dave got satisfaction from his acts of service. When cancer limited what he could do, I just thought he missed being physically active. But, it quickly became clear that his inability to continue serving made him feel less valuable as a person. So when he was sick on the couch or was in the hospital, perhaps he felt he wasn't doing enough to serve others.

I never knew Dave to have self-esteem issues; he always appeared confident. Yet, as he received this revelation about God's grace, he was set free. Dave realized while it is good to serve, we can't earn God's favor. We already have it because of Jesus. I was so appreciative that Uncle Gary took time to explain this to Dave. His call felt like an instrument of God's perfect timing. Once again, He had come through for us.

And, as I discovered what was on Dave's heart, I also decided to stop doing and soak up God's grace. Symbolically, I put away the Joseph Prince book. When I pulled it out weeks later, I read with renewed vision. Instead of trying to get something, such as healing and answered prayers, I read with gratitude.

I hadn't known Dave was struggling before, and I was so thankful he now was at peace. I also understood that even if he didn't beat cancer, God's grace was more than enough. Believe it or not, that meant way more to me than healing. In this instance, I viewed Dave's spiritual condition as more important than his physical state of being sick or well.

Soon, Dave left for his CT scan. Unfortunately, the technicians were unable to complete it that day. Once again, his gut was so full there was no room for the contrast he was supposed to swallow. Less than twenty minutes after going down for the CT scan, Dave was wheeled back to his room. I had planned to eat a late lunch in the cafeteria but hadn't even left the room yet. A few minutes after Dave returned, the surgeon entered his room. What he said next was everything we had wanted to avoid.

He said, "I'm sorry to say this, but we have to go into surgery."

My heart skipped a beat. "What...now?!"

The surgeon nodded. "Yes, now."

I gripped Dave's hand, not wanting to let him go.

"We don't have any time to waste. We have to go in and see what's happening. But without surgery, a bowel perforation seems inevitable. I'll need you to sign some paperwork, and then we'll take Dave down." Dave and I looked at each other, unsure of what to say.

After a slight pause, the surgeon continued, "I have to say… I'm guessing we'll find another blockage and more cancer. It's possible Dave won't come out of surgery alive."

There were many risks associated with having three major surgeries in less than a year.

"Can we have a moment to talk about this?" I begged.

"Yes, but only a couple of minutes. I'll have the nurse bring in the forms before we head downstairs."

The surgeon left, and I sat down on Dave's bed. This could be our last moment together.

"I don't know how we'll make it if you die!" I cried.

Unfazed, Dave spoke gently, "You'll be fine, Hon. You're strong, and you will do a great job with Lydia." That was just like Dave, always thinking of other people.

"Thanks," I said tearfully.

"But I am a little worried about my mom," Dave went on.

"I know," I said. "It would be tough on her, too. You've been an excellent son to her, calling her each week and checking in with her."

Dave looked at me and asked softly, "Will you take over calling her for me?"

I squeezed his hand and said, "Absolutely, yes! Of course, I will." I would have stayed in touch with Cynda anyway, but it brought Dave extra comfort when I confirmed this.

We talked a few more moments before the nurse came in. Beyond my initial shock and hesitation, we never questioned whether to go to surgery. While we would not have chosen it, we knew our options were limited. The situation was risky both ways, surgery or not. At the very least, we might finally get some answers regarding the pressure building up in Dave's gut.

Chapter 12

"But we have this treasure in jars of clay to show that this all-surpassing power is from God and not from us. We are hard pressed on every side, but not crushed; perplexed, but not in despair; persecuted, but not abandoned; struck down, but not destroyed."
2 Corinthians 4:7-9 NIV

As Dave and I waited for him to be taken to surgery, we tried to cram so much into such a short time. We briefly reviewed plans for Lydia, and Dave reminded me of his password list, among other things. Once more, I asked him if he had any funeral preferences. He confirmed his choice for cremation. As we looked over the surgery paperwork, I noticed the mention of a possible colostomy. "Oh, no. Not again!" I thought.

Dave's nurse, an older lady, was compassionate. She gently answered our questions but was mostly quiet as she prepped the hospital bed to go directly to surgery. As the transport team came for Dave, we were both somber. I kissed him and said a tearful goodbye.

"I love you, Dave," I said, not knowing if I would ever see him alive again. I tried to be brave while he was there with me, but I broke down in tears as soon as he was gone. Dave's nurse hugged me and brought me some water to drink. I sat in the room alone for several minutes, stunned and unsure of what to do next.

Soon, I remembered Lydia at the drop-in daycare. I called my friend, Sara, and asked her to stay at our house with Lydia so I could be with Dave. Then, I picked up Lydia at daycare, drove home, and called my parents to give them an update. Mom and Dad started packing right away and made plans to leave before midnight. The twelve-hour trip prevented them from being there during the surgery, but they had already been preparing to come up for an extended period.

The distance had been difficult for them, but instead of coming every month for a few days, they had prepared for a lengthier stay. I also asked my parents to call some of our 'prayer warriors' to let them know Dave was in surgery. I didn't have the time or energy to call everyone or provide an online update, especially with so many unknowns.

Next, I called Cynda. She hadn't even been home a week from her last visit with us. I hated to have to tell her Dave was in surgery again, but I wanted her to know she was welcome. She was glad to hear my parents were on their way and made started making plans to come again. I also notified Paul, Dave's supervisor, of the need to go to surgery.

Then, I gathered a few personal items for the hospital and realized I had unintentionally skipped lunch. I didn't have much appetite, but I made a peanut butter sandwich for later. When Sara arrived, I quickly showed her where everything for Lydia was. She was already familiar with our house since she often came to visit.

"Thanks so much, Sara. I cannot tell you how much I appreciate all your help."

"Lydia and I will have fun," she said, as she hugged me. "I'm happy to help and can spend the night if needed. Is there someone who can sit with you in the waiting room?"

"No, I don't have anyone to sit with me, but that's okay," I replied. "I have peace and know God will take care of me."

I kissed Lydia goodbye and drove back to the hospital. My supernatural sense of calm gave me courage. In part, I kept thinking about Dave's conversation with Uncle Gary. He had finally understood that God's love for him was what gave him value. The peace that had washed over Dave brought me comfort, too.

As I walked into the surgical waiting room, I noticed a handful of other people scattered around the room. I checked in at the receptionist's desk to see if there were any messages for me. By this time, Dave had probably been in surgery for close to an hour. There were no updates.

Around 5:00 p.m., the volunteer receptionist left for the night; her shift was over. I knew from experience to answer the phone when the receptionist was not present. That way, the surgical staff could communicate with us while we waited for updates. I took it upon myself to answer the phone over the next few hours.

One by one, each person in the waiting room got a call to come for his or her loved one. Soon, I was the only one left. I hadn't received any surgery updates. I grew a little worried, not sure if no news was good news. However, during that time, I had a few calls and texts from friends and family. Aunt Mamie and Uncle Charlie called to check in and pray with me. Then, around 9:30 p.m., Dave's surgeon came to find me and give a report.

"Mrs. White, Dave made it through the surgery, and he did as well as could be expected."

"Thank you, Doctor," I said quietly, relieved yet still very cautious.

"We didn't fix everything we wanted to, but we did what we could." With a sigh, he continued, "Dave has cancer all over, little spots peppered throughout his gut. It doesn't look hopeful."

I nodded my head slowly, overcome with sadness. This was not what I wanted to hear.

"The team is going to finish doing what we can in there, but we won't be able to sew him up tonight. There's too much damage and too much risk. We're going to leave his gut open for a couple of days, and then try to close it once the swelling goes down." He answered a few questions before heading back into surgery.

Of course, I had mixed emotions. I was disappointed when the surgeon confirmed Dave had another colostomy (this time a different kind), yet I understood it was needed. The surgeon also cautioned Dave might not make it through the night. At the same time, I also had a sense of peace, knowing God was with me in the situation. I could not predict what would happen, but I knew He was in control.

Once again, I had a calming sense God had prepared me for this moment with my work history. Years before, I had a similar patient whose gut could not be sewn up after an extensive operation. That man had a transparent protective material covering his intestines and other internal organs while his skin, abdominal muscles, and fascia (connective tissue) rested. I didn't ask, but I assumed that's what they did for Dave, too.

I texted Sara a quick update and checked on Lydia (now asleep). Around 10:30 p.m., the phone rang with an update from one of the nurses.

She said, "We are taking Dave to a room in the intensive care unit (ICU). It's going to be a while because we are still stabilizing him, but I wanted to give you an update."

Half an hour later, at 11:00 p.m., the phone rang with more news.

"We are heading to the ICU now, Mrs. White."

"What should I do? Can I come to see him?" I asked. I wasn't sure what the ICU policy was on late-night visitors.

With a soft sigh, the nurse replied, "You know, if I were you, I would consider going home to get some sleep."

I agreed, knowing I needed to keep whatever strength and energy I had.

"I just hate leaving him here by himself."

"Dave won't know you are here. He is sedated on a ventilator. Let us get him through the night, and things might look better tomorrow."

When I heard that, my heart sank; I had not thought about him still being sedated! I had seen many patients on ventilators before—but it was hard to envision my young, strong, and loving husband on one.

I had a lot of questions, but I knew I needed to make a decision. "Okay," I said. "I think I will go home and be back first thing tomorrow."

On the way home, I called to update my parents. They were loading the car and planning to drive through the night.

"We should be on the road within the hour." Dad said, "We hate that you have to go through this alone, but we are on our way!"

"Are you sure you want to drive through the night?" I asked.

"Yes, we would have left sooner, but we had to finish a few last-minute tasks," Mom said, "We love you, and we'll see you around lunchtime tomorrow!"

After I arrived home at 11:30 p.m., I briefly updated Sara, and then she left. I checked on Lydia, before promptly going to bed. Since March, I had been sleeping with my phone next to my bed, just in case. That night, I wanted it to be nearby in case Dave's nurse called. I wasn't sure what the morning would bring.

The next morning, on Friday, my alarm went off, and I woke up to the stillness of my dark bedroom. I opened my eyes and pondered what the day might hold. It was so quiet without Dave. Suddenly, I remembered the events of the night before. As I assessed the day, I knew I needed to stay focused on the Lord.

I read my *Jesus Calling* devotional, and also looked up the corresponding Bible verses. Verses in Isaiah and 2 Corinthians talked about how we are vessels designed to display God's glory. I realized our weaknesses, like little cracks, are opportunities for God's power to shine in our lives. These verses brought me comfort and strength. It was just what I needed.

Soon, I felt at peace and knew there was nothing else I could do except bravely face the day. After I checked on Lydia, who was asleep in her crib, I called the nurses' station at the hospital for an update. Dave's nurse told me he remained sedated, but he was stable. Grateful, I wrote down his room number and the ICU visiting hours. Then, I showered and got myself ready to face the day.

Around 8:00 a.m., I dropped Lydia off with Jackie, who graciously offered to watch her for me. Once again, I was torn between Dave and Lydia, but I knew Dave needed me most. With a hug, Jackie said, "Oh, leave her here with me, Nat. We're praying for you!" Even now, I can't fully express how grateful I was for her consistent help. She was such a blessing to me!

On the way to the hospital, I grew nervous about seeing Dave while he was on the ventilator. After I parked, I made my way inside. I had been to many critical care units through my professional work experiences. Still, it turns personal when you are visiting a loved one—especially a spouse—in uncertain times. I had never been to this ICU before and did not feel prepared for what I might find!

By the time I stepped off the elevator, I was nearly in tears. I might have appeared calm, but inside I was almost sick to my stomach. I was anxious, and I hadn't seen Dave since kissing him goodbye the day before. Trying to contain my feelings, I focused on my surroundings.

On my left were the doors of the ICU separating it from the rest of the floor. On my right, there were two small waiting rooms across the hall from each other. There was a bathroom nearby and multiple patient rooms down the rest of the hall. Mustering my courage, I turned left.

As I pushed through the ICU doors, I noticed the nurses' station was in the middle, with several individual patient rooms surrounding it, making a square. I quickly looked for someone to point me to Dave's nurse or his room. As I walked to the nurses' station, I noticed another dietitian named Ava. I was surprised because I hadn't realized she worked in critical care.

Just one year before, Ava had served with me on the local dietetic board as we planned a state convention. Shortly after that, Dave had come home sick. Had it really been almost a year since this chaos started?

I walked over to say hello to Ava, who was sitting and working on a computer. When she saw me, she said, "Oh, Natalie! How are you doing?"

Immediately, tears started flowing. Then, Ava jumped up, came around her work station, and wrapped her arms around me in a tight embrace. I started shaking, feeling relieved to be able to cry on her shoulder. Her compassion struck me, as I didn't know her that well.

Indeed, it truly felt as if Jesus Himself was hugging me. I could envision His arms around me, pulling me close, like never before. Then, after I calmed down a few moments later, I asked about Dave's nurse. Ava pointed her out, but she was busy in another patient room.

"I was just reviewing Dave's chart before I go check on him. Do you want to go in there with me?" Ava asked. Especially in critical care, nutrition plays a vital role.

"Oh, yes, thank you. That would be great," I replied, instantly relieved to know Dave was in good hands. Also, I was grateful God had provided a friend, so I didn't have to go alone.

Ava led the way to Dave's private room and walked around his bed on the far wall. I was somewhat hesitant but just took it one moment at a time. Ava checked on the TPN rate, which had been restarted after surgery. Then, she gave me an overview of Dave's medical and nutritional status. I asked a few questions and took it all in. Ava was patient and respectful, understanding how difficult it was for me.

It's hard to describe how Dave looked. He certainly didn't look like himself with his breathing tube and equipment all over his body. His six-foot-two frame seemed extra-long on the bed. I stood on Dave's right side and spoke to him softly, letting him know I was there, but I was unsure if he could hear me. I touched his right arm delicately but didn't want to cause him any more pain or sensation.

After a few minutes, Ava needed to get back to work. She asked if I wanted to go to the waiting room down the hall. I agreed. In hindsight, I could have probably found a chair and stayed with Dave in his room. However, I knew he needed to rest, and the thought didn't occur to me then. At that point, I didn't have an agenda; I was just going with the flow. I knew I could not handle this trauma on my own, so I was trying to stay in tune with Jesus for support.

Ava pointed me in the right direction, and I went to sit down. I texted Jackie an update before checking in with my parents, who were still on the road. Then, I observed the other people waiting, too, though I didn't talk to anyone. What would I even say? I felt a little numb, unsure of what to do with myself. Mainly, I spent time silently praying and listening for any internal cue or word from the Lord.

I checked my phone and Dave's phone for incoming messages. At about 9:30 a.m., Dave's phone rang. "Hello?"

"Hi Natalie, it's Joe."

As soon as I heard Joe's voice, I remembered he wanted to meet with us. Dave had recently agreed to go on short-term disability, but he had not been able to sign the paperwork before his emergency surgery. Joe was following up with me so I could proxy-sign the documents. We decided to meet in the hospital lobby, within the hour.

I could use a change of scenery, so I decided to take a walk and wait in the lobby. I wanted to make it easy for Joe, but I also didn't want him to see Dave on the ventilator. As I made my way downstairs a few minutes later, I reviewed how we got to this point. A couple of weeks before, Caterpillar had requested Dave's oncologist, Dr. Lloyd, fill out documentation about his long-term prognosis. They wanted his professional opinion regarding the likelihood of Dave returning to work.

I didn't know it then, but Dr. Lloyd had given Dave six months or less to live, saying he would not recover or return to work. (I had requested an extra copy of that paperwork but couldn't bring myself to read it until months later.)

When Joe approached Dave about short-term disability, we didn't know what Dr. Lloyd's note had said. I only assumed Joe was handling Dave's case according to protocol. When Dave and I had discussed the information, we felt it was the best option. He could take time off without penalty for up to six weeks. After that, I wasn't sure what would happen.

So, as I sat in the lobby, waiting for Joe, I prayed for wisdom. "God, show me what to do, and please guide our conversation." A few minutes later, Uncle Gary called me back from the day before. I explained I couldn't talk long because I was meeting with Joe. I also thanked him for what he had shared with Dave about God's grace the day before.

Uncle Gary encouraged me with some Scripture verses and prayed for me. It was perfect timing. He finished praying, just before Joe arrived with another man, who was the plant manager.

My heart pounded, and my stomach churned, as I saw the two men from Caterpillar. It was surreal filling out the short-term disability paperwork while Dave was sedated and unaware. I felt timid but tried to smile and hold my head high. These men were extremely kind and spoke well of Dave. They were more concerned with how we were than with the forms.

"How are you doing, Natalie?" Joe asked. "Do you need anyone to help around the house?" At the time, Joe lived down the street from us and had helped clear snow once or twice after a blizzard.

"Thanks, but I think the house will be okay." I went on, "My parents are coming today." I also explained that Dave might need more surgery.

"Well, we're all praying for Dave and hope he pulls through." Joe continued, "If there is anything you need, please don't hesitate to ask."

"Thanks, Joe," I replied, with tears welling up in my eyes again.

I didn't want to admit to them how bad off Dave actually was. Though in hindsight, they had probably already read the poor prognosis from Dr. Lloyd. At the time, I wanted to protect Dave's job. I now understand, per Caterpillar HR's previous statement, his employment was never at risk. Still, I was growing more cautious about sharing information and updates in general.

Ironically, the previous year, Dave had earned a rating of '1' on his performance review for Caterpillar (the highest, on a scale of 1-5) based on several factors. It came with a good bonus and made his supervisor, Paul, very proud. And now, here we were with Dave on life support. It was hard to believe the contrast. When he was sick, Paul, Joe, and others were kind to give us the benefit of the doubt based on Dave's work ethic and character. We also knew God was gracious to provide for us despite our calamity.

After meeting with Joe, it seemed time stood still. My parents, Tom and Debbie, arrived in town around noon. I gave them directions to the hospital over the phone, and they met me in the lobby a few minutes later. They hugged me tightly, and I felt peaceful again, as if everything would be okay with them present. I hated that they had to come under such dire circumstances, but I knew they wouldn't want to be anywhere else.

Soon, Mom and Dad walked with me into Dave's ICU room. I'm sure it was tough on them to see him on the ventilator because they loved him like another son. On our way to the waiting area, our friend, Pastor David, stepped off the elevator and joined us. The larger waiting room had more chairs and windows, but we chose the smaller room across the hall because it was empty. This room had a couch, two chairs, and a lamp, it was a little dim, but for some reason, it was comforting to me.

It just so happened that day, April 5th, was my parents' 38th wedding anniversary and Pastor David's birthday. I was honored they all would spend time with me in the hospital, especially when they'd typically be celebrating. As we all caught up, we told funny "Dave stories" to pass the time. In my family, that's what we do. The mood was both sad and sweet; we faced uncertainty, but we trusted God with the outcome.

As the four of us sat in a little circle, I shared a Bible verse I had read that morning. I mentioned 2 Corinthians 4:6-9 (NIV), which says: "For God, who said, 'Let light shine out of darkness,' made his light shine in our hearts to give us the light of the knowledge of God's glory displayed in the face of Christ. But we have this treasure in jars of clay to show that this all-surpassing power is from God and not from us. We are hard pressed on every side, but not crushed; perplexed, but not in despair; persecuted, but not abandoned; struck down, but not destroyed."

I also recalled that Jeremiah 18:6 states God is like a potter, and we are the clay. These two verses converged in my mind, and I had the sense that God was doing something significant in me. "I've been thinking today how I am like a clay vessel," I explained, full of emotion. "And I want God to use me for His glory." I shared my awareness that people would be watching my reaction in the coming days, regardless of what happened. Those verses felt like a rallying cry calling me to a new level of steadfastness and grit.

I knew God could work through my brokenness, and I resolved to let Him use me in whatever way He determined. Whether Dave lived or died, I wanted to let God's light shine through my weaknesses. This experience seemed like our worst trial yet, but despite the pain I was feeling, I knew other people were fighting their own battles.

For whatever reason, it seemed people had been taking their cues from us over the last year. How we handled our challenges gave them the courage to stand firm in their own trials. No one knew the depth of my struggle with doubt and fear, but we had tried to point them to God instead of ourselves. Even with Dave in the ICU, I didn't want to wallow in self-pity or cause anyone to falter in their faith.

Dave and I had felt God was carrying us through, and so I chose to keep persevering. We would never have chosen this path or platform, but now I resolved not to waste the opportunity to be a godly example. Of note, at this point, I no longer fought with doubt. It was as if I was running the race of faith for both of us (Hebrews 12:1).

I still didn't know what would happen—and I hoped Dave would make it—but I was relying on God's sovereign plan. He would get the glory from our story, as we turned to Him in our darkest hour.

Later, I picked up Lydia from Jackie's house. Mom watched her for the next several days while I spent most of my time at the hospital with Dave and Dad. It was a lot to ask, but I was grateful for my mom's help so I could focus on my dear husband! He needed all the support he could get.

Chapter 13

"The Lord will fight for you; you need only to be still."
Exodus 14:14 NIV

On Saturday, April 6th, Dad and I went to the hospital again. Dave remained on the ventilator without much visible change, but the surgeons were happy to see reduced swelling. We spoke with another surgeon about the next procedure he needed. Dave's nurse said she was one of the best, and I found her to be rather direct but kind and genuine. Because Dave was unable to speak for himself, this surgeon asked for my input. I was thankful Dad came, too.

The surgeon led us to a dimly-lit consulting room, only big enough for our three chairs and a side table with a small lamp. The surgeon began compassionately, "I know this is the worst feeling, and it doesn't look good. However, Dave has been stable for the last two days. He is young, and he appears strong."

These were good signs, and I started to feel a little more hopeful.

"I want you to know we are doing what we can to help Dave and make him comfortable. I have reviewed his surgical records, and it appears we have two options." The surgeon went on.

"Dave's insides are in bad shape. His intestines are speckled with cancer, and there is a lot of scar tissue from his previous surgeries. I don't have much tissue to work with, in sewing his abdomen back together," she explained. "So, you decide. Do you want me to try and sew the fascia together, or just the external skin layer?"

The first option would take longer and be more extensive. It was risky and could result in Dave's death. The second option—sewing together the bare minimum—would at least create a semblance of normalcy. However, I wondered if Dave would be able to function well if his abdominal muscles weren't intact.

"What do you think, Dad?" I have always leaned on my dad's calm strength, wisdom, and overall steadiness. Together, we asked questions and discerned between the two options. We considered different scenarios and what Dave would want. He was always so active that it seemed not having his muscles fully intact would be a hindrance. Without the surgeon pulling together the fascia, Dave would have limited mobility in his core.

I also thought, if the situation were flipped, I would want him to do everything in his power to help me live the best life I could. In the end, I decided to have the surgeon sew up both layers of Dave's abdomen so his muscles could function fully.

"I want you to do everything you can to help him have a normal life if he comes out of this," I said firmly. Even though his condition was severe, I didn't lose hope. I had left the outcome in God's hands, regardless of what happened, but I was still Dave's advocate. We scheduled the operation for the following day.

During these few days, I wrestled with many 'what ifs' about the future. I faced many fears, especially about being a widow and a single parent. I also had to make many decisions on Dave's behalf. I needed time to process my feelings, but it was difficult for me to do this alone. I appreciated my parents acting as a sounding board and helping contain my wild emotions.

Mom also took it upon herself to make meals and complete household tasks, like dishes and laundry. In some ways, she was doing double duty because she was taking care of both me and Lydia. As such, Mom didn't come to the hospital every single day, though she came as often as she could. Instead, she prayed for Dave while she cared for Lydia, cooked meals, and managed the house. Having her oversee these daily needs was such a blessing.

All of my energy was going toward Dave, though Lydia needed me, too. I tried to spend time with her every evening, but by that time, I was spent. Often, I would get up early, get myself ready, check on Lydia (still asleep), discuss options for the day with Mom, and then leave for the hospital. It wasn't ideal, but it was necessary. I knew Lydia would be okay in the short-term with all the attention she was getting; my main focus at the time was Dave.

Cynda arrived that Saturday afternoon. Because my parents were sleeping in the guest room, she decided to stay in a nearby hotel. The next day, on

Sunday, Mom stayed home with Lydia, while Dad and I drove to the hospital together. Cynda joined us in the surgical waiting room. It was my fourth time there in less than a year. This operation didn't take long by comparison to the others—at most, perhaps a couple of hours. Afterward, the surgeon came out to talk with us.

"Well, Dave made it through the surgery. I did what I could. But, you know, there is cancer everywhere. Therefore, the outcome will be limited at best." The report was grim, and she didn't expect Dave to last long. She continued, "I give him two days to live. If I were you, I would call the family in to say goodbye." We sat there in shock. I didn't know what to think.

But after the surgeon left, the three of us discussed a plan to call our loved ones. In the meantime, before they all arrived, Dave remained in the ICU. He was weaned off the ventilator that afternoon, though he still needed oxygen. Dave was sleepy due to all the pain medication in his system, but I was surprised at how active his body was! A few times, he moved his arms and legs as if he was trying to get out of bed. Dave kept his eyes shut and didn't speak, yet he moved around so much I thought he would start pulling at his surgical wounds.

Whenever he moved too much, I tried to calm him down. "Dave, I'm here. You need to be still and rest. You've had surgery, and you need to take it easy." Then, his body would relax, and he might sleep again.

Dave had several local visitors and a plethora of medical staff coming in at all times. That extra level of monitoring is crucial in critical care; however, we had very little private time together, just the two of us. As he became more aware, the physicians and nurses told Dave all that had happened over the previous few days. Of course, it was his right to know the details, but I was concerned he would be discouraged by the poor report.

So, I tried to limit his exposure to the negative feedback by asking the physicians to let him rest. I hoped they would talk with me instead so that I could filter the information into smaller, more manageable chunks. I soon grew irritated because no one seemed to understand my desire not to burden Dave with such grave information.

After the nursing shift change that Sunday, I started to realize Dave's care plan was not overly aggressive. Everyone provided thorough care, of course, but it seemed like they were only taking comfort measures instead of planning other options. No one communicated with us directly, but I deducted the only plan was to send Dave home to die. I felt a growing sense of unease.

I woke up on Monday, knowing I had to make some more tough decisions about Dave's care. Dad and I arrived at the hospital, yet, once again, we were unable to talk much with him. I had a sinking feeling in the pit of my stomach. I needed to discuss something with Dave but didn't know how or when. We hardly had any time alone to reconnect, pray, or confer.

As I prayed about what to do, I asked, "Dad, can I talk to you about something? I need your advice." I had been wrestling with my thoughts and feelings for a couple of days and hoped maybe Dad could help. I could have also discussed this with Cynda or my mom, but they weren't there at the time.

Sensing my concern, Dad said, "Sure, let's go get some coffee."

Walking out of the ICU, we came upon the elevators. Dad suggested we go to the small waiting room again. There was a coffee machine, and we could be close by if the nurses needed us. To me, it was dark and cozy. Since we were the only ones there, we had privacy, which made me comfortable. Dad poured each of us a cup of coffee, and we sat down near the only window in the room. He used my family nickname, and said, "So tell me what's on your mind, Mim."

I took a deep breath. "I'm thinking about all the possibilities...like if Dave doesn't make it. I'm considering what I would need and what I would do. If he dies, Lydia and I will still be here. And if that happens, like the doctors are sure it will, I feel the need to protect our hearts right now."

My dad nodded his head slowly, as if trying to understand my point.

I explained, "You see, when we moved here, we didn't know what to expect. Being so far from family, we built our house to be a sanctuary, a refuge of sorts. If we had a bad day or the winter weather was unbearable, at least we could come home to a comfortable house."

I paused briefly. "If Dave dies, I will need that refuge and protection. I will need our home to be a safe place for Lydia and me."

Dad was listening. "Mmhmm. Go on."

"This is what I am struggling with: I can't have Dave coming home to die." I was relieved to acknowledge this difficult decision out loud. At the same time, I felt like a horrible wife. What kind of wife would say she didn't want her husband coming home? But I knew my limitations, emotionally and physically.

I didn't want any negative energy or emotions in our home. I also knew I could not care for Dave as well the nurses in the hospital could. I already had my hands full with Lydia. During the first two surgeries, Lydia wasn't mobile. Now, at sixteen months, she was walking all over. She was in full-on exploration mode, and she required even more attention and redirection!

"I don't know if Dave will understand," I continued. "I don't want to hurt his feelings, but I need to guard my heart, too. I need to have good memories of Dave at home, so it's a happy place for Lydia and me. Also, I think he will get better care here in the hospital."

All year I had been conflicted between meeting Lydia's needs and Dave's. I couldn't help both of them at the same time. If Dave came home and Lydia accidentally got into his medication or otherwise got hurt, he might have to wait for me to help him (or vice versa).

Discussing this with my dad helped me voice my thoughts and validate that it was okay to feel this way. He encouraged me to be honest with Dave. He also agreed with my logic that it would be nearly impossible to care for him on my own.

On our way back to see Dave, the elevator opened. As Cynda stepped into the hall, we paused so I could explain my preferences to her. Thankfully, she agreed with me. She said, "Yes, I understand. I think that's a smart decision."

Gently hugging her, I said, "I appreciate your support, Cynda. This is really hard for me; I can only imagine how it is for you."

As we drew closer to Dave's room, we saw that his nurse was still working. I told her we'd go downstairs for lunch and be back soon. We walked down to the cafeteria and bought some food. I didn't have much appetite, but I attempted to eat something small.

Suddenly, I felt a strong urge to go up ahead of them to see Dave. I had only been gone for about twenty minutes but felt the need to hurry. When I walked in, I was surprised to see several doctors surrounding Dave's bed and discussing hospice with him! What's more, I was shocked to hear him agreeing with them! I was distraught for several reasons.

First, Dave and I had never discussed hospice as a real option; no one had ever brought it up to us after Dr. Lloyd first mentioned it over a month before. Second, the medical staff discussed hospice with Dave when he was alone (again!!). I felt they intentionally excluded me from the discussion when we preferred making big decisions together as a team. And third, I didn't believe Dave was coherent enough to make a life-or-death decision like that on his own.

Dave was easy-going by nature, and he had virtually no medical knowledge before he became sick. So, when he agreed to go on hospice, perhaps he accepted it as the only option presented. As I stood by Dave's bed, I thought, "Is he going to abandon us? What about our family and our marriage? I know I can't make Dave fight for his life if he doesn't want to. But what are we going to do? I'm not ready to say goodbye!" I was crushed.

While I was upset with the physicians, I didn't address the issues at that time. I was not sure how to handle the situation, and Dave was my priority. Yet, in my opinion, this was a major mistake on their part. In all of my years as a professional, I had never come across this situation.

A patient should never be isolated when faced with such dire decisions. If they had included both of us in the conversation, perhaps hospice would have been acceptable. Instead, they left me completely out-of-the-loop, which only made me wary and defensive.

The medical staff had never given us much reason to hope, but Dave had received adequate medical care overall. Still, I grew apprehensive after the physicians cornered him without my presence or knowledge. Suddenly, I felt the need to protect him. The seeds of distrust were planted, and I no longer felt comfortable leaving Dave by himself.

Within a few minutes, Cynda and my dad returned from eating lunch downstairs. I filled them in, saying, "Dave decided he wants to go on hospice." I didn't tell them I felt he was coerced into it!

Then, Cynda, who is a strong and bold woman, challenged her son as only a mother can do! Knowing we had been relying on God for direction, she came at it from that angle.

Cynda cut directly to the point, "Well, David, what is God telling you?"

Dave weakly replied, "God's telling me that it's better for my family if I'm not here."

I couldn't believe my ears! I was already on edge, but that comment pushed me over. Maybe Dave had peace about dying, but I felt we had to leave it in God's hands. He couldn't just give up that easily! So I did the best thing I could think of—I yelled at him!

Without a second thought, I said, "I love you, Dave, but what you're hearing is a lie!"

My voice grew even louder. "God does not tear apart families! He puts together families, just like He did with us! God does not give up on us! He is for us and not against us!"

I continued, "Satan is a thief and a liar! He only comes to steal, kill, and destroy! But Jesus came to give us abundant life. He saves, restores, and heals!"

As I continued, more and more passion poured out.

I said, "If God decides to take you, that's on Him! We won't argue with or be mad at Him! But, we're not giving up on you, so don't you give up on us! You fight for your life and do not give up!"

Catching my breath, I went on with more compassion, "I understand that you're in pain, Dave. That's normal, and you've been through so much! No one would deny there's a lot that needs to be healed. The doctors keep telling you that you have two days because they are expecting you to get an infection. But you don't have an infection! Every time you spike a fever, we pray, and it goes down. So, you need to keep fighting!"

I continued, "You are on a lot of medicine, and that may be affecting your thoughts. But, when you think about giving up, you think of that precious little girl of yours." Suddenly, tears poured out as I said, "Lydia deserves to have a dad, and if you die, I will have to give her an answer someday as to why you're not here. And, I want to be able to tell her that you did everything you could to be with her."

I knew I had to say some of these things because, to me, it was a matter of Life or Death. I didn't want to lose respect for Dave because he gave up. I also wanted Lydia to have closure and know she was loved. I wanted her to be able to honor her father and appreciate his legacy.

Thankfully, Dave came around quickly and agreed. "Oh, you're right, you're right. I'm sorry, Hon. I'm sorry for almost giving up. I do want to fight it out."

"That's okay," I told him, grabbing his hand. "I'm not mad at you really, just mad at the lie you believed."

Even now, I have no doubt Dave would have died within two days with an infection if his mindset hadn't changed. As it were, only a few minutes had passed, but the doctors had already had his code status changed in his medical chart. That angered me, too, which only made me more determined to protect Dave.

I could envision something happening to him in the middle of the night while I was at home—Dave wouldn't have had a chance before they let him go! So, I made them reverse it because, at least then, they'd give me the heads-up.

I was adamant. "I want you to change him back to being full-code. We have not agreed upon the 'do not resuscitate' (DNR) status. You should have never let him make this decision without me!"

The staff was surprised, but they did as I asked. Not wanting to rely on their follow-through, I asked his nurse to show me the written record after it was complete.

Rejecting hospice and the DNR status was a very personal decision. I know many compassionate hospice nurses, and they do an excellent job caring for their patients. Hospice is an appropriate option for many people, but for us, it felt like giving up. Spiritually, I felt called to stand our ground, to not give up any territory. Cancer was an attack on our family, and hospice felt like defeat.

On the other hand, in college, I completed a rotation with hospice and loved it. Contrary to my reaction in the ICU, I do believe people have the right to die on their terms, if at all possible. And, if I had not been able to change Dave's mind, I would have gone with his wishes and honored his choice. But first, I needed to remind him of what was at stake—the future of our family.

So, by yelling at him, I questioned Dave and confronted what I felt was a lie. I advocated for him when it seemed the medical staff was ready to write him off. As it was, Dave's nurse went to get other members of her team during my speech. They overheard me yelling and were moved to tears, saying it was the most touching thing they had ever heard!

When I finally got to speak with Dave alone, perhaps a half-hour later, the medical staff still had no plan regarding what to do with him. They were sure he would die within two days; therefore, they were not considering any longer-term goals or plans. I wanted to be upfront with Dave and discuss what we might want or need before something was decided for us. So, I took the opportunity to explain my concerns with him coming home.

Standing by his bed, I said, "Dave, I have something else to tell you. I did not tell you this before because you were on the ventilator, and then we've had hardly any time to ourselves."

"Okay, what is it?" Dave asked calmly.

"You know how we built our house to be a refuge in case things turned out different than expected here. Well, we certainly didn't plan for you to get sick; and if you die, I am going to need our home to be a safe place."

Bravely, I went on. It was now or never!

"I would have to do most of the work of caring for you myself, but I can't provide the same level of care as the nurses. Now, you have more wounds, tubes, and medications with very little strength to help me. Plus, our insurance won't cover as much Home Health services as you'll need."

I continued, "I am already maxed out at home, taking care of Lydia, the dog, housework, snow, and bills. Lydia requires a lot of hands-on attention, and I'm worried she'd get into all your medical equipment."

I knew, in my heart, Dave needed to stay in the hospital. If he ended up dying, it needed to be away from our personal space so that I could move forward in peace. I didn't want to be reminded every single day of his death.

Tearfully, I explained, "This is hard for me. I'm so sorry, Dave, but for my sake, you just can't come home. I don't want you to die there."

Dave was quick to respond. "Oh yes, I agree," he affirmed, wholeheartedly. "I don't want to cause you any extra pain. And, you are right about Lydia. I don't want her to get hurt. You've already had to stop her several times from pushing the buttons on my bed and morphine pump! I'm happy to stay here, as long as you are with me," he confirmed.

I was relieved that Dave took it so well. After that, we explained our reasoning to the staff. Then, they switched gears and were more supportive. With Dave's renewed desire to fight for his life, his physical health also changed. Almost immediately, he no longer needed oxygen and came off some medications. Being too good for ICU, that same day, he was transferred back to the oncology floor.

Interestingly, everyone noted how good Dave looked. He had been so pale and weak in critical care, but the minute he moved out of the ICU, even on the elevator, his strength improved dramatically! His color returned from extra pale to normal. Dave's energy and mood improved, as well as his grasp on his condition. It was a night and day difference, one I would not have believed if I hadn't seen the change with my own eyes!

By Monday night, our family started trickling in, and we appreciated having their support. I am sure their presence and encouragement gained us several days, which then turned into weeks. Contrary to the doctors' predictions, Dave didn't die within two days, but grew stronger!

Dave's sister, Brooke, had dropped everything to fly in from Florida. His brother, Kevin, and his Aunt Beth (Cynda's sister) drove through the night to reach Fargo by mid-morning. My siblings came as soon as they could. Charlie and Mamie flew in from Ohio, and Dave's dad also flew in for a few days. With my parents in our guest room, my siblings camped out on couches or air mattresses in the basement. Dave's family, and Charlie and Mamie, stayed in hotels just down the road. The more, the merrier!

With the turn of events, Dave was in a jovial mood. We all piled into his small hospital room, and Cynda recounted my speech for everyone. She was so proud of me and said I could have easily won an Emmy for all I had said! We also filled Dave in about all he had missed.

Later that night, I posted a Facebook update:

"4/8/2013 9:19 pm

Dave update #25: Dave is now out of the ICU and in a regular oncology room. We have been on that floor quite a bit this past month, so we know our way around. Dave is strong and has his head in the game. He has renewed purpose and will to fight! I am SO thankful right now...for all the love, encouragement, prayers, friends, and family rallying with us both now and always. After all, it is NOT the medical report we look to but to Jesus Christ, who has the final say on Dave's life… He sees the end of things from the beginning, and yet is with us at the same time!! Praise God!"

I didn't mention how much of a battle it had been. I asked for prayer but didn't have the energy to provide more details. I was doing my best to remain positive and not give in to fear.

Chapter 14

"But he said to me, 'My grace is sufficient for you, for my power is made perfect in weakness.' Therefore I will boast all the more gladly about my weaknesses, so that Christ's power may rest on me."
2 Corinthians 12:9 NIV

Dave and I were grateful to have our loved ones with us in Fargo. With approximately fifteen people there for support, the sadness soon turned into the joy of a family reunion! We had started this journey on our own, but now everyone was here to help. I felt at ease, letting others take a shift to stay with Dave so I could rest. Cynda, Charlie, and Mamie joined the daytime rotation, while Dad and my father-in-law, Denny, sat with Dave overnight.

Mom and Livi brought Lydia to the hospital most days. Dave's sister, brother, and aunt, along with my brothers, also visited frequently. By the end of the week, though, almost everyone returned home. Charlie and Mamie stayed for about ten days and were helpful all around. Several others helped cheer us on, too. Dave's coworkers and our church friends came to visit. Also, people from around the world were praying for us.

At first, Dave seemed to regain some of his strength. He even received some physical and occupational therapy. He was able to walk around a mile up and down the hallway on his best days. His cheerfulness was contagious. Even Dr. Lloyd, Dave's dour oncologist, was smiling as he saw Dave regularly walking the halls. I was so proud! However, around the third week of April, it seemed his physical and mental status peaked, and then slowly, he started to decline.

On April 18th, Mamie and Charlie brought Dave some decorations for his hospital room before they flew home. One item stood out. It was a black and white wooden memento that said, "God Give Me Guts." We got a good laugh out of that because Dave needed healing and all new guts! The message served as a reminder for me to pray for courage, too.

For a few days, I had been growing concerned about our upcoming appointment at the Mayo Clinic the following week on April 23rd. My parents had left the day before, so I was grateful to have Charlie and Mamie with us for support. I broached the topic in front of them because I valued their input, and I knew it would be similar to my parents' advice.

"Dave, we are supposed to go to Mayo Clinic next week. Do you think it's wise to go to your appointment?" I asked cautiously. I wondered if I would be able to drive him safely there.

"Well, I don't think I could travel in our vehicle," Dave replied. "It's not the most comfortable anyway, and I don't think I could sit up for the full five hours."

"What do you think we should do?" I asked.

As we sat there, we all brainstormed options. But after more discussion, Dave and I agreed that going to Mayo Clinic didn't feel like a good option. There wasn't much they would be able to do with Dave still having surgical wounds. Plus, if he had a medical emergency, getting back to Fargo might be problematic. As soon as we decided against it, I called to cancel the appointment. Doing so, I was surprised at the tremendous peace I experienced.

Charlie and Mamie prayed with us, and then they left for the airport. But, as we said our goodbyes, I had a sinking feeling that our protective safety net was disintegrating. We were on our own again. Dave, however, didn't seem to be worried.

Later that week, we were talking as he sat up in bed. He was cheerful and calm as we spoke about all that had happened since his diagnosis. It was indeed a whirlwind of drama, but we could see God's faithfulness.

"You know, we've had a lot of ups and downs," Dave said with a big smile. "But in all, it's been a phenomenal year—God has been so good to us!" His words struck me, and I knew he was right. It had been a wild and crazy year, but God had done so much more than we could have imagined. Mine had been a struggle with fear and doubt, while Dave's had been more of a physical battle, but we had survived nonetheless. As we reflected on this, we praised God.

And then, within a few short days, Dave started to forget even the simplest of things. It was as if our families' presence had formed a boundary to limit the fallout of his cancer and surgeries. With them all keeping watch, we were secure. Dave had rallied! In their absence, however, his condition deteriorated, and it was evident that he had taken a turn for the worse.

For instance, the hospital protocol was for the nurses to ask the patient their name and date of birth every time they received medication. But soon, Dave started having moments where he couldn't recall the correct information. On more than one occasion, his reply was, "Ummm...oh, I know this... but I can't remember." Perhaps his confusion was related to the buildup of toxins in his body as his body started to shut down. He always perked up after getting blood transfusions, but no one offered any support or explanation for what was happening.

While Dave maintained his positive attitude, I was apprehensive. So, with my supervisor's permission, I cleared my work schedule to spend as much time with him as possible. I still occasionally brought Lydia in to see Dave, but as a toddler, she required constant supervision. Thankfully, Jackie offered to take Lydia nearly every day.

Of course, I wanted Dave to be healed, yet I had to face reality. While I wasn't wholly fear-driven, as I was previously, I had a lot of questions. My response was to spend more time praying and sometimes bargaining with God. I held onto hope but did not sense Dave would survive. Looking back, I see now that this back-and-forth struggle was a part of me coming to acceptance. The chaos of cancer had been my focus for so long; I had never considered how to live without Dave.

One night, I spent about an hour downstairs in the lower level of my house, again pacing to help me think through some intense emotions. I cried and poured out my heart in frustration and weariness. I listed several issues and gave the Lord time to answer me. "God, Dave can't die! What are we going to do?! How am I going to live without him? How am I going to sell his car and truck?"

The Lord reminded me of Dave's gentle spirit. He had a sense of confidence and trust since the beginning of this trial. We had been facing the unknown during that time, too, but then we were in it together. Now, I was facing the likelihood of life without my dear husband.

But then, Dave's voice came to mind from a previous conversation: "If

I die, sell my truck. Sell my car! Don't hold onto anything because of how I would feel about it."

I knew I needed to trust God to provide for me.

My next complaint was even more near to my heart. I am close with my dad and could not fathom Lydia missing out on everything good fathers typically bring into a child's life.

"God, Lydia needs a dad! What about her?!"

Finally, I asked a bigger question, aimed directly at God. "And Lord, what are people going to think about You, if Dave dies?!"

Of course, God is not weak, and He doesn't need to defend His record. Yet, we had been hoping He would heal Dave, and that had not happened. After getting it all out there, finally, a sense of peace came over me. I didn't know how it was all going to work out. I wasn't entirely sure if Dave would live or die. But, I had a resolution. "I will just cross that bridge if I come to it, and God will help me."

Day by day, Dave was growing more tired and weak. It was heartbreaking seeing him unable to accomplish many of the physical tasks he had done with flying colors a day or two earlier. If someone had mentioned what I could expect, I might have taken it in stride. But no one explained anything. So, within a few days, Dave grew confused to the point that I asked for an evaluation to understand the cause.

On the morning of his evaluation, I dropped Lydia off with Jackie and cried, "I don't know what to do! It's like Dave is forgetting everything!" With a hug, she comforted me and prayed for me.

At the hospital, one of Dave's therapists came to conduct the evaluation. After introducing herself, she kindly explained how she was going to conduct the test. Then, she asked, "Hi, Dave, what is your name?"

"Dave." He said. I breathed a sigh of relief.

"Can you tell me your wife's name?" she asked.

"Natalie," Dave said, grinning as he looked at me.

The therapist asked several more questions. She covered counting, colors, the days of the week, and more. "Okay, Dave, can you list five words that start with the letter 'F'?"

"Food...field..." Dave paused, thinking. "Fieldmouse..." He couldn't think of anything else. I tried my best not to prompt him, but it was painful to watch.

While Dave's periods of confusion were not always consistent, they were discouraging. Just nine months before, he was calculating his input and output rates for the nurses! For as long as I had known Dave, he had always been an excellent problem solver. He often did complicated math in his head, but now couldn't even recall the days of the week in order. Dave was known for his attention to detail. And, just two months earlier, he was notified of his patent for Caterpillar!

As much as I longed for him to be well, I slowly started to think of the alternative. Dave was at peace and had no outstanding requests. Occasionally, he still attempted to walk, but mostly spent time resting. Dave appreciated visitors; though, more and more, he mainly wanted me to be present. "Will you just stay here with me, Natty?" As the days merged one after another, I knew we could not keep this up for much longer.

Something had to give. I could not keep missing work to sit and stare out the window with Dave, as much as I wanted to spend time with him. I could not keep asking friends to watch Lydia without eventually wearing out our welcome. With its four-hour limit, drop-in daycare was not a long-term option, but Lydia was not able to stay in the hospital all day either.

One day, as I tried to reconcile my wishes with our actual circumstances, a quiet thought formed in my mind. It slowly occurred to me, "Maybe we are walking him into eternity." The weight of those words stayed with me, and I determined to help Dave walk whatever path lay ahead.

I had mixed emotions, but I kept them to myself and didn't share my hunch with anyone. My goals were to make my dear husband comfortable and spend time together. I didn't want to miss anything and found myself, once again, memorizing every detail I could.

During the last full week of April, we got word that our health insurance company was starting to balk at the medical bills. In their view, Dave's progress, or lack thereof, didn't warrant the high level of care he was receiving. Having worked in healthcare for many years, I understood the process and the questions.

On Friday, the 26th, Dave and I had a late-afternoon meeting with a pain management physician and the oncology case manager to discuss his situation. I felt uneasy going into the meeting because the decision would affect Dave directly.

My parents had returned for another week-long stay. Livi, Cynda, Charlie, and Mamie also had come for another visit, so Lydia was quite content. Their continued prayers and support gave me an emotional boost. I was nervous, but I felt a strong urge to advocate for Dave and protect my heart. While he had received adequate care, it felt like the administrative staff was ready to kick him out. No one at the hospital used those words specifically, but it seemed they were growing tired of us.

When the physician and the case manager walked into Dave's room, I was sitting in a chair near the window. The physician remained standing, noting that he had another meeting and would need to leave soon. We had talked to him at length over the last few weeks, so we felt comfortable with him. Friendly and soft-spoken, we trusted his input, even if he didn't fully comprehend our reasons for refusing hospice.

The case manager drew Dave's curtain halfway shut. Then, she grabbed a chair from near the door and sat down at the foot of the bed. She adjusted her scarf and put on a smile. I knew she was trying to appear friendly, but since she had only talked with us once before, I didn't think she understood our position.

She started off pushy, "Dave's insurance company is starting to ask us questions about the amount of care he requires. So, we need to make some decisions on another, more acceptable placement." She jumped right to the issue of financial reimbursement, as if that's the only thing that mattered.

Annoyed, I remained firm and reiterated that I could not care for Dave alone. "I understand if Dave needs to go somewhere else because of insurance, but he needs more medical care than I can manage on my own." At this point, he required round-the-clock care!

The physician kindly explained, "We could give Dave pain medications that are easier for you to administer at home. There are options like suckers containing medicine that he could use for pain relief..." He explained the side effects, which included possible cardiac arrest.

Having already been over this at other times, I looked at Dave and then interrupted the physician. "No. That won't work. It's way too risky for us. Besides, our daughter could accidentally get into it, thinking it was food." I watched Lydia, of course, but I clearly would have my hands full with providing care for both her and Dave. I didn't want to take any chances!

Furthermore, I felt the need to establish boundaries for myself. I didn't want Dave to die at home, leaving me with sad memories there. We had tried to explain this to the medical staff, but it felt like no one truly listened to our concerns.

As we started discussing other options and facilities, I felt nauseous. It seemed as though they just wanted to boot Dave out because his case was hopeless in their eyes. Hospice was brought up, but we declined. Again, it wasn't that hospice was a terrible option. I just felt they had not handled the topic well. If they had approached me separately and with even an ounce of compassion, perhaps I would have felt differently. But, they kept blindsiding us at the most inopportune moments!

I had grown so defensive and protective of Dave that, at this point, I felt our situation was beyond a calm intervention. Then, the case manager huffed and asked pointedly, "So, just what are your expectations for Dave?" She continued, "We're trying to provide the best care we can, but the insurance company needs to see a certain level of progress here. And based on what the physicians are telling me, Dave's condition is not improving."

At that moment, I could envision the drama Dave's case must have been causing behind the scenes. I had participated in many care plan meetings over the years, and I'm sure we were creating quite a buzz! I had sat with many families in similar situations, but I had handled them with care and compassion.

Just a few months before, I had held an elderly lady's hand while we discussed her husband's need for hospice care at the nursing home. I had offered her a tissue and wiped my own tears, too, as I saw parallels with our medical journey. Had this case manager done the same for me, I would have been much more open to her suggestions. But that didn't happen. She offered no conciliatory olive branches and didn't appear to be on our side.

Thus, my response was a little heated, though I spoke as calmly and evenly as I could manage. "I'm sure you think we're in denial—or delusional! But I have worked in healthcare for many years. I am not naive." I took a deep breath and grabbed Dave's hand.

Then, I explained, "I understand the insurance process, as I have participated in a ton of care plan meetings over the years. And yes, we know Dave's going to die unless God heals him miraculously. You keep telling us that!! But, it seems like you are all giving up hope! It feels like you are writing him off, just wanting him to get out of your system as if he is a bother to you."

I was upset but stood my ground. "Dave is still here, a human being in need of care, and I don't appreciate you treating him like a problem to be solved!" Resolutely, I said, "If the insurance company says we have to leave, we will. But, for the last time, I cannot take Dave home. So I need you to find another place for him."

At this, the case manager stuttered and back-tracked. "W-w-well, there is one place that might take him." She said, "It's considered a step-down facility because they don't do as much care there. It's technically a rehab program, but maybe they will take Dave anyway." She continued, "We will have to check with insurance first, but that might be the best compromise."

"Yes, that sounds good," I said. "Please look into it and keep us posted." Of course, Dave was not in a position to do much rehab, but it seemed like it might work. After they left, Dave thanked me for sticking up for him. I told him I wasn't trying to be obstinate; I just wanted a reasonable option.

I went on, "I hope this new place is an answer to prayer. We'll see what they say." A little while later, I joined our family at a restaurant for dinner and gave them an update.

The following week, my parents left again promising to return soon. I felt better about them leaving this time as Dave had been approved to go to the step-down facility across town. He didn't meet much of their admission criteria, but we were thankful for the option. It was only about ten minutes from home. I felt at peace because things seemed under control.

I couldn't have been more wrong.

That weekend, on Saturday, May 4th, Jackie once again watched Lydia for me while Dave was transferred to the new facility. His case manager arranged a ride in a special van through the local ambulance service. For a small fee of about ten dollars, the van would take Dave to the new location while he sat in his wheelchair! Dave and the driver shared a first name.

David, the driver, was extremely kind and friendly. Even now, I recall his warmth and hospitality. He and Dave talked all the way from the oncology floor, through the hospital, and to the van. When Dave was wheeled outside for the first time in over a month, his weight loss and pale skin were much more evident. He looked sick and weak, but he was content. He had a large blanket on his lap and a huge smile on his face. Dave was able to stay seated while the hydraulic lift loaded him into the van.

I knew this placement was the best compromise, but it also felt like we were rocking the boat. I followed behind the van in my vehicle. I noticed the driver drove at a steady speed and gently navigated the curves. He drove smoothly around potholes and stayed in the same lane almost the entire time. I was grateful, and yet the whole experience was surreal.

When we arrived, I was disappointed and unimpressed. The entire unit was only one floor, rented from a larger medical building. I had heard of this rehab network before when I worked in central Illinois, but this facility was dilapidated. In addition to needing a remodel, Dave's room was tiny. There was only room for his bed, medical equipment, a box fan, and a small folding chair. I moved around the bed to the window so I wouldn't be in the way.

Dave's nurse seemed very young and inexperienced. She appeared jittery and unsure of herself. She didn't leave me feeling very confident in her abilities. When Dave's morphine pump kept beeping, I asked if the nurse could fix it. "Oh, I just haven't gotten to it yet!" She laughed anxiously. "Hahaha, hmmmm, I wonder how this goes. Something isn't working here."

I had a pit in my stomach, though I tried to remain positive. I prompted the nurse, "Do you think you could call someone to help?" Silently I prayed, "God, I know You have a good plan. This is where insurance says we have to be. Please keep Dave safe."

I unpacked Dave's belongings to pass the time, though many of the items seem superfluous now. Since March, he had only worn hospital gowns and pants, and non-skid socks. Out of habit, I hung his street clothes in the closet. These included his Columbia winter coat, a t-shirt, a grey sweatshirt and sweatpants, socks, and shoes.

Looking back, I don't know why I didn't just take these items home. It never occurred to me that Dave might not need them, after all. I also arranged his glasses case and hearing aid case on a little bedside tray, just in case he decided to use them. Soon, I kissed him goodbye, so I could run a couple of errands before picking up Lydia.

Later that afternoon, I returned with Lydia. She was cranky with me because I would not let her run around. The room was so small that I held her while I leaned into the windowsill. At seventeen months, Lydia squirmed and sought her independence. When she hit my arm in anger, Dave grew stern. He told her, "No, Lydia. You need to respect your mom." Even though she was little, his quiet admonition was effective.

Heartbroken, Lydia's bottom lip quivered, but I was grateful Dave came to my defense. Indeed, it was probably the only time he had the chance to discipline her as a father. It was bittersweet, but I was proud of Dave and glad he supported me. Soon after that, we said our goodbyes for the evening. Lydia was growing tired and even more upset, and I needed to get her home. I just hated leaving Dave all alone in this rundown facility.

Chapter 15

"But the Lord is faithful, and he will strengthen you and protect you from the evil one."
2 Thessalonians 3:3 NIV

At about 4:00 a.m. the following morning, on Sunday, May 5th, my cell phone rang and startled me awake. I jumped out of bed to answer. It was Dave.

"Hi, Babe, what's going on?" I asked urgently. Stumbling down the hall, I turned on the kitchen lights.

"Hi, Natty, sorry to wake you up," he said calmly. To my surprise, Dave was cheerful and clear as ever! "I don't want you to worry, but I have to go back to the hospital for monitoring. I was given too much morphine, about five times what I should have received. Now, my heart rate is too high, and they want to give me a detox medication."

"What?! I don't believe it! They overdosed you?" I was shocked. "How could that have happened?!" I was happy to talk to Dave, of course, but I was nervous he would have a sudden adverse reaction. The apparent negligence made me angry, as well.

"I'm not sure. But, I wanted you to hear my voice and know that I am okay." It was Dave's inclination to always think of others. What a dear man!

He went on, "Also, they said there's no need to rush. The ambulance will be here soon to transfer me, but it will take a while for them to get me back to the ICU and do the detox. You might as well take a shower and then meet me there. That way, Lydia can get more sleep. It might be a long day."

"Okay," I sighed. "I'll shower and then get Lydia up and fed. I love you!" If it had been an absolute emergency, I would have gone immediately. But I knew Dave was right; everything probably would take a while. So, I used that time to shower, pray, get Lydia and all her gear ready, update the family, and prepare for the unknown.

By 7:00 a.m., I met Dave in the ICU. At this point, he was very lethargic and didn't want to talk. Ironically, he didn't seem confused. He was getting both the detox drug and a unit of blood. I'm not sure if the blood transfusion was because of low blood counts or if it was needed to help dilute and clear out the morphine.

Of course, I had Lydia with me, because it seemed too early to ask friends for help, and some of them would be headed to church anyway. Daycare was not open on Sundays, so that was not an option, either. After a few hours, the detox was complete, and Dave moved back to the oncology floor.

Over the next few days, one thing remained constant: Dave's huge smile. He was in a good mood most of the time and went with the flow. By this time, he was well-known there for his gentle, optimistic outlook. Dave didn't mind when the staff had to change his bedding or gown. Over the last year, he had grown accustomed to most of the poking and prodding, too.

Dave had few cares and was eager to socialize with anyone who walked in. In fact, the nurses and CNAs consistently requested him as a patient. If they were not assigned to him, they would pop in to say hello! In general, Dave took every day in stride and was happy. Since his level of pain was rising, his medicine was a constant now. But, he didn't mention the pain or discomfort often.

I tried to be with Dave as much as possible. Most days, we just sat and enjoyed each other's company. Nothing else seemed as significant as just being together. Dave usually sat in his bed, but sometimes, he had the energy to sit in a chair and look out the window. One morning, as I walked into Dave's room, I noticed his eyes were shut, but he looked content.

"Hi, Dave! How are you?" I asked, taking off my winter coat. The snow was melting, but it was still chilly outside. Even in early May, snow was a possibility.

"I saw a robin!" I exclaimed, finally happy to see a sure sign of spring. After a little while, our conversation turned to Lydia. She was changing so fast that it seemed essential for me to give Dave daily updates. At this point, I was struggling with how Lydia would be affected by our cancer journey. I trusted God that anything was possible, but I knew the situation was grim.

"Dave, does it bother you that you might not get to see Lydia grow up?" I asked gently. His answer surprised me, but it helped ease my own heart.

"You know, I'm okay with it." He said calmly. "I'd love to be here, of course, but I had some sort of dream or vision, and it helped me."

"What do you mean, Hon?"

With a peaceful smile on his face, Dave said, "Well, I saw a girl, who I believe was Lydia. It was like she moved through different ages, and I was able to see what she looked like as she grew."

"Wow, that's amazing," I said, unsure of what else to say.

"Yeah, it was like I could see her when she started school and then when she was around twelve." Dave went on, "Then, I saw her when she was a little older, like in high school or something. She was doing different activities, but somehow I knew it was Lydia."

I was glad Dave was at peace regarding Lydia. I'm sure it must have been sad for him at first, and I'm so grateful God gave him that gift.

I had hoped we could stay in the calm environment that the oncology floor provided, but soon, Dave's health insurance dictated his move back to the less expensive rehab facility. I was still upset when the hospital case manager and I finally discussed what had happened. She explained that the dosing calculations for each facility were different. Perhaps that explains why no one had caught it.

Much to my chagrin, on Thursday, May 9th, Dave transferred back to the rehab facility. Just before this, the rehab case manager also called to explain what happened from their perspective. She apologized for the error and said they would double-check all of Dave's orders when he arrived.

To me, that wasn't enough!

"Well, I understand accidents happen. But an overdose is unacceptable—he could have been killed!" I continued, "Besides that, my concern isn't just for Dave, but for all the other patients! Dave's nurse that day didn't appear to know what she was doing. It might not have been her fault, but having her take care of Dave makes me very uncomfortable."

The case manager replied, "We won't put Dave in her rotation. But, please give us a chance to do better. We will talk about this issue at our next staff in-service."

Reluctantly, I agreed to give the facility a second chance. What other option did we have?! This whole experience made me tense and strengthened my resolve to protect my husband. Once again, we hired the small van to transport Dave, and I followed him across town that afternoon.

My parents returned to Fargo the next day, Friday, May 10th. I was so glad to see them after all we had been through that week! Once again, Mom held things together at home, while Dad and I alternated sitting with Dave. I usually sat with Dave during the day while my dad spent the nights watching over him, reading to him when he was awake, and praying for him while he slept. Cynda came to visit for the weekend, as did Livi and Paul.

On Saturday, there was a special event at Caterpillar, called Family Appreciation Day, which I had always enjoyed. This time, I wasn't sure if we should go, but after some discussion, my family and I felt it was important to show up on Dave's behalf. I suppose I wanted to remind people he was still a part of Caterpillar, even though he had not been there in a couple of months. Together, we had agreed for him to go on short-term disability for six weeks, but that time limit was almost complete.

We had about a week left of that special status, and I wasn't sure what would happen after that. I didn't know if Dave would be put on long-term disability or lose his position entirely (though now I understand his job was secure). To some people, it may seem unnecessary to be worried about Dave's career when he was close to death. However, his job was our primary source of income, and the potential loss was disconcerting.

When we arrived at Caterpillar, Dave's supervisor, Paul, took us on a tour of the plant, showing us everything Dave had done. In addition to leading a team, he had been responsible for organizing the new assembly area. Just a few months earlier, Dave had found great joy in this project. He had often come home excited to tell me about his day. I heard about the giant cranes and specialized equipment he ordered to make the assembly area more efficient.

Months earlier, I hadn't fully understood what Dave had meant, but seeing the cranes and the equipment in person was impressive. The scope of what he had done was inspiring!

"Wow! Dave's so smart!" I said, in awe. Everyone laughed.

A man named Jay, said, "Yeah, I signed off on all his paperwork, but I didn't know how—or if—it was going to come together. I couldn't envision it, but Dave sure could!"

Throughout the tour, which probably lasted less than half an hour, I teared up thinking about Dave and how proud of him I was! Along the way, his coworkers stopped to smile at us or nod in our direction. Some of the men joined us on our tour, pointing out specific projects they had helped Dave complete. Everyone was happy to see little Lydia, too.

"I wish Dave were here to see how much people love him," I thought.

The next day, Sunday, May 12th, was Mother's Day, the second one that Dave was sick. That morning, Cynda spent time with Dave while everyone else came to church with me. I put on a brave smile, but it was all I could do. Once again, we skipped the child dedication ceremony. We had briefly considered it when Dave was doing better, but the timing was never right. Missing this event was one more reminder of our life now. This was not how I had envisioned life as a young mom and wife!

Regarding a special Mother's Day gift, I didn't expect anything from Dave. He had barely been out of bed for at least two months! I had resigned myself to muddle through the day as best I could. However, behind the scenes, Dave had texted my mom for help. At some point, he asked Mom to pick up a card for me and to buy me a gift certificate to my favorite massage place. She bought two Mother's Day cards, and let Dave choose the one he liked most. He wrote a message to me and signed his name.

Later that afternoon, we went to see Dave. We all crowded in his tiny room, most of us standing because there was only one chair. My mom handed me the card from Dave. "What's this?" I asked curiously. I thought she was just trying to make my day a little brighter.

"It's not from me. Your sweet husband wanted to make sure you had a Happy Mother's Day." Mom said with a gentle smile.

Pleasantly surprised, I opened the card only to have my heart break a little more. As I read the card, I did my best not to show my sadness—but the words were indecipherable. Dave tried to explain it, but the words in his mouth also came out jumbled.

I could not understand him, but said, "Thank you, Dave. I love you so much." He smiled as I kissed his cheek, humbled that he would remember me when he was so weak and sick. I had been dismayed about the unfairness of the day, but Dave had been thinking of me!

On the morning of Monday, May 13th, Livi and Cynda each returned home to Illinois. Livi flew directly home, having already said goodbye to Dave the evening before. But, Cynda drove to rehab to see Dave before she left. She only stayed a few minutes; Dave was so sleepy, and she had a ten-hour drive ahead of her. On her way out, Cynda asked him, "David, is there anything you want me to bring when I return?"

Previously, Dave might've asked for a magazine or something like that. But at this point, he was not talking much beyond a simple yes or no. Remarkably, Dave's words to his mom were clear and profound, "I just want Jesus." When Cynda relayed this to me several days later, I was in awe. After all Dave had been through, he was focused and firm in his faith. He didn't complain or ask for relief. He just wanted Jesus.

That day, I drove to work in Dave's three-quarter-ton truck because my vehicle was in the shop for repairs. We had been having trouble with it ever since getting hit from behind, nearly six months before. I talked with my coworker about Dave and gave her a brief update. I didn't stay at work long, but I checked my email and did a few other small tasks. I had cleared my schedule and didn't accept any new patients during this time. Then, I went to see Dave.

On the way, I prayed, "God, we need you. Please show us what to do." Dave's short-term disability was expiring at the end of the week. By nature, he and I were planners, so not having any sense of control or a financial plan was tough.

It was growing difficult, impossible really, to schedule or plan anything with Dave so sick. My brother, Patrick, was getting married Memorial Day weekend, about two weeks away. I was afraid if I left to attend the wedding, Dave would die while I was gone, or he would wake up and question where I was (how could I leave him?). Of course, Dave was sleeping when I arrived at the rehab facility. I discussed my options with my dad, who had been sitting with him. Then, I called my brother in Illinois.

He picked up immediately and asked how we were doing. "Hey, Pat, we're hanging in there." Then, I continued. "I'm calling because I don't think we're going to make it to your wedding. I just can't leave Dave." Patrick understood, of course, but missing his wedding was not a choice I wanted to make.

A few months before, during the dreadfully long winter, Dave and I both sensed that change was coming. We had hoped and prayed for healing, but ultimately, we just needed an answer—any answer—to our prayers. It felt like we were in limbo, and we could not maintain that pace much longer. Gradually, I grew aware that Dave's languishing in a hospital bed, in pain and inactivity, was not part of the 'abundant' life Jesus died to give him (John 10:10).

Initially, when Dave was diagnosed, he had implied that his quality of life was essential to him. My goal had been to make sure he survived so that he could be present for Lydia and me. But as time wore on, I could see Dave was right. He would've never been satisfied to lie around with limited capacity. He had always been so active! Slowly, my stance also changed. I finally understood we could not accept anything less than total physical healing.

To me, it wouldn't be enough if Dave were cancer-free and did not need artificial means of life (pain medications, g-tube for drainage, TPN for nutrition, and his second colostomy). His surgeries had also taken their toll. Dave's gut had significant damage from all the cutting and rerouting his operations required. Even without cancer, he likely would have had ongoing complications. Thus, I started to accept the inevitable.

We had been praying for a miracle, but perhaps the miracle God gave us was the gift of extra time together. In April, the doctors had given Dave two days to live after his third surgery. But it seemed God had overridden that term on our behalf, giving us five-and-a-half additional weeks together.

Indeed, if Dave had died within two days as his physicians predicted, this would be a much different story. But in the end, we needed miraculous physical healing from cancer—or Dave needed to receive a better, more complete healing from Jesus in Heaven.

It might seem presumptuous to think I could ask or expect something big like this from God, all or nothing. But, He is a big God! And, I had grown in my relationship with Him to know His strength and my position. I had gone from fear to faith, learning, firsthand, that God is not swayed by my perceived cracks in our relationship. He is ever-faithful and constant.

God does not feel threatened by my emotional outbursts, nor does He turn His back on me when I am inconsistent. No matter what I threw at Him, I knew He could handle it, not because of my merit or lack thereof, but because He is good.

Moreover, I knew God loved Dave more than I ever could, which was a lot! I understood He wanted what was best for Dave, but He also knew what was best for Lydia and me. God could heal Dave—no doubt. But, I didn't give Him an ultimatum. I simply gave God the space He needed to do what was best for all of us, even when it didn't make human sense.

To be clear, I was not demanding God do anything drastic to heal Dave. I just wanted God to be God. No longer was I basing my faith on the outcome. I tried to take each moment as it came, trusting that God had a greater plan. Through this time, it was crystal clear that none of our plans amount to anything without God's input, help, and presence.

At this point, I spent most of my time with Dave, often watching him sleep. In those quiet moments, I reflected on our cancer journey. As we grew closer to the one-year mark of his first operation and diagnosis, I considered all we had learned and experienced. That year, we had canceled many important plans and disregarded people's expectations of us.

We had simplified our schedule so my dear husband could rest, skipping anything that wasn't necessary. We had continued certain activities when Dave felt up to them. But, it was quite freeing to pare down our commitments, and I'm grateful we prioritized spending time together as much as we could.

I also kept thinking about Dave, lying on what was essentially his death bed. He wasn't thinking about how much money he had made or if he had been successful at work. Dave wasn't concerned about food, clothes, or other belongings, either. I concluded that when everything is stripped away, very little truly matters at the end of one's life.

For me, it boiled down to these two questions: Did I know Jesus? Did I love people? Each of us has to answer for ourselves, as they require personal commitments. Yet, Dave exemplified these concepts, which would continue to occupy my mind in the coming months. Pondering how his experience unfolded gave me something to focus on when it often felt like everything else was meaningless.

As tough as it was to get through each day, sometimes nights were worse. For much of April and May, when I slept, I had the same dream on repeat. I dreamed that Dave came home in the middle of the night as if he had just walked out of the hospital and driven home, completely well. Dave would be in our closet with the light on getting dressed in a navy blue t-shirt and pants. His excitement to be home always woke me up from my dream within a dream.

"Natty, guess what! I'm healed!" he would say.

Oh, how I wanted that to be true. But instead of waking up to Dave, I woke up to a dark room, alone in my bed. Then, I would get up and prepare for another long day.

On Tuesday, May 14th, I attended a professional meeting in the evening while Lydia stayed home with Mom. Perhaps I was grasping at a sense of normalcy. I was antsy because this last meeting of the season was the only one I had managed to attend all year. Twice I had planned to network with other dietitians but instead stayed home at Dave's request. To think, a year before, I was planning a state convention, and now I was unable even to attend meetings!

My friends were happy to see me, and I gave them a brief update. Then, after the meeting, I went to the store to pick up a few groceries. Yet, as I wandered around with my cart, I suddenly felt compelled to go see Dave. I wasn't sure exactly why, but I felt it might be an urging from the Holy Spirit. I had planned to go home after the store, but I wondered if God was giving me a chance to say goodbye to Dave. I had mixed feelings about this, but I didn't want to miss the opportunity—one I might never have again.

I quickly checked out and tossed the groceries in the passenger seat. Then, I drove to see Dave. It was around 7:45 p.m., and I arrived at the rehab facility around 8:00 p.m. Though it was late, I walked purposefully inside. As the elevator door opened, I noticed the entire medical floor was quiet. Someone at the front desk looked in my direction but didn't say anything. I did not take offense, and since Dave had been accidentally overdosed on morphine ten days prior, I didn't feel like talking to anyone anyway. I walked down the hall to Dave's room. His door was half-open.

"Hi, Dave," I said quietly. He mumbled a slight hello, but he didn't open his eyes. "I came to visit after my meeting tonight. Lydia's at home with my mom." I continued to make small talk, briefly telling him about my day. I asked about his day, but I didn't get much response. Dave merely made a few small murmurs whenever I asked him a question.

I only stayed for about half an hour because Dave was not interacting much. I kissed his cheek, knowing it might be the last time I ever did that. The thought saddened me, but I also felt peaceful. I prayed softly, "Lord, we've done everything we could the best we know how. The rest is up to You." Gently, I squeezed Dave's hand and said, "Goodbye, Dave. I love you so much." He didn't respond or reply, but I knew he loved me.

I quietly left Dave's room and walked back to the elevator, not paying attention to anything else. As I left the building, I was somber. I didn't want to lose Dave, but I also knew it might be for the best. Intuitively, I felt something important had happened to me, but I couldn't quite describe it. Perhaps it was the resolution of letting go. I sat in my car for a little while, contemplating it all. Then, I drove home.

Lydia was already in bed when I pulled into the garage, but Mom and Dad were still up and had been praying. I told them about my meeting, going to the store, and seeing Dave. I didn't share that I had said goodbye, partially because I was still processing it myself. Then, I went to bed, exhausted. Dad went back to sit with Dave for a few hours, but he came home around 2:00 a.m. I was sleeping, but he told my mom that Dave was pretty much unresponsive at that point.

Chapter 16

"For to me, to live is Christ and to die is gain."
Philippians 1:21 NIV

The next morning, Wednesday, May 15th, I woke up around 7:00 a.m. Based on my intuition from the night before, I had a sense of needing to prepare for the day. I didn't know what might happen—but I wanted to be ready. I showered and checked on Lydia, who was asleep in her crib. A little while later, Mom and I were talking in the kitchen as we prepared our breakfast and coffee. Dad was downstairs, sleeping after a late night with Dave. Everything seemed calm, and I tried to keep an open mind. Still, I could not shake my sense of apprehension.

As I glanced out the window, I could tell it was going to be a beautiful, sunny spring day. But nothing could prepare me for the call from Dave's rehab case manager at 9:00 a.m. In an urgent voice, she told me, "Mrs. White, Dave is in cardiac arrest. You need to come quickly."

"Dave's in cardiac arrest?!" I repeated what she said, out loud, so my mom could hear. The case manager confirmed the news and explained the paramedics were there. She reminded me Dave was still a full-code status, meaning they were trying to keep him alive.

Suddenly, I realized why I had fought so hard to keep the full-code status: If Dave stepped into eternity that day, I would be present. I had been excluded so many times throughout his treatment, but the full-code status meant I would be included in the final decision. We had been married on a cruise ship five years earlier, promising to be faithful 'till death do us part,' and now the best way I could honor Dave was to be there for his final breath if it came to pass.

So, when the case manager asked if I wanted them to keep working on Dave, I said, "Yes, do everything you can!" While it might sound unrealistic, it bought me enough time to get there. I felt like 'we' needed to go down fighting, but I didn't want to make the final call. I knew God could do anything, and I deferred to Him. If Dave died that day, I'd do my best to move forward however I could manage. But I wasn't going to lose hope!

After I hung up the phone, I jumped into high gear. Mom called down the stairs to wake Dad up. "Tom, get up! Natalie needs you! ...Tom!!"

Dad didn't respond fast enough, so I ran down the stairs yelling for him to wake up. I banged on the bedroom door. "Dad, wake up! We need to go! Dave's in cardiac arrest!"

As I ran back up two flights of stairs, I called Pastor Bob. I'm not sure why I called him first, but I am so glad I did. Later, I learned he had been in a meeting. But, instead of being annoyed at the interruption, he immediately picked up. When I told him about Dave, he calmly said, "I'm on my way!"

While I waited for Dad to get dressed, Mom tried to keep me calm. I felt a little panicky. She prayed for me while I prayed for Dave. I knew the odds were slim he would survive, but I wanted to lift him up anyway, leaving the outcome in God's hands.

Dad drove to the rehab facility, and neither of us said much. I was glad this building was closer than the main hospital we'd been at for much of the year. We parked and walked quickly inside. At the same time, I had the surreal feeling that everything was in slow motion and crystal clear. I remember the hanging baskets outside, the cool breeze, and the bright sun.

As we stepped off the elevator, we turned the corner and saw a small crowd of people at Dave's door. As we drew closer, his nurse met me and introduced herself.

"Hello," I said. "Can I see Dave?"

"They are working on him, but you can peek inside."

As I leaned into the room, another crowd of people stood around Dave and his bed. In all, approximately fifteen medical and emergency personnel had rushed to help him. The people outside his room were milling around, probably waiting to see what else was needed, but the ones inside were doing CPR. I saw a man pumping Dave's chest with his hands. A woman pumped air manually through a breathing tube in his mouth while counting. Others held various tools and equipment.

It was disturbing to see, but I wanted to bear witness to what was happening—not because Dave wasn't receiving proper care, but so I could understand what he was experiencing. I wish I could have held his hand, but of course, that was not possible. Soon, I had seen enough. I turned back to the nurse, who quickly introduced me to the head physician working on Dave. He paused to give me a brief update, and I reiterated that I wanted him to do everything he could.

Then, Dave's nurse pointed us down the hall to a small waiting room. Not knowing what else to do, Dad and I complied. The waiting room was rather barren and uninviting. There was a handful of old, beat-up chairs, magazines, and very sparse decorations. With the bright fluorescent lights, it was not comforting at all! Dad and I sat together next to the door.

Before Pastor Bob came, a different clergyman tried to comfort us while we waited. I know he was trying his best, but his chatter was an unwelcome distraction. He went on and on about some unrelated topic, but I just wanted to be alone with my thoughts! Not wanting to be rude, Dad talked with the man, while I silently prayed for wisdom and help. I was trying to stay focused on the Lord, attentive, and listening for any word of comfort or direction I might receive.

Minutes later, Pastor Bob arrived, and I felt relieved. Maybe that's because the other clergyman left! But with Dad and Pastor Bob there, I knew, whatever happened, I would be alright. These two men were trustworthy and had been walking with Jesus for decades. I knew they wanted the best for Dave and me, just like our loving Heavenly Father.

Still, I don't think anything can adequately prepare someone for moments like these. Around 9:30 a.m., the head physician came in. He was apologetic but a little detached.

"Mrs. White, I'm sorry. There was nothing more we could do for your husband."

"Thank you, Doctor," I replied. In my mind's eye, I instantly saw a huge steel door slamming shut. I could almost feel the thud and hear the echo. Internally, something clicked, and my heart jolted within me. Dave was gone.

Dad, Pastor Bob, and I sat silently in the waiting room for a few minutes. I don't know what was running through their minds, but I was at a loss.

Dave had left, and I could not follow. I felt deep sadness, shock, and forlornness—but I also felt relief. Only 364 days had transpired from Dave's diagnosis to his death, but it felt like a lifetime had passed. It was hard to believe.

I thought, "I am a widow at thirty years old. Never in a million years would I have expected this." But, I also knew Dave was no longer in pain.

We had been praying for an answer, and we had received one. We had done everything to stand firm in our faith and persevere. I was proud of Dave, but it was not at all the answer I had wanted. "What are we going to do?" The thought kept circulating, as I sensed the finality of the situation. I felt sick to my stomach. What I had hoped would happen, hadn't.

I knew I had to keep moving forward, but what did that look like? Dismayed, several thoughts rolled through the sudden fog in my brain. "Do I have to go through this, Lord? What about all our plans and dreams? What about Lydia?"

What seemed like a possible end to our agony, wasn't. Instead, everything shifted to even more extreme levels. And now, I had to figure out life. Alone. Without Dave, who had always been so steady and reliable.

Dad and Pastor Bob did their best to be lighthearted, but there wasn't much to say. A few minutes later, I stood up and asked to see Dave. I was allowed to go into his room, but what I saw was rather unpleasant. It was as if they had abandoned Dave's body as soon as his heart stopped and left their equipment in place. His nurse could see that I was upset. Gently she said, "Let me clean him up, and I will call you in a few minutes."

I went back to the sterile little waiting room in silence, unsure of what to do with myself. About twenty minutes later, the nurse called me back in. This time, my dad and Pastor Bob came, too. There was only standing room at this point. The room was so small, and we had no reason to sit down anyway. Dad stood on one side of the bed, with his back to the small window. Pastor Bob and I stood on the other side.

I didn't know what to say or do. Who does in a situation like this? Dave looked so peaceful. I laid my hand on his arm, noting that his body was already growing cold. As I stood there by the bed, I prayed silently about what to do. I knew my life would never be the same, but I slowly gained clarity on a few key matters.

Within moments, this came to mind: "If I am going to get through this, I'm going to need God's help." When I had yelled at Dave to fight for his life, just weeks before, I had said that I would not be mad at God. And so, while I still held onto Dave's lifeless body, I chose to cling to the Lord and not turn away in anger.

Years before, in high school, I lost a dear friend in an accident. God brought me through that horrible time, and I knew He would be faithful again. I didn't know how things would turn out—but I knew God was with me and for me.

As I pondered life without Dave, everything became very simple. This nightmare had ended, and Dave's pain and suffering were gone. My days back and forth at his bedside were over. But, what I hadn't expected was this new set of circumstances. For me, being a widow and a single parent was uncharted territory, though I was able to make some preliminary decisions.

While some people decide to move right away after such a loss, I felt it was prudent to stay put and let things settle down for a while. I knew there would likely be many changes ahead, but for now, I needed to focus on taking care of myself. I avoided putting extra pressure on myself to make big decisions, like moving.

As I stood next to Dave's body, even in my shock, I also felt a firm conviction to be involved with PLACE. I knew I needed to continue volunteering at church, though I was not in a rush to do so. Of course, it would take some time to regain my sense of direction. I also thought, "I'm going to need some mom support." Lydia and I were in for some big adjustments!

Soon, we all walked back to the waiting room. The nurses needed to finish prepping Dave's body, complete some paperwork, and call the funeral home. While we were still in the hallway, Pastors David and Ischee arrived. Pastor Bob had called them, and they came as fast as they could. When Pastor Bob said he needed to go, I was grateful these dear friends were there.

Just after this, Dave's nurse came to ask some questions about how to proceed. "Who would you like for me to call to pick up Dave's body?

Which funeral home should I notify?"

I had heard of one or two funeral homes through my previous job at the nursing home, but none of them stood out. Suddenly, I could barely breathe or focus on the decision at hand.

"I don't know. Do you have any ideas?" I asked.

The nurse, an older lady, compassionately suggested a funeral home in Moorhead, just across the Red River in Minnesota. I thought about it for a moment and asked Ischee for her input as a pastor; but she was also unsure. Then, the nurse said something which surprised me.

"They took care of my parents, husband, and son." She continued softly, "I've trusted them with my entire family."

I was comforted and had peace that she understood what I was feeling, having had so much loss in her life. I felt strengthened when I considered God had chosen this woman to be Dave's nurse that day. Also, I realized, if needed, I could avoid driving by the funeral home because it was conveniently out of my way. I confirmed my choice and thanked Dave's nurse for her help. Silently, I prayed, "Thank You, Lord."

Then, Ischee and I joined her husband and my dad in the waiting room. We sat in silence for a few minutes. Then, Dad spoke up, a little reluctantly. "Well, I guess we should make some calls. I will call Debbie to let her know."

Before he stepped into the hallway to call Mom, we coordinated a basic list of who to call with the news. Soon, my parents called my siblings and extended family. Everyone was so sad. Upon hearing Dave had died, my sister broke down. Livi was so upset she left work early and made plans to fly out the next day.

I remained in the waiting room with David and Ischee. The bright lights and mismatched furniture were disorienting, so I closed the large black door, hoping at least for a little privacy. I thanked my friends for being there. Then, with a sigh, I said, "I should probably make some calls too, starting with Dave's mom. But how do I tell her about her son?"

None of us had any answers.

A moment later, I dialed Cynda's number. She had been home for only two days. I listened to the phone ring, still not knowing what to say. I hated calling with such devastating news when she was at work. To my surprise, she picked up the phone on the second ring.

"Hello!" Cynda said cheerfully. "I'm just leaving my weekly brunch with my friends. Normally we meet on a different day, but we had to reschedule it this week."

I silently thanked God for His grace. Cynda would have support after what I was about to say. I took a deep breath before speaking.

"Hi, Cynda. I'm glad I got ahold of you. I was afraid you'd be at work. I'm calling because, well, Dave died this morning. He's gone."

Cynda had started to back out of her parking space, but then I heard her pull back in and turn off the car. "Oh," she said tearfully.

"I'm so sorry, Cynda. Are you okay? I don't want you to be alone."

After a brief pause, Cynda replied with a cracked voice, "I will just go back inside and tell my friends. They will want to know."

I'm so grateful her friends were present to comfort her. Even then, I could see God working in the situation to make it a little better.

I called Dave's dad next; he seemed to keep his emotions to himself. I'm sure he was heartbroken, but he didn't say much other than asking me to keep him informed about the funeral arrangements. Then, I called Paul at Caterpillar and left a message to call me back.

Next, I called my friend, Jackie, to tell her the news. "Hi, Jackie. I'm calling to let you know that Dave died this morning."

She replied, "Oh, Nat, I'm so sorry." Her husband, Dean, worked at Caterpillar with Paul.

"Jackie, you can tell Dean, but please make sure he talks with Paul before he tells anyone else. I'm waiting for Paul to call me back."

I wanted Paul to know first out of respect for him. He was a great supervisor to Dave and the reason we came to North Dakota in the first place. Besides that, we were good friends with him and his family. I knew he would take it hard.

I called some of my friends in our neighborhood. I wanted people to be aware, but it also helped me to talk about it. Everyone I spoke with was in shock. Ischee and David had called some of our church friends. Soon, my phone started ringing with condolences in between calls. Sara and Krystal called, as did Aunt Mamie. She said that she and Uncle Charlie were packing their suitcases so they could fly the next day.

I also called my friend, Katie, who shared the news with her parents, Jan and Craig. I notified several of my prayer warriors, including our friend, Jean, in Illinois. She called her three sons (Andy, Jake, and Sam) and a couple of Dave's other friends. I knew they would be so sad because they had grown up with Dave and were very close.

Soon, Paul returned my call, after Dean had intercepted him and informed him. Paul's voice shook on the line. "I'm so sorry, Natalie. Wow, this is hard to believe. We told everyone about Dave, and they are all upset. He was so loved." I sighed, both incredibly sad and proud. Paul continued, "We're putting together a list of people who want to bring food over. Do you mind if a few people stop by?"

"Thank you, Paul," I replied. "That would be great."

For the last several weeks and months, I had been focused on the cancer crisis. It had taken so much effort to survive the daily chaos that I hadn't considered what to do if Dave actually died. I had known it was a real possibility, but now I didn't quite know how to proceed on this new path. Nonetheless, I was grateful for everyone's support as I suddenly realized I would have a lot of guests in the coming days. The food was very much appreciated!

After spending a few hours at the rehab facility, most of it on the phone, Dad and I left. The funeral director had come for Dave's body, and already I was feeling the separation. I don't recall what time it was because time just seemed to stop. We didn't say much on the way home.

When we walked in the door, Mom embraced me and gave me a bowl of her homemade potato soup, which was comforting. Then, Jackie and her daughter, Grace, brought over some food as well. She brought two rotisserie chickens, salad, and dessert.

"This is what we Norwegians do! We eat!" she said. Later, she hugged me, saying, "Oh, Nat, you are so brave. Thank you for being such a great example for Grace. She's watching you turn to the Lord and sees how you are handling all of this. We love you!"

Tearfully, I thanked her. Her words meant a lot to me.

Throughout the day, I had several calls and texts from friends and family all over the country. Paul's wife, Kristen, dropped off a huge cooler of ice and drinks. Quincy, one of Dave's coworkers, brought in several platters of sandwiches and cookies. I thanked him for coming and for bringing food.

Tearfully, he said, "Oh, we're making a big list in the shop. There will be other people bringing over more food. I just wanted to bring this right now. We sure are going to miss Dave." I hugged this man I barely knew, grateful for the wonderful people at Caterpillar.

At some point, I made Dave's death 'Facebook official.' I posted a picture of Dave and me two years prior (May of 2011) when I was pregnant with Lydia. I didn't have the heart to say too much, but I did write: "This morning, my beloved, David, went home to meet our loving Savior, Jesus, face to face. Thanks for all of your thoughts and continued prayers. They are greatly appreciated." Within minutes, I had several comments and condolences. I'll never forget the overwhelming love I felt from everyone.

Various people came to the house, including friends in our small group, and later, Pastor Bob, Dean, and Jackie. We sat outside on the deck sharing funny stories about Dave. We laughed, cried, and prayed.

That night, after our guests left and the house grew quiet, I looked at the bookshelf where I had placed the "God Give Me Guts" sign from Aunt Mamie and Uncle Charlie weeks before. I already knew I was going to need a lot of courage, so I prayed, "God give me guts!" Then, I thought, "Perhaps the sign was meant for me all along!"

Chapter 17

"I remain confident of this:
I will see the goodness of the Lord in the land of the living."
Psalm 27:13 NIV

The next morning, Thursday, May 16th, I woke up with a dull headache. I hadn't slept well, but I knew I needed to get out of bed. Then, it hit me: Dave would never again sleep beside me. For weeks, I had dreamed that he suddenly appeared at home in the middle of the night, healed. The look on Dave's face matched only his excitement when Lydia was born. I had hoped for a miracle, but now, those dreams seemed somewhat perplexing.

Then, I considered the dreams could have a different meaning. In my mind's eye, I could envision Dave's excitement at being free from all his pain and suffering, more alive than he ever had been on earth. "Natty! I'm healed! I'm home!" What a glorious sight that must've been! I was comforted by these thoughts but understandably sad for my loss.

Yet, how could I want anything different for Dave? I knew he was healed and did go Home. It just happened differently than I had wanted. And, I realized the problem was not God's failure to come through but my expectations.

That morning, my parents and I planned to meet with George, the funeral director, to finalize the funeral arrangements. We had talked briefly on Wednesday when he had picked up Dave's body. Now, we needed to figure out the details.

Thankfully, Jackie volunteered to watch Lydia for us; it was a blessing knowing she was in good hands. As soon as we parked in her driveway, she ran out of the house to grab Lydia, so we weren't delayed. Jackie also volunteered to pick up my sister from the airport since we didn't know how long we would be.

Then, I drove with my parents to the funeral home. After my parents walked inside, I stayed in the car for a moment. My heart was heavy, yet I could feel my pulse racing. I prayed, "God, help me. Please. I don't know how I am going to do this."

Next, I opened my car door and stepped out. My hands were clammy. Taking a deep breath, I prayed for strength and put one foot in front of the other. "Lord, I need you!" I whispered. All I could do was depend on Him. When I finally reached the entrance, the funeral director welcomed us inside. Another pastor from our church was there, too.

As we greeted George, I felt calm. He was so kind and gracious. He even was tearful at times and apologized. He explained, "My son is the same age as Dave."

My mom later asked, "How are you able to do this day in and day out? You make it look seamless, but it must be so difficult."

His response stood out, yet it was a confirmation that I had chosen the right place. He said, "Well, I grew up in the family business, and I've been doing this for over thirty-five years. For me, it's a calling. It's how I can help people during their great loss." He gave us a brief tour and took us to his office.

While we were at the funeral home, I tried to keep it together and not cry too much. We had a job to do, and it was good to focus on something concrete. My main goals were to honor Dave and bring God glory. Dave's only preference was to be cremated because he felt it was an economical choice. It also solved a potential future challenge. If Lydia and I ever moved away from Fargo, we wouldn't be able to visit his grave if we held a traditional burial.

Once again, I relied on my parents. As we discussed all the options, I asked my dad to give the eulogy for Dave. He had delivered a moving tribute at his mom's funeral years before, and it had quite an impact. I trusted whatever he felt compelled to share would be just right.

Mom helped me with other decisions. Together, we chose a dark blue urn for Dave's ashes because it was simple and masculine. Still, we decided to rent a casket for the funeral to keep the traditional feel. Other decisions included times for the visitation and funeral, how the service should go, and details for the obituary. I chose a handsome picture of Dave and decided to write the obituary at home so I could think about what to say.

I thought of songs for the service and immediately wanted the classic hymn, "It Is Well with My Soul," because during other trials, it has always reminded me to keep an eternal perspective. I couldn't think of other songs on the spot, but the pastor gave me his cell phone number so I could call him later when I made my decision.

When George brought up the funeral location, deep down, I felt the service should be at our church. However, I didn't mention this because I was still processing mixed emotions. I was afraid I would always be thinking of Dave's funeral during worship time. I didn't want to feel sad and lose focus on the singing, praying, or even the sermon. So, I let fear win and opted to have the visitation and the service at the funeral home.

Later in the afternoon, Mom and I picked the flowers out for the casket piece at a local flower shop. Together, we chose a simple white color scheme with calla lilies, carnations, and other flowers. We also requested different types of greenery, which gave it a woodsy feel. I was grateful for Mom's input and her years of experience as a florist. Dave always had an eye for aesthetics, and I knew he would approve!

The next day, Friday, May 17th, I woke up around 7:00 a.m. thinking about what to write for Dave's obituary. As soon as I woke up, I said, "But God, Dave was so young!" Then, in my heart, I felt the Holy Spirit speak to me, "The purpose of life is not to live to be one hundred years old, but to know Jesus and to bring as many people to Him as possible."

That clarification gave me such strength and peace. Certainly, Dave walked with such grace that his life and his death were an example to many. He showed the love of Jesus to everyone. I was so proud of him!

A few minutes later, I called the pastor I had met at the funeral home. I requested a few classic hymns, including "Victory in Jesus," because I felt like we had received victory after all. I wanted Dave's funeral service to point people to the overwhelming triumph we have in Christ. Despite life's ups and downs, we can trust Jesus because He is good.

An hour later, as Mom made breakfast, I sat at the kitchen island to write Dave's obituary. I wondered, "How can one or two pages sum up Dave's whole life and our life together?" Together, Mom and I brainstormed ideas as I wrote about our marriage and Lydia. I wrote about his love for Caterpillar and his coworkers.

I also wrote about Dave's warm smile, kind and generous spirit, and servant's heart. To me, these were his best qualities and what I wanted people to remember about him. After that, I emailed it to the funeral home. From there it was distributed to the local newspapers and our hometown newspapers in Illinois. It was posted on the funeral website, too.

Then, as family started to trickle in, I felt myself go on autopilot. My sister flew in first, followed by Charlie and Mamie. They bought food, laundry detergent, and toiletries, knowing we would need them in the coming days. We had received a lot of food and beverages already, and with the influx of people and supplies, I had no clue where to put everything! But, every time someone did something kind for me, I credited it back to God.

Cynda, my brothers, their girlfriends (now wives), and brother-in-law, Paul, all arrived next. Cynda had driven alone, but the others had carpooled and driven through the night. As everyone arrived and got settled, I wanted to make sure they had everything they needed.

It was comforting to have my loved ones stay at my house. Being the hostess gave me something to focus on, and I didn't mind all the commotion. I set out sheet sets, sleeping bags, and a couple of air mattresses for everyone. It was a little crowded, but no one seemed to mind.

That weekend, I went to Target with Mamie and Livi. They had a list of items to buy, but I just wandered around with them. I found a placemat for Lydia and bought it on a whim. It had a mommy octopus and baby octopus, which somehow felt symbolic. It was just the two of us now. Yet despite my emotions and circumstances, I somehow knew we would be okay.

As the weekend wore on, I was surprised when more and more family came. I will never forget how many people showed up to see us. As I took in all the loving support, I felt the courage to keep moving forward. I was honored that so many of my favorite people would come, though I'm sure I looked a little like the proverbial deer in the headlights.

Periodically, I went to my bedroom for a minute so I could be alone and just breathe. As an introvert, I needed a quiet space to think and process all that was going on. Standing next to my bed, I recalled something God had said to me as we started the cancer journey one year earlier. I had felt the Holy Spirit speak to my heart, "I'm going to use this to show you just how much I love you." A year ago, I had wondered what that meant, and now, I could see how much God loved me. This was measured not just in answered prayers or provision, but by the number of people supporting me!

By Saturday, I had at least fifty people coming in and out of my house. (I stopped counting after that!) As I looked around my living room, kitchen, and dining room, I enjoyed watching different sides of the family catch up with each other. Some people alternated between laughing and crying as they reminisced about Dave and other family members they missed.

On the other hand, Lydia was ecstatic to receive so much attention. She played outside with cousins and other relatives like nothing was wrong. I'm grateful she was so little and didn't understand what had happened. As I watched Lydia innocently playing, I felt a strong urge to protect her. Tearfully, I thought, "I'm Lydia's only remaining parent. I need to do the best I can to let this grief run its course, so I can help her process her own grief someday."

Overall, I took every moment head-on. I didn't allow myself much time to stop and think. Externally, I felt I had to be strong and keep it together. But inside, I was floating along, disoriented, with no real grounding. It was as if the floor had dropped out from under my feet, and I had nothing to hold onto to keep me steady.

At times, it felt like I was in a dream, but I no longer felt as if I were in a nightmare as I had when Dave was sick. His battle with cancer had seemed as if it would never end. Now, I found myself in a new situation, one I didn't know how to handle. I had nothing to compare it with, so I could only take it as it came. At the time, I couldn't think of anyone else who had lost a spouse so young. It would take a while for my new reality to sink in.

A number of friends and family had come to show support, and it seemed like everyone was watching me to see how I would react. I was an inadequate example on my own, but I hoped to point people back to Jesus' peace and strength. I could sense the collective grief around me—in Fargo, online, and around the world. At the same time, it was touching to see Dave's life had mattered to so many people.

On Sunday, May 19th, we prepared for the visitation, which was scheduled from 5:00 p.m. to 8:00 p.m., that evening. During the day, I felt a little frenzied, though I had no real obligations. I had already written the obituary and planned Dave's services. To my relief, Aunt Mamie and Livi stepped in to organize photos of Dave for the evening event. They ran errands and relayed information to family members who were on their way.

Lydia tagged along with various family members, happily unaware of the circumstances. Occasionally, someone would ask for my opinion or needed me to make a simple decision. But overall, it was difficult to connect my thoughts and think straight with all that was going on. Thankfully, my only real choice was what to wear to the visitation and funeral!

That afternoon, I decided upon a knee-length blue dress I had bought at Target. Then, I drove to the visitation with Livi and Lydia. When we arrived at the funeral home, George took us to a private area so we could rest or step out of the public view as needed. Then, he led us through a lobby and showed us where we could place some pictures of Dave and fun family memories.

Next, George took my parents and me into the chapel to see Dave. Previously, I had asked for the casket to remain open for a short period before the public came at 5:00 p.m. I felt it was important to see Dave again, but I was nervous. Lydia, dressed in a frilly pink sundress with tiny white polka-dots, stayed for the moment with others in the hallway. I wanted to see him first and would bring her in later.

Immediately, I noticed flowers everywhere. The chapel seemed smaller because it contained at least twenty-five flower bouquets! I didn't have time to read the cards until later, but family, coworkers, church friends, childhood friends, college friends, and neighbors had all sent flowers and condolences. Mom held my hand as we walked closer to the casket. I was grateful for her calming presence.

Seeing Dave was surreal. I thought, "I've been to many funerals, but now it's my husband who is lying there in the casket! How is this even possible? We were supposed to grow old together..." In some ways, I was forced to acknowledge Dave was gone, which provided some closure. He would not be coming back.

At that moment, I was tearful for my loss, but I felt grateful for the way Dave had lived his life. I was glad the cancer struggle was over, even though Lydia and I were beginning a different journey without our loving husband and father. We hadn't planned for this! And now, we had to learn to walk this new path alone.

As I stood there with these mixed emotions, I was instantly pleased with the outfit I had picked for Dave to wear. I had chosen a combination of clothes he had enjoyed wearing: a long-sleeve black collared shirt with white pin-stripes, layered with a black argyle sweater vest. I had matched these up with a dark grey pair of khakis and Dave's black dress shoes.

A few minutes later, my family, Dave's family, and a few close church friends came into the chapel. We had them come an hour early, around 4:00 p.m., so they could see Dave one last time while the casket was open. It brought me comfort to talk about Dave and his death with those who knew us best.

Then, my mom quietly suggested it might be good for Lydia to see Dave before everyone else arrived. I found her playing with others in the lobby and scooped her up. I whispered, tearfully to her, "Lydi, let's go see Da-Da." At the sound of my voice, she stopped squirming. Perhaps she sensed my intense emotions.

I held Lydia in my arms and walked down the aisle to the casket—only five years before I had walked down another aisle toward Dave. How different things were then! Gathering all my courage and choking back tears, I said, "Lydi, this is the last time we'll see your daddy for a while. We sure will miss him, won't we?"

My parents and sister stood a few steps behind me to offer encouragement and support if I needed it. I had little expectation that Lydia would know what was going on—but it seemed like the right thing to do anyway.

It was a difficult afternoon, but I remained calm. I wanted to honor Dave's memory with grace and dignity, knowing there would be plenty of time to fall apart later. Then, around 4:45 p.m., I heard a commotion in the lobby. I left the chapel to see what was going on. With a sharp breath, I could barely believe my eyes.

Some of Dave's best friends from Illinois were there, along with several Caterpillar friends and coworkers. Then, my mouth fell open as even more aunts, uncles, and cousins trickled in! Most of them had driven all day. Incredulously, I hugged several people and thanked them for coming. It was wild to see so many familiar faces simultaneously!

It meant so much because I know how much time and money it takes to fly or drive and reserve a hotel on short notice. Many of these relatives and friends had small children, so the fact they came was quite generous! I was grateful for their sacrifices in my time of need.

A few of these people also trickled into the chapel to see Dave. Others used the time to catch up with people they knew or peruse the pictures Mamie and Livi had placed on tables in the lobby. As I surveyed all the dear people around me, I immediately grew less sad.

I had expected our local friends and coworkers to come, as well as our immediate families. But I did not expect such a large turnout from everyone else! The small funeral home lobby suddenly felt like it was going to burst at the seams. I was in awe. George, on the other hand, seemed a little panicky.

Wiping his head with a handkerchief, he said, "Based on the large group already here, I expect several hundred people tomorrow. Logistically, we can't have that many people here. We are going to have to move it to the church. I'll call and confirm it all if that's okay with you."

Ironically, days before, I had felt the funeral should be at the church, but I was afraid to speak up. I hadn't wanted negative memories of the funeral at my place of worship. I didn't want my feelings of loss and sorrow to overshadow times when I should be focusing on the Lord. However, I immediately sensed God's blessing and grace in how He set the scene. It was a little easier knowing He was walking with me, preparing the way.

"Of course, Dave's funeral should be at the church," I thought to myself. By the time George spoke to me, the move to our church seemed like a God-thing, so I was excited to see what else He had planned. I was glad now because more people could attend and hopefully gain closure as we grieved together.

We quickly adjusted the plan and notified everyone of the change. Then, I ran an idea by my mom, who was standing with me. "Mom, we need six pallbearers. Do you think the CAT guys would do it?"

She said, "Oh, yes, that's perfect. Dave would be honored!"

So, as each of the men came to the visitation, I asked them to help the next day. Paul, Dean, Mike, and Deven were some of Dave's closest Caterpillar friends. They quickly agreed. To round out the six men, I also asked Matt and Owen, who were friends from church.

Then, George reminded me, "Mrs. White, you requested that at 5:00 p.m., we shut the casket before opening the doors to the public." He asked, "Is that still what you want to do?" I confirmed my choice, and he went to make sure my request was carried out. Dave had always taken good care of himself, and I didn't think he would want everyone to see his dead body.

The casket piece, filled with beautiful white and cream-colored flowers, was placed in the middle of the closed casket. On either side of those flowers, there was a photo of Dave. The first picture was a studio photo of the three of us, taken just six months previously, after Lydia's first birthday. Even though Dave was sick, he looked happy and healthy. It was our last family photo where we all looked our best, so it was very special to me.

The second picture was one of my favorites of just Dave. I had taken the snapshot on vacation a few months before Lydia was born. We had gone to a laid-back, rugged part of Wyoming south of Yellowstone to visit a friend I met in college, through another friend's family.

Wyoming holds a special place in my heart, as my friends and I went out there on a number of exciting trips over the years. We went swimming in hot springs, canoeing on a river, hiking in the mountains, and camping under the stars. We enjoyed hunting, fishing, and off-roading escapades. We searched for antelope, bears, elk, prairie dogs, and other wild animals. We told jokes, played games, sang songs, and had many inspiring conversations out in those wide open, remote spaces.

I could always relax and be myself in Wyoming. Combined with all the fun I had there, it seemed natural to share that with Dave! He wasn't keen on fishing because he had not had much success previously. But, on the day we went, he caught the majority of the fish! Dave looked so alive and happy as he held up the trout we caught for dinner. The bright blue sky and reservoir-lake provided a beautiful backdrop for the picture. It was one of our best adventures together.

And now, seeing the picture on top of Dave's casket helped me remember all the good times we shared. Though I was missing him, I was glad we prioritized that Wyoming trip as we would not be going to Alaska for our ten-year anniversary, like we originally planned.

Soon, our families, coworkers, neighbors, and church friends were lining up in the hallway outside the chapel to pay their last respects. I loved hearing how many people Dave's life had touched, even locally. Most people commented on how much they loved Dave, how he helped them, and how they would miss him. Of all the people who came to the visitation, Dave's supervisor, Paul, stands out.

He had arrived with his wife, Kristen. When it was their turn to greet me, Paul's eyes filled with tears as he hugged me tightly. He and Kristen had become good friends, but I didn't expect such a reaction. Stunned, I looked at Kristen, who nodded and smiled with tears in her eyes, too.

Paul struggled to compose himself, but soon he started praising Dave. He mentioned how much he loved working with Dave and having him on his team. Paul explained it wasn't going to be the same without Dave. Many other Caterpillar employees also came and said similar things. It was extraordinary to see so many emotional men!

That evening, as we returned to the house, I was amazed. The evening had gone even better than I could have imagined. I was relieved to get through the first event, but I was even more thankful that God worked everything out for me. I felt honored to be Dave's wife when everyone spoke so highly of him. It brought me much comfort despite my sorrow.

Chapter 18

"I lift up my eyes to the mountains—where does my help come from? My help comes from the Lord, the Maker of heaven and earth."
Psalm 121:1-2 NIV

On Monday, May 20th, Dave's funeral was scheduled for 3:00 p.m. at our church. The morning was spent running small errands. There was a sense of anticipation, but I was also uneasy. Again, I wanted to be brave, but I didn't know how I was going to make it through the funeral. I knew we had to proceed, though I wished it was over already.

Throughout the day, I withdrew to my bedroom to collect my thoughts. At one point, Livi noticed and followed me. After I explained how I was feeling, she hugged me and helped me pick out a dress. I settled on my favorite knee-length black dress and cardigan with black shoes.

I don't generally like being the center of attention, but I knew many eyes would be on me that day. Thankfully, I had a lot of support! Livi dressed Lydia in a dress my mom had bought for the occasion. It had a full skirt covered in light yellow and blue flowers on a white background. Lydia wore a white cardigan, and I parted her hair with small barrettes.

Whenever I looked at her, all I saw was a beautiful, innocent toddler at her daddy's funeral. Her outfit and a full head of curls made her look like a little doll. She twirled around with cousins and laughed at all the attention she received. But to me, it was a little heartbreaking.

Around 2:00 p.m., we heard a knock on the front door. To my great surprise, Kim and Ginny, two dietitians from Chicago, walked in the door. We had studied nutrition together in college and remained good friends. On Monday, they raced to Fargo and arrived just as we were preparing to leave for the funeral. I was nearly floored to see them!

"What?!" I shrieked. "Oh, my goodness! I can't believe you girls are here!" They had been present at our cruise wedding, the start of my marriage with Dave, and now they were present to witness the end of our marriage five years later at his funeral.

Ginny gave me a big hug and said, "We couldn't imagine missing this, Nat. We really wanted to come!" I was beyond grateful.

Kim also hugged me and whispered in my ear, "Ginny drove like the wind to get here!"

I laughed and thanked these dear friends who had made such an effort to come. They rode with Livi, Lydia, and me to the church. I sat in the driver's seat, still taking an active part in the day, but I paused after I started the car. I had been to church many times, but this was a new experience. The significance of the moment weighed on me.

"You guys, I feel like I'm going to be sick." They all encouraged me to take it one moment at a time. Livi offered to drive for me, but after a few deep breaths and a quick prayer for strength, I was able to drive.

Before the service started, Pastor Bob joined all of our extended family in a large room for a short prayer before the service. Then, he walked us into the sanctuary to the first two or three center rows reserved for us. I briefly glanced around, noticing even more flower bouquets than were at the visitation. Seeing a large crowd boosted my confidence, as well.

I found out later, approximately four hundred people attended Dave's funeral, including some neighbors, a few of my coworkers, and church friends. Also, Caterpillar had shut down parts of their local facility so people could attend if they wanted. I recognized several faces among Dave's coworkers from both North Dakota and Illinois!

During the service, our friends, Pastors David and Ischee, read some Scripture verses. Then, we all worshiped together. I had requested certain songs that, to me, felt more like statements or personal anthems. In addition to "Victory in Jesus," we sang an updated rendition of "Tis So Sweet to Trust in Jesus." We also sang "Give Me Jesus" as a reminder that Dave's faith had not wavered. As we sang, I noticed the pianist had tears in his eyes. I had wanted Dave's funeral to be a celebration, and it was quite a moving experience indeed.

My dad had agreed to speak that day, and what he said was perfect. He shared a few funny stories about Dave, highlighting his servant's heart and his good nature. Dad also addressed the fact that we had been praying for Dave's healing—but he had died instead. Of course, life doesn't always work out how we hope and pray.

Regarding faith, some people might say ours was too small or that God failed us. But we didn't see it that way. We count on Jesus Christ for the final Victory, even when we don't understand. We trust that God is good and always has a plan for us, not because we deserve it, but because of His wisdom, love, and grace. As Dad said, "We don't have to have all the answers to walk by faith."

After Dad sat down, Pastor Bob joked, "Well, I don't have anything left to say!" Then, he reiterated how Dave had walked with the Lord and was faithful to the end. Just about everyone present had personally experienced Dave's kindness. He had helped so many people with projects or minor emergencies! Pastor Bob explained that Jesus was the source of Dave's love for other people.

Pastor Bob also mentioned the fact that Dave had only lived thirty-four years. He made the parallel that Jesus was also in his early thirties when He died. If Jesus had lived to be an old man, he certainly could have performed many more miracles. But that was not His sole mission. Similarly, God had a specific purpose for Dave's life. We may not understand it, but we can trust God saw it through to completion (Philippians 1:6).

Next, Pastor Bob called two men to the podium for a special presentation. In all, Dave had worked nine years at Caterpillar. Chris had been Dave's supervisor in Illinois, and Paul was Dave's supervisor in North Dakota. These men came forward to honor Dave posthumously for his contribution to the company. Each man spoke about his work ethic and character.

Chris mentioned the patent Dave had earned for one of his gear designs. He explained what it entailed, and then he and Paul jointly gave the plaque to me on Dave's behalf. I was a little shaky, but I proudly stood up and walked to the platform to receive the award. Chris smiled and warmly shook my hand. Paul greeted me with another emotional hug.

Pastor Bob made a few closing remarks, and we closed with one of my favorite songs. As we sang "It Is Well with My Soul," I raised my hands as a declaration of worship and surrender. I knew I had years of intense grief work to do. Yet, at that moment, I chose to see beyond my pain, trusting that eventually, the Lord would bring something good from this situation. So, I willfully gave God free reign, remembering that I am just a vessel to be used for His glory.

Then, the six pallbearers came to transfer Dave's body out to the hearse. Together, the men picked up the casket and carried it up the center aisle of the sanctuary. I followed along with all the family. Then, everyone else gathered with us in the lobby, where Pastor Bob said a few final words. My heart felt like it was in my throat, and I could barely breathe.

Knowing Dave's body would be cremated, the finality of this goodbye was strong. We would not be going to a cemetery. As the pallbearers walked toward the outside door, I suddenly felt compelled to reach out and touch the casket as it passed by. I wasn't really thinking; it just felt right.

Immediately after the service, we had a light reception of cookies and punch in the church gym. Perhaps everyone expected me to stay in one spot and cry, but I wanted to make the most of the opportunity at hand. Even in my grief and shock, I was grateful to be surrounded by friends and family, who otherwise would have never been all together at one time.

Many people were from out of town, and I wanted to thank each of them for coming. Therefore, I spent my time walking from table to table greeting everyone. While doing so, I noticed some people were nearly beside themselves with emotion and tears. Several people told me, "I'm a total wreck! I don't know how you are going to get through this!"

I probably looked calmer than I felt. I was quick to acknowledge the people in my support system, but I also said, "If you see anything strong in me, that's Jesus!" I wasn't sure how I was going to make it without Dave, but I knew I could make it through with Jesus. He had been faithful to walk with us during cancer, and I knew somehow He would heal my heart again.

Unexpectedly, I started feeling rather cheerful as I moved around the room. I was relieved the service had gone so well, even better than I could have planned. By God's grace, instead of feeling sad, I found joy in the number of people who had come. It was refreshing to see everyone.

One of Dave's coworkers told me, "That was the most uplifting and encouraging funeral I have ever been to!" I was glad Dave's funeral had such an impact. I was also grateful a friend was able to videotape the service. I haven't yet watched it because I don't have the energy to relive those memories. But, I am glad to have it for Lydia's sake if she is curious in the future.

Later, I talked with nearly a dozen of our Caterpillar friends from Decatur, Illinois, who had made the trip. I was honored to see them and invited them over to the house so we could catch up. I wrote down my address for those who could make it.

Evening came, and I again counted over fifty people in my home. We used every single chair I could find! I pulled chairs from the office and folding chairs out of storage. The weather was finally getting warmer, and some guests went outside to use the patio table and chairs. That night, someone generously ordered pizza for the entire crowd. I could envision Dave walking around to see if anyone needed a chair or perhaps a refill. How I missed him!

Sometimes, I felt myself withdrawing to my bedroom again so I could regroup. It was at least 10:30 p.m. before the last of my guests left. I was worn out, yet continued processing all that had happened and how many people had been present.

Instead of going to sleep, Mom, Cynda, and I started opening cards and tracking any gifts so we could thank everyone. Some people had supported Dave's favorite charities in his honor, per my request. Others sent money to be put toward a college fund for Lydia.

At one point, I said to Mom and Cynda, "Look at this! These stacks of cards are from people at Caterpillar. Based on the handwriting, it looks like the men wrote in the cards, not their wives." It was touching these men would take it upon themselves to write out such heartfelt words. It's just not something men often do! It was extremely comforting to see how much everyone loved Dave.

The next day, May 21st, our friends and family started to head back home. Some of them had left Monday after the funeral because they needed to work the next day. But, many people decided to leave bright and early on Tuesday. Life has a way of moving us forward, but I didn't know what that meant for me. Everyone else was able to return to their normal lives, but mine would never be the same again.

That day was also bittersweet because Dave's cremation was scheduled on the same day Lydia turned eighteen months. I'm not sure anyone else made the connection, but I kept thinking of all that had happened while she was so little. We could not have crammed in more drama if we had tried! On the one hand, I was grateful she would never recall the chemo and chaos. But I was also sad she would never remember her daddy and the wonderful man he was.

As everyone in my support system began to leave, I started to realize how much help I was going to need. My parents were packing up after spending nearly a month at my house. Charlie and Mamie were still in town, too. They all stayed another day to help me clean up a bit. As I put away all the chairs and reorganized my house, I felt a little lost. Dave had always made sure everything had a place.

Carrying a box downstairs, I started to cry, thinking to myself, "How am I going to fix things when they break? How can I maintain this house by myself? I don't know what I am going to do without Dave." Tearfully, I walked back upstairs to put away some pictures. As I stood at the kitchen island, my chest tightened, and I felt a sharp pain in or near my heart. With a hand on my chest, I took several deep breaths.

Uncle Charlie noticed this and walked over to me. Drawing close, he hugged me and let me cry. "My heart hurts," I sobbed.

He nodded sympathetically, "I know, Natty. I know."

Then, I remembered that his first wife, my aunt, had died of cancer years before. I was grateful he could understand what I was going through. After a few minutes, we talked a little more. Giving a brave smile, I said, "Grief stinks!"

Later that day, Mom and Mamie asked what I was going to do next. My brother, Patrick, was getting married the next weekend, on Saturday, the 25th (Memorial Day weekend). After some discussion, I decided to go to Illinois for the wedding and to recuperate a bit. I had no other agenda other than taking some downtime. My mom could help with Lydia, and I knew I would always regret missing my brother's wedding if I didn't go.

Wednesday, May 22nd, was one full week after Dave had died. The funeral director, George, brought over his ashes and a few other keepsakes. He expressed his condolences and asked if there was anything else he could do for me. I could sense his sorrow over Dave, though they had never met.

"You've been so kind, George," I replied. "Thank you for all you've done for us. I'm so glad you were there to walk us through this process."

Trying to pack for Illinois was challenging since I couldn't think clearly. Also, I hated to leave Fargo without Dave because it just felt wrong. Yet, it forced me to recognize the empty feeling in my heart. The next morning, I followed my parents back, though I took a slower pace with Lydia. I drove about ten hours to Rockford, Illinois, near Dave's hometown of Belvidere. I briefly visited some friends on the way.

My sister-in-law, Brooke, and her husband, Dale, were staying at Cynda's house with their family before returning to Florida. Space was limited, so Lydia and I went there to visit everyone but stayed overnight with other friends. I was grateful for my friends' hospitality, and I was glad to be in familiar, peaceful surroundings.

At this point, I only wanted to be near people who already knew the details of my story—those who would shower love on me and not require any explanations. I didn't want to talk about cancer, Dave's death, our choices, faith, or anything complex. I just wanted to decompress.

The next afternoon, I finished driving to my parents' house with Lydia. We stayed in Illinois for about ten days. In some ways, it felt empowering to drive all that way with Lydia by myself. I was sad and in shock, but I kept putting one foot in front of the other.

On Saturday, we drove about an hour-and-a-half to Springfield, Illinois, to celebrate Patrick and Melissa's wedding. Thankfully, I was able to keep my composure as I met everyone. Melissa's family was gracious and warm. When I met Aunt Becky, the hostess, she hugged me and said, "You are so brave, and your daughter is just beautiful. We are praying for you!" It was touching that she would acknowledge me and my situation.

"Thank you so much," I said, trying not to cry. Becky didn't have time for a lengthy discussion, but I was thankful she was aware of my pain.

Naturally, I couldn't help but think of my wedding. My marriage with Dave had turned out to be quite an adventure! However, I didn't allow myself to dwell on my feelings that day. I tried to be a part of the celebration and not detract from the joyous occasion. Just because my marriage had ended didn't mean I wasn't happy for Patrick and Melissa. I wanted to honor them on their special day, not make it be about me.

During the reception, I greeted and talked with people at my table, more or less like I normally would. That evening, as we were leaving, I took Lydia in my arms and grabbed a balloon. We walked out to the sidewalk, and I asked her, "Do you want to send Da-Da a balloon?" This seemed to catch her attention. I whispered a tearful, "We love you, Dave. We miss you so very much." Then, I released the balloon and watched it float to the sky.

The rest of our time in Illinois was intentionally low-key. During the trip, I visited more family and a few friends, such as our old neighbors from when we lived in Decatur. They had been encouraging us from afar throughout that year but had not made it to the funeral.

One day, we met a dear family friend, a widow named Sandy, for lunch. Her husband died unexpectedly when her three sons were young. She always makes me laugh, and, that day, she cheered me up quite a bit. Sandy also gave me some tips about grief; she validated what I was feeling and said it would get better eventually. Seeing her lightheartedness after everything she'd been through inspired me to take her advice.

Soon, it was time to return to home. I had to work and needed to get affairs in order. Mom said she could come with me, but I replied, "Oh, you don't have to do that. I think we'll be okay." I didn't feel like entertaining anyone, and in some ways, I just wanted to be alone in my grief. I see now that would have been the worst thing for me.

Instead, Mom told me, "I want to come; it's my job to take care of you and make sure you are alright. Let me do this for you. I can help with Lydia and anything else you might need." For emphasis, she added, "I've already told your dad I will be gone for two weeks!"

I didn't realize just how much I would need my mom's support, but it turned out to be such a blessing! We drove back to Fargo on Sunday, June 2nd, and as soon as we left, I was glad Mom hadn't listened to me telling her I was okay! I was grateful not to have to be alone with my thoughts and an active toddler. We drove for several hours, talking about Dave, grief, and how things would be different now.

Then, somewhere in the middle of Wisconsin, the engine of my Santa Fe started knocking. We were along I-94, at least six hours from Fargo (around halfway). I noticed we were losing speed, yet we were able to coast to a gas station nearby before losing power. We called my dad for advice.

Dave and I had planned to buy a different car, but then he grew too sick. Thankfully, Mom stayed with Lydia in the car while I checked various fluid levels and topped them off with supplies from the gas station. Dad talked me through my options. I didn't want to pay for the car to be towed several hours back to North Dakota. Also, I didn't want to get stuck in Wisconsin for several days if something was seriously wrong.

Fortunately, after cooling down for about half an hour, the car started working again! I was grateful my mom was there; otherwise, I would have had to keep track of Lydia while I tried to fix the car. We drove cautiously and made it home that evening. I was exhausted from twelve hours of driving, not to mention the emotional turmoil of arriving home without Dave.

As if that were not enough, the next day, my car broke down again! This time, I barely cleared a main intersection in Fargo before pulling off the road. Seeing smoke rising from my engine, I called the repair shop for a tow. The mechanic confirmed the spark plugs and a few other components all needed to be replaced. He said it was good I was not on the highway when it happened. I silently thanked God for keeping us safe the day before!

I called my dad back in Illinois as well as our Caterpillar friend, Dean, for input. The mechanic was knowledgeable and had always done right by us. But without Dave to oversee the work, I wanted to make sure the costs were reasonable. I was suddenly aware of how easy it would be for people to take advantage of me.

Later, the mechanic mentioned he found some other damage he thought was related to when we were hit from behind six months before. Surprisingly, he was able to submit an insurance claim. Therefore, the repairs were fully covered, and I received a refund check in the mail to reimburse me for the original repair fees. It seemed like another way God was taking care of me! I was able to drive Dave's truck while the repairs were made, so that was helpful, too.

It has been said mothers know best, and in my case, it was true. I thought I could handle things on my own, but I didn't realize how much effort grief required. Mom was a great help in those first weeks of adjustment. She understood I needed to get out and start doing normal things. I would have preferred to stay home and isolate myself, but one afternoon, she suggested we go out for lunch before running errands and getting groceries.

A few minutes later, as we walked into Noodles & Company, I was overwhelmed. As silverware hit the plates around us and glasses clunked onto each table, I thought, "It's so loud! Do none of these people care that Dave just died?!" Everyone kept laughing and enjoying their meals, totally unaware of my internal trauma. I didn't want Mom to feel bad and kept all of this to myself. I didn't have much appetite and took home most of my food to eat later.

Next, we went to Walmart. Mom offered to take Lydia with her so I could focus. I had not made a list because nothing sounded good to eat. Thus, I just roamed up and down each aisle and found things I liked 'well enough.' When I turned a corner and saw Dave's favorite salad dressing, I whispered, "Oh, Lord, this is so difficult!" Who knew something as simple as ranch dressing could cause such emotional pain?

I wanted to leave, but I could not find Mom and Lydia. "This was not a good idea to split up! Where are they?" I thought. I found them a few minutes later in the jewelry section, but in the meanwhile, I forced myself to pick up some other essential items.

Eventually, grocery shopping at our usual stores became too painful, so I gave myself permission to switch stores. This helped me get into a new routine, though my budget took a toll. My focus shifted from saving money to finding peace and joy. I spent a little more money at other stores, but it seemed worth it at the time and helped me move forward emotionally.

One afternoon, Mom, Lydia, and I went to a plant nursery. She bought some cheerful flowers to decorate my front step and entryway. Also, she planted a cherry tomato plant for me, hoping to encourage me. It was a thoughtful gesture, but sadly, the poor plant didn't fare well! In my grief, I often forgot to water it. The mighty wind knocking it over didn't help. By midsummer, what remained of it was propped up against my deck railing, dry and withered!

Day after day, I walked by the tomato plant in a daze. In some ways, it represented my life quite well at the time. But soon, I noticed there was fruit. Despite appearances, my poor tomatoes were hanging on! And that's when I saw God's grace at work. Everything changed when I realized I didn't have to do it all myself. God was helping me.

After a while, I took a picture of the resilient tomato plant because it inspired me. I reflected, "I must look like this plant, down and out, a little worse for the wear. But, God is still at work." I had no clear plan at the time, but I knew He would make something good out of it all if I didn't lose hope (Jeremiah 29:11). His grace was covering me!

Part III

Grief and Moving Forward

Chapter 19

"Come to Me, all you who labor and are heavy laden,
and I will give you rest."
Matthew 11:28 NKJV

During the two weeks Mom stayed with me, I returned to work and tried to resume some sort of a routine. My friend, Debbi, and I shared an office, and I was grateful I didn't have to sit alone. I only worked a couple of days a week, but the commitment provided me with much-needed structure. It was helpful to focus on other people and tasks instead of on myself. I was comforted knowing so many of my coworkers attended the funeral and were supportive.

One coworker, a nurse, pulled me aside to tell me her husband had died suddenly when her four children were young. I hadn't known she was a widowed, single mom, but she was so kind to share her story. I readily accepted her advice, which included some pointers on grief and how to explain things to Lydia as she grew. Seeing that she was smiling and doing well gave me hope that someday it would be easier for me, too.

One afternoon, Mom and I heard a song on the car radio, which became an instant favorite. Soft and slow, "Lord, I Need You," by Matt Maher, resonated with what I was feeling. The lyrics emphasized that we need Jesus every hour. I paused at the stop sign and reflected, "I need Him every minute!" I knew I needed to rely on the Lord for strength, especially when I felt vulnerable without Dave or a plan. The song went on to say Jesus is our defense. This caught my attention because I felt like people wanted answers I couldn't provide.

In my mind's eye, I envisioned a courtroom where Jesus was on my side, standing up for me. It brought me peace, despite the uncertainty I faced. I decided to let people think whatever they wanted about God and Dave's death. Really, even if he had been miraculously healed, the idea that his cancer could return would have hung over our heads. I typed up the lyrics as a reminder and put them next to my bathroom mirror, where they remain even now.

Still, there were several surprises those first few weeks after Dave died. Suddenly, my life had gone from 'we' to 'me.' Even just finding the right personal pronouns to use was an adjustment. Was it our house or my house, Dave's truck or my truck? Should I refer to Lydia as our daughter or my daughter? Everything had changed, but I knew if I let God take care of me and order my steps, He would make everything right in the end.

In the meantime, however, I sought to resolve Dave's accounts and personal estate. With Mom's help on the home front, I was able to make progress in closing various legal matters. First, I made an appointment with the attorney we used to draft our will. The attorney explained the probate process, which is necessary after someone dies. I was nervous because we had never signed the document, but the attorney assured me it would be okay.

We revised the will, sadly removing Dave's information, which was no longer valid. I was a little anxious until I signed the updated version a week or so later. In my grief, I was sensitive to the fact that all the parenting responsibilities fell on me now. But as soon as I signed the paperwork, I felt relief that I had a plan in place for Lydia's future. I knew that's what Dave would have wanted, too.

Then, when I notified the bank that he had died, they immediately froze our joint account, which I did not expect. Thankfully, I had withdrawn a small amount of cash to get groceries beforehand. But, I couldn't access my account to pay bills until I provided his death certificate and created a new account. Of course, that took a few days and was rather inconvenient!

Next, I made a list of all the household bills that needed to be transferred to my name. As I explained my situation over the phone, most of the technicians were kind and expressed their condolences. Still, I had to pay several account transfer fees even though they were only taking Dave's name off the account. It didn't seem fair, though I didn't feel like arguing with them. I knew they were only doing their jobs, but all of this cost me a lot of time and emotional energy!

Of note, one thing that brought me comfort in this process was Dave's password list, which he had created for me. Amid all the stress and grief, I was encouraged to know he had prepared for the worst-case scenario. As I worked to close his estate, it was a little easier since I had all the information I needed in one place. I didn't have to spend time or tears looking for it.

Dave's paycheck had funded over ninety percent of our budget since moving to Fargo, and I soon felt the blow financially. I had enough money to stay afloat for a little while because we had been able to build up our savings. But still, I was unsure about what to do long-term. So, I turned my worries into prayers, no longer allowing fear to get the best of me.

My prayers were constant. "Lord, how am I going to afford to live in this house? Do I need to move? God, please give me wisdom and show me what I should do!"

I immediately pared down my expenses, not wanting to spend money needlessly. Taking over the budget had been heart-wrenching at first, but now I praised God that Dave was able to guide me through the process. Back then, it had been a painful burden, evidence he was going downhill. Now I saw all that practice had been a blessing in disguise as God prepared me for the unknown.

I spent some time considering how I was going to earn more money. I prayed, "God, will I need to work full-time now? Should I go back to school to get a higher-paying job?" I already had earned my Master's degree, but I wondered if it was enough. However, the thought of working full-time or going back to school seemed impossible.

Over and over, I calculated the costs and time. I determined I would need to work approximately sixty hours a week to cover my household budget, full-time daycare costs, etc. I had always enjoyed school and had been a good student. However, I knew school would not be a good fit because of the time and focus it would require.

Both options, working more and going back to school, sounded miserable because I needed to recover. On the other hand, I was committed to doing whatever it took to survive and take care of Lydia. So, I decided to trust the Lord at a deeper level. I prayed continually, "God, You are Jehovah Jireh, My Provider. Please help me figure this out. I don't know what to do to make ends meet, but I trust You, Jesus."

I gave myself a grace period of one year before making any significant financial decisions. It seemed wise to wait before making choices that would affect our future. Waiting also gave me emotional space to grieve. In my case, I didn't want to regret selling my house or anything else. Some people feel compelled to make other decisions, but for me, my home was a comfort and a haven. Our families were very supportive, though they would have probably preferred to have me closer so they could help me more.

Additionally, I had taken candid pictures of Lydia and Dave together at home, but I wanted her to have a sense of context, which is not always seen in a photograph. For instance, I wanted to point to the built-in cubby holes Dave had made and show her a picture of them together during the building process. Since Lydia was so little, I knew it might take a few years before she was old enough to grasp all that had happened—so staying in our house made sense for the time being.

Then, one day in early June, I heard from Paul at Caterpillar. He called to check in and asked me to come to the office. He wanted to give me Dave's personal belongings after they cleaned out his desk. Paul notified me that Joe, the HR manager, wanted to meet with me, too. We agreed to meet the next morning.

Mom, Lydia, and I went in Dave's truck because my car was unreliable and kept having trouble. Plus, it just seemed right to take the truck there one last time. When we arrived, I was a little anxious. I wasn't sure what Joe might need to discuss. We lived in the same neighborhood at the time, but I didn't know him or his family well.

I texted Paul to let him know we were in the parking lot. Then, he and another man brought Dave's personal belongings directly to the truck. I could have carried everything out after our visit, but it was kind of them to help us. They each brought a box of items, which included some notebooks, binders, pens, and a few remaining business cards.

Afterward, I thanked them, and we all walked inside together. It was so strange to be at Caterpillar without Dave. In the lobby, Paul gave me an envelope and said, "I wanted you to have this, too. Inside there are a few emails from Caterpillar employees in our other locations. Also, when they were clearing Dave's work laptop, the IT guys sent their condolences."

I looked inside the envelope and saw five or so pieces of paper. Dave had offered technical support to various Caterpillar facilities, including offices in England and Singapore. It moved me that, while they couldn't attend funeral, the employees had sent notes. After Paul led us to Joe's office, he hugged me and said to let him know if I needed anything.

Mom and Lydia came with me as Joe welcomed us into his office. Then, he shared some valuable information with us. We discussed details regarding Dave's employment and how much he had contributed to the company. Joe also gave me information about Dave's life insurance policy. He gave me a brochure with the phone number to call and advised me on how to start the process. We thanked Joe for his help, and he reiterated how much Dave would be missed.

As we were leaving Joe's office, other employees stopped by to say hello. It was touching to hear people talk so highly of Dave. Mom and I were in awe. Our time at Caterpillar was healing, and we were grateful for the compassion and encouragement we received.

Back at home, we read the notes in the envelope from Paul. Dave had met so many wonderful people when he traveled for work. Thus, Mom and I were inspired as we read emails from all over the world, including Chile and Australia.

One man in India had written about the impression Dave had made on him. When the man came to work at the local Caterpillar facility, Dave befriended him and helped him acclimate to the new environment. Dave helped him find an apartment and rent a vehicle. They enjoyed eating lunch together on several occasions, too. Despite cultural and religious differences, Dave's kindness and generosity spoke volumes.

Within days, I called the life insurance company using the information from Joe. It would take a few months for all the paperwork to be approved, so it was good I didn't delay. Somewhere in the process, I also made an appointment to get my own life insurance policy. In my emotional state, I was worried something would happen to me. I couldn't bear the thought of leaving our precious daughter all alone.

I also called the local Social Security office to report Dave's death. I scheduled a phone appointment to fill out some paperwork for survivor benefits, which are primarily for the young children of deceased workers. George, the funeral director, had encouraged me not to wait because some of the forms are time-sensitive. The amount of money each family in this situation may receive varies based on several factors. There are certain stipulations, but since I had not been expecting any help, I was humbled to see it as God's provision.

I was grateful, but it took me a few months to accept the concept of receiving Social Security survivor benefits. I was raised to work hard, pay my way, and help others, so it wasn't easy to admit I needed this help. There was no way I could've managed on my own, however. Without those benefits, I envisioned my income quickly falling below the poverty line.

While I did have certain assets and some savings, I didn't know how everything would end up. Social Security provided some relief, but it did not fully replace Dave's paycheck or solve all my problems, so I continually had to reprioritize. I still had to make decisions about health insurance (expensive COBRA policy or go without) and paying for the funeral, which was still costly though we had made conservative choices. Would I be in the red or in the black? It felt wise to hold off making any unnecessary financial decisions that first year of grief.

Cynda also reminded me that since he was sixteen, Dave often worked three jobs to earn money. At some point, I understood that, although Dave had worked so hard, he would never have the opportunity to draw Social Security retirement benefits. For me, it was an answer to prayer. All Dave's efforts would benefit Lydia and me instead.

It's no surprise that being a single mom is demanding. Many single moms work multiple jobs to provide for their families, for example. Similarly, widows also struggle, and I certainly had unique issues of my own as I was in both categories. In those early days without Dave, grief made my situation seem impossible. But as I processed all of this, I saw a whole new level of God's grace.

Jesus already did the most difficult work on the Cross. Through His death and resurrection, He has provided all we need to live for Him. Ephesians 2:10 says, "For we are God's handiwork, created in Christ Jesus to do good works, which God prepared in advance for us to do." I found deep comfort in knowing God is the Master Planner. He has good plans for my life, and I just have to walk them out. This often requires courage and commitment, but I can rely on His strength and provision.

Finally, in those first weeks of grief, I had to make another big decision. It seemed that grief and motherhood took all my energy, and I soon realized I could not care for our dog in the capacity she deserved. Britain, a beautiful golden retriever, was basically a sixty-pound lap dog! She always wanted to be close-by.

I often had to carry Lydia or push her stroller during Britain's daily walks. Britain had boundless energy and always wanted to race ahead, so this took considerable effort and coordination when the weather was good. I knew when winter came, it would be impractical at best. Plus, Lydia was growing fast and needed my full attention.

Then, I remembered how much my brother, Patrick, loved Britain. He loved petting her and always gave her extra attention. He and his new wife, Melissa, had said to let them know if I needed anything. So, after praying about options and discussing it with my mom, I called Patrick and Melissa to ask if they would take the dog for me. They quickly agreed.

After Mom's two-week stay came to an end, we met Dad about halfway in Eau Claire, Wisconsin, so I didn't have to drive so far. We brought Britain along, and then she made the trip to Illinois with my parents. It was bittersweet as I hugged our beloved dog goodbye, though I knew she would be happy. "Thanks for being such a great dog, Brit," I said with tears in my eyes. Dave and I had gotten Britain when she was two years old, so it felt a little like I was giving away a child.

On my six-hour drive back home, I was emotional but prayerfully worked through my grief. "How could my life have changed so dramatically in such a short time? First, Dave, and now, Britain is gone." Finally, as I pulled into my driveway, I resolved to keep moving forward.

My dear friend, Katie, arrived on Tuesday. We had been college roommates at NIU, and she eventually ended up in Montana. Katie couldn't attend Dave's funeral because of the short timing, but now, she flew in and stayed five days with us. Katie hadn't been to Fargo before, so I enjoyed showing her around. We tried out new restaurants and some familiar ones I had enjoyed with Dave. I was relieved I could be myself with her and not have to pretend I was okay.

One day, I called Paul at Caterpillar to ask if I could bring Katie to tour the facility, which had been a significant part of my life with Dave. Paul quickly agreed and personally took us through the building. Along the way, other friends and coworkers came to say hello or join the tour. The massive facility was impressive, but Katie was also intrigued by how much everyone loved Dave.

Back in June 2010, three years before, Dave had brought donuts into the office to share with the team on his first day. Because he hadn't had a chance to say goodbye, it seemed fitting to bring donuts as a final gesture toward his coworkers. In delivering the donuts, Katie and I were able to see where Dave's desk had been. I had never been to this part of the facility, so it helped me to envision him happily at work and brought me a sense of closure.

During her visit, Katie also volunteered to help me around the house. I had her clean out Dave's truck, which was in the driveway. I had decided to sell it because each time I saw the big, white truck, I would think, "Oh, Dave's home!" I would get excited, only to be hit by a wave of deep disappointment as I realized, "No, Dave's not home." The emotional weight was growing too much for me.

Around this time, our Caterpillar friends, Mike and Becca, offered to let the truck sit in their driveway instead. This and Katie's offer to clean it for me lifted a burden and brought healing. Selling Dave's truck had been one of my bargaining points when he was sick. Yet, through this experience, I let go of any anxiety and let God work on my behalf. It would have taken me a while to figure out all the details on my own, but He motivated these dear friends to help me.

Much later, I called Katie to ask what she remembered about her visit (to help with this book). She said, "I was amazed at how quickly things came full circle. You would be talking about this excruciating emotional pain, but within minutes, you would be praising God for what He had done for you."

"There was only one time I wasn't sure if you would be okay," Katie told me. "We stayed up talking late, and one night, you started crying and didn't stop for several minutes. I didn't know what to do! But eventually, you felt better, and we talked about it. You were so sad, but you were also grateful." After hearing this, I recalled the many nights I cried myself to sleep that first year.

Chapter 20

"Give your burdens to the Lord, and he will take care of you.
He will not permit the godly to slip and fall."
Psalm 55:22 NLT

It is common to feel a spectrum of emotions after the loss of a loved one. I experienced this, too. On the one hand, I felt relief, not that Dave was gone, but because the cancer part of our journey was over. Then again, I felt uncertainty because I had to come to grips with my new reality being far different than what I had thought—and much like what I had feared. But with time and a little rest, I realized I was not the only one to have lost someone.

Other people have faced similar situations, or even much worse scenarios, and survived. As I pondered my emotions, I thought, "These things happen, and somehow, people get through them. If they can do it, then I can, too." I knew it would be challenging, but instead of giving in to fear, I trusted God to lead me, help me, and heal my broken heart.

I also knew God didn't owe me anything, including answers. Nowhere in the Bible does it say life will be easy or free of trials. On the contrary, Jesus Himself suffered greatly and said we would have trouble, too (John 16:33). But, I could have peace knowing I had His power and strength to get through the immense grief. So, I let go of any false expectations and clung to Jesus. In His presence, I found hope like an anchor, strong and sure (Hebrews 6:19).

Three years earlier, Dave and I had come to Fargo for the very first time to scout out the area before accepting his new position. Together, we drove around and explored the community. As we neared the northern end of town, looking across fields as far as our eyes could see, I began to have an odd feeling. However, I could only describe it to Dave as, "I feel like my right arm is cut off." Of course, since I am right-handed, it would be a significant adjustment if I had to do everything left-handed!

Back then, I chalked it up to nerves. But now, without Dave, the feeling came again. Suddenly, I understood that he had been like my right arm.

Dave had always been so reliable. Yet without him, I needed to learn an entirely new way to live. At first, everything I did took so much effort and required me to change my habits. I had to learn different ways to solve problems and ask for help. Thankfully, it became easier with time.

In the early stages of grief, I had several moments of ambivalence. Sometimes, I felt both fierce and fragile simultaneously, and at other times, I didn't know how I should feel. Generally, I just prayed and processed these feelings on my own. In my discomfort, I wanted to do something to alleviate my pain or get through it faster. It was rough, and I often felt like running away and ignoring it altogether. Even so, I knew I needed to face the pain, not hide from it. So, I decided to be present with my emotions.

Similarly to how I would talk to a friend in need, I learned to sit with my grief until it felt better. In my mind's eye, it was as if I was sitting on a park bench and the hurting part of my heart—grief—came over, needing a place to sit. I could get up and move away from the pain, or I could give those emotions space on the bench.

It was tough to process my complex emotions, but I tried to treat myself well and give myself grace. In those moments, I might pray about what to do, sing to encourage myself, journal my thoughts, or reframe my feelings and experiences.

Sometimes the feelings would be fleeting, and at other times, it took several hours or days to process. But later, when the timing felt right, and I had gained perspective, I shared what I had learned. I talked with my family, friends, neighbors, pastors, or anyone who would listen! I also posted some of these insights online. The healing process took a lot of emotional work, but I have not regretted giving myself time to grieve.

Early on in the grief process, I made a connection between how I felt in high school after my friend, Seth, died and how I felt after losing Dave. Of course, there are many differences in what happened; however, the traumatic sense of grief was the same. I was able to use what I had learned previously as a template for processing Dave's death. In a way, it felt like redemption.

I also asked a professional Christian counselor about grief support classes and counseling. I was not sure I needed her help, but I wanted to do whatever was necessary to heal. She did not have a specific recommendation for me but reminded me that Jesus Christ is the Wonderful Counselor (from Isaiah 9:6). She implied that if I let God take care of me, He would make sure I had the closure and healing I needed. He would bring wholeness as I walked closely with Him. Based on my previous experience with grief, I knew she was right.

Prayerfully, I understood I had to let grief run its course, however ugly it was and however long it took. In high school, I had tried to avoid my pain through busyness. I often chose to bottle up my grief and internalize it. Now, I decided to clear my schedule of anything unnecessary so that I could grieve appropriately. (That may look different for each of us.)

I allowed myself the freedom to share the burden of grief with those I trusted, those who cared deeply about Lydia and me. I also chose not to fake feeling fine if I wasn't. If I didn't feel happy, I wasn't going to force myself to carry on as such. I didn't have to make everyone around me feel miserable, but I also could be honest with myself and others. I could share my feelings and let other people provide feedback when needed.

When people don't deal appropriately with intense emotions, they have a way of resurfacing in other ways. This may include post-traumatic stress, addictions, poor decisions, or regrets. Some people never move beyond their grief. It's like they get stuck and are stunted from future growth and happiness. I didn't want to deal with any of these delayed reactions for both Lydia's sake and mine. I wanted to keep moving forward.

Because she was so young and had no understanding, Lydia was somewhat protected from the worst parts of cancer and grief. She would not remember the trauma Dave and I had endured. Still, I didn't know what emotional needs Lydia might have later on. Thus, I resolved to deal with my grief in healthy ways so that I could be emotionally available for her when she needed me.

Through our cancer journey, I had learned to choose faith as my default instead of fear. When we choose to trust and follow Jesus, we can live victoriously. Victory, for me, meant I finally understood what it meant to be unafraid. Within days of Dave's death, I reached a crossroad. I've heard it said that around ninety percent of the things we fear never happen. Well, all of my worst fears had come true: Dave *did* die.

Yet amazingly, I discovered when everything in my life fell apart, God Himself was holding together what remained. "The eternal God is your refuge, and underneath are the everlasting arms..." (Deuteronomy 33:27). When I felt like I was free-falling into despair, the Lord caught me. By faith, I saw everything that truly mattered to me was secure. I had peace Dave was safe in Heaven. He had made it! We, too, had been through the fire, but Lydia and I were doing well. By God's grace, we had survived. That doesn't mean it was easy, however.

For several months after Dave died, the early evenings were particularly tricky. Previously, Dave usually came home from work around 5:30 p.m. He would walk through the door, greet me, and tell me about his day. How I missed that! I also noticed Lydia would get cranky, even with a snack. So, to push through that time, I started taking her to the park in our neighborhood in her little red wagon. We would stay around forty-five minutes and then walk home and have a later dinner.

I thought it was a good idea to go during our dinner hour to take my mind off of Dave. Yet, what I hoped would provide relief brought another challenge. I had assumed other families would be at home eating at that time. Instead, I saw several dads playing, chasing, and pushing their kids on the swings. To my dismay, this only reminded me of Dave's absence.

To be polite, I would briefly say hello to the families and make small talk about the weather. But, I also found myself explaining why we were there—trying to cope without Dave. It seemed necessary for me to clarify that Lydia did have a dad, but he had died. Of course, no one would likely have noticed anything unusual if I hadn't mentioned it! At the time, I continued to wear my wedding rings.

Soon, it became awkward because none of these strangers knew how to respond to my grief. After a few days of going to the park, I realized I was trying to defend myself out of fear. They probably weren't judging me, but I let myself feel that way. Thankfully, with much prayer and reflection,

I remembered Jesus is my defender. Eventually, I decided the opinion of strangers should not matter to me.

To avoid having these embarrassing conversations with strangers, I resolved not to explain myself unless it came up naturally. I applied this basic rule when I went to the park, the grocery store, and even church. On occasion, I did have the opportunity to share about Dave with someone I just met. This included when I felt God wanted to use my story to comfort another widow, for example. We still went to the park before our evening meal when the weather was good, but we also started listening to the radio during dinner.

Eventually, wearing my rings on my left hand became a burden—a painful reminder of what had been. Nevertheless, it felt easier to wear the rings and keep up the appearance that I was married (unless asked, of course). It was difficult to see myself as a single mom, and I didn't want to be stereotyped according to social stigmas I perceived. My pride told me my situation was somehow different.

But as I worked through my grief, I clung to Psalm 68:5 which says, in part, "God is a father to the fatherless and a defender of widows." I re-evaluated my position after I felt the Lord whisper to my soul, "Natalie, I'm asking you to trust Me with this."

I knew He could make it right in due time, whether I remarried someday or not. As a result, I then decided to keep my rings on because I treasured them and wanted to honor Dave's memory. It felt like a big breakthrough and helped me accept my new status as a widow and single mom.

Still, it is interesting how grief manifests differently for each person. In my case, I wanted to hold on to certain sentimental items but purge others that were too distressing to keep. Seeing Dave's toiletries, like his toothbrush and toothpaste, bothered me. The upstairs bathroom has his-and-her sinks, and it pained me, knowing he would never again stand there to get ready for the day. It helped me to clean out Dave's items so Lydia could take over his sink as she grew.

I wrestled with what to do with the rest of Dave's belongings. During the last week of June, I donated his hearing aid and batteries to the hearing clinic where he had been a patient. The clinicians were saddened to learn of Dave's death but grateful for the items I brought. His hearing aids went to an overseas medical missions group, and all the hearing aid batteries went to local schools. I also donated his glasses at a grocery store drop box. It eased my pain, knowing these necessities would go to good use.

Deciding what to do with Dave's clothes and books was more complicated. To me, they represented who he was, his essence. Instead, I permitted myself to keep them as long as needed and put no time limit on my emotions. I struggled with what to do with everything because if I got rid of them, it would have seemed like Dave never existed. So I decided to wait until I felt more at ease. Until then, I categorized other household items into groups. I created piles of things I wanted and could use, things Lydia might want as she grew, and items I could donate at a later date.

Then, during the first week of July, Dave's mom came to visit. We congratulated each other for having made it through the first month-and-a-half without him! In part, I felt my grieving success was due to the amount of support I had received. I had friends, neighbors, coworkers, and church family checking in on me and helping as needed. And as I reflected on the situation, I could see God lining up my mom, Katie, and now Cynda, to stay with me, so I didn't have to be alone.

Cynda stayed through the 4th of July, so it gave us something to celebrate. It was hard to believe that only a year before, Lydia had been a baby and Dave had just finished his first round of chemo. What a difference a year had made in our lives!

During her visit, Cynda and I had several conversations about grief. We discussed how Dave's death affected us personally and as a family. I also affirmed my intent to keep Dave's family as a part of Lydia's life. I said, "Cynda, you will always be special to me. Even though Dave's not here, you are still my mother-in-law. We're family, and you can't get rid of me that easily!" It felt good to laugh despite our pain.

By this time, I had started to make a few subtle changes in the house to improve my mood and support my new routine. I needed something to cheer me up, and Cynda helped me find three new rugs for the living room and entryway. Britain's sharp claws had torn up some of the stitching on the old rugs, and replacing them seemed reasonable since she had gone to live with my brother, Patrick.

Soon, life slowly started drawing me forward. I could not feel sorry for myself for too long because my toddler needed me! Lydia didn't care if I was sad, nor did she understand the grieving process! But she did need me to get up, pay attention to her, feed her, change her, love her, and more. It was difficult, but it was also a blessing to think about and care for someone besides myself. I tried to be thankful and take each day as it came.

For me, grief and moving forward often happened in tandem. As I grieved, I made small changes to make life easier. As I moved forward, I muddled my way through each awkward moment. Slowly, over many months, I gained more self-assurance and energy. At the same time, I struggled in other areas that were previously important to me.

When it came to eating healthy foods and physical activity, I had no motivation at all! Even though I was a dietitian, I started to question certain ideas. "Why even bother eating fruits and vegetables? Dave did that! Why exercise? Dave was always so active but got sick and grew weak anyway."

I barely had any appetite or desire to cook—thanks to the grief—but I knew we needed sustenance. I decided to give myself grace and make the best choices I could at the moment. I continued to eat nourishing foods, but kept our meals simple. Sometimes, I even ordered takeout to make life easier on myself.

I also began to reconsider other areas of life, like saving for retirement. Dave did that too, and it seemed unfair that he would never use the money he saved. However, I understood this had a greater impact beyond Dave. For example, Lydia and I could still benefit from his wise financial decisions.

Over the summer, I even questioned the meaning of life and wondered why I followed God. "Why am I still here? What's the point? Do I only follow God because that's what my parents taught me? Or is there a personal reason I need Him?"

As far as I was concerned, I had already concluded that God exists without a doubt. His continued faithfulness was evident! This period of questioning was different. It wasn't a question about if God was with me, but whether I needed a relationship with Him.

During this time, I met a friend from church at the park in our neighborhood. She had grown up as a pastor's kid and was both confident and open-minded with spiritual matters. She patiently listened to me talk while our kids played. That morning, my friend asked me, "Natalie, how is your relationship with God? I'm sure you have a lot you are working through."

Grateful for this timely question, I answered, "Wow, thank you so much for asking!" I hadn't expected her query but understood it gently got to the heart of the matter.

"To be honest... I'm not sure what to make of it right now. I'd appreciate your prayers, though." I continued, thinking out loud. "You know, I'm not mad at God that Dave died—we left that decision up to Him—but I am trying to decide what my relationship with Him is supposed to look like now. I'm a little confused because everything I was praying for didn't come to pass like I had hoped. I know Jesus loves me, He's made that clear in so many ways, but I'm working through what to do with that on my end. It feels really unfair."

I still struggled with the sting of my new reality.

Thankfully, my friend wasn't fazed by my words and kindly challenged me to keep working through it all. She prayed for me to have clarity and reminded me, "Natalie, that's okay! It's totally understandable to feel how you do! But don't forget you can ask God those questions directly. He loves you and is able to handle any doubts you have. As long as you keep pursuing this relationship and don't give up, it will be okay. Just keep talking to Him about it. He will walk with you through the pain and confusion."

Her nonjudgmental answer was precisely what I needed. I knew she was right. I didn't need to rush through the process or make any rash decisions. I could take it day by day, knowing the Lord was patient with me. He didn't ask for more than I could give, yet I sensed He was near. At the time, all I could do was come and tell Him how I was feeling. So, I clung to Him with all I had. Through this, I started to see grace in a whole new light.

I have always been somewhat task-oriented; I love to-do lists, sticky notes, plans, and goals. Though, in my grief, I felt overwhelmed by the extra responsibilities, which Dave used to handle. It was a burden to keep the house in working order, pay the bills, discipline and take care of Lydia— not to mention going to work, preparing food, and trying to sleep. Yet, during this time, God's serenity filled my heart.

Slowly, I had the strange sense I was in a spiritual safe-place, like Frodo in Rivendell at the end of JRR Tolkien's *Lord of the Rings* trilogy. It was a supernatural calm, one I cannot adequately describe. Rivendell doesn't do it justice! Just like Frodo, I had survived this major battle and needed to rest and regain my strength.

Soon, I realized I didn't need a plan—I needed to recuperate. I continued to deal with the strong emotions that came with profound grief. However, I started to feel spiritual peace and weightlessness and brightness. In my mind's eye, I had the sense that everything was going to be okay. Psalm 17:8 mentions how God hides us in the shadow of His wings, and I felt like He was nestling me close to Him for protection and comfort.

Of course, this security made me trust God more, and I wanted to dwell in His presence, to stay close to Him. I knew, eventually, my heart would heal enough to take on other things. But in the meanwhile, I let God do the heavy work. I rested in His presence, and that was enough. I prayed to see the situation from His perspective so that I could discern a path forward.

Eventually, I concluded that I needed God because His grace and love changed my life. During Dave's cancer battle, I had struggled with trusting God and with fear in general; I questioned His goodness and even His existence. Before Dave's death, I strained to feel God's presence. However, after he died, I experienced a new level of God's grace and love. He was especially kind to me that summer of 2013. How could I not want Him in my life?

Some people might say if God is good, why did Dave get sick and die? Well, I don't have all the answers, but that is something I dealt with, too. As Jesus mentioned, the sun shines and the rain falls on both the just and unjust (Matthew 5:45). God does not tempt us or send evil upon His followers (like Satan does), but sin is a part of the world we live in. We still have to deal with the consequences. Yes, Jesus came to save us from all that, but our choices do carry weight and our hearts often lead us astray. Thankfully, with Him, we can withstand temptation and overcome evil with good (Romans 12:21).

Because God's ways and thoughts are higher than ours (Isaiah 55:9), He has a much broader perspective than we do. Indeed, God has set eternity in our hearts (Ecclesiastes 3:11), which means that we were made for more than what this world has to offer. While our lives are only a brief mist which quickly fades away (James 4:14), what we do here is an investment in the life to come. It matters.

Even in the Bible, we see lives filled with both tragedy and triumph. People like Job, Joseph, and Hannah all trusted God amid their struggles, and they saw His faithfulness in the end. I am inspired by their examples because they never stopped moving forward!

In my case, I have already seen God use cancer and death to refine my character, surrender me, and grow me. Furthermore, I know He will continue to redeem the broken parts of my story, turning them around for my good and His glory (Romans 8:28). Yes, there is a considerable amount of faith involved, but that's okay. Trust is vital in any relationship.

Trials can strengthen or destroy even the best relationships. For instance, in our marriage, whenever Dave and I disagreed, we had a choice to make. We could choose to avoid the problem or resolve it. We felt our relationship was worth preserving, so we did everything we could to make it work. We allowed for each other's differences and forgave quickly. Through those choices, our relationship grew and trust was maintained.

Similarly, I could see cancer and grief in light of my relationship with God. I chose to let these trials draw us close instead of letting them push me away. At any rate, I can point back to many personal encounters or times where God showed up in my life. I can see a trail from where we've walked together over time. Because of these experiences, I do trust that God is good; He collects my tears and won't waste my pain (Psalm 56:8). I believe He will make it up to me in the end—whether in this life or the next.

As I drew closer to the Lord, I tried to resolve other questions, too.

"God's got to have a bigger purpose for me...beyond being married to Dave. But what is it?" There is a tendency in marriage to lose one's self (at least to some degree) as two people are shaped into one unit. Yet, with much prayer and reflection, I saw that even though I had been a wife, I was still me.

It wasn't easy to distinguish where I fit in, though. At times, I felt isolated and alone. I mourned because I could no longer attend couples groups, but with a toddler, joining a typical singles group wasn't practical either. I had to find out who I was again.

I was twenty-five years old when I married Dave and thirty when he died. Thus, I've been single a lot longer than I was married! This understanding was helpful when I began doing many of the same things I had done before marriage. That included spending time with friends, spending time outdoors, and reading. I also used the time to draw closer to God by searching my Bible for insights.

As I dove into the Bible, I read the old, familiar stories with new eyes. Whenever I noticed a passage with a widow, I took note! In 1 Kings 17, the prophet Elijah went to stay with a widow in the village of Zarephath. She was preparing a final meal to share with her son when Elijah asked her to feed him first. I paraphrased the story here, but I love that just when she was ready to give up hope, she was given something to do. Life wasn't easy for this widow, but God gave her meaningful work and blessed her for doing it.

In my grief, I often questioned if I had anything left to contribute. But, when I read what Jesus said about the widow in Luke 21, I was encouraged. He commended the woman for her generosity, though other (more wealthy) people had given more. She gave only two small coins, but it was all she had. It was a timely reminder that even though I didn't feel like I had much to offer, my life still had value to God. My life held meaning and purpose, but maybe it was just different than I had envisioned. In time, I began to have a renewed sense of hope.

As I looked for ways to serve others, I started to see the Lord use me in a variety of ways. For as long as I could remember—even when I was a child in grade school—people would come up to me and ask for prayer or advice. Yet, I was surprised when suddenly a large number of people began seeking my input for their problems. I started tracking how many people I interacted with, and it quickly grew to around forty people per week!

For whatever reason, I could relate to their pain, even though my experience was different (2 Corinthians 1:3-5). It was uncanny, and I thought to myself, "I'm the one grieving right now, but I am comforting them! Do they not realize that I need to heal, too?" At the same time, I was glad to be of service, and dealing with other peoples' problems helped me keep mine in perspective.

As I coached people through different scenarios, I was encouraged, too. I saw God using my pain, and in a way, His grace in my life was spilling over to bless others. As I shared lessons learned, I was refreshed, too. Overall, I saw these requests for help as a way to keep working in my strengths. I was grateful God could still use me.

Chapter 21

"You keep him in perfect peace whose mind is stayed on you, because he trusts in you."
Isaiah 26:3 ESV

August marked the end of my third year in Fargo. Yet, when Dave and I moved into our house, we never could have imagined just how much life would change in such a short time! Thankfully, this month was full of new experiences that helped me heal emotionally. I saw evidence of God's grace sprinkled throughout my daily interactions and choices.

After two months of praying and test-driving cars, I decided to buy a different vehicle. I had stalled because grief made me question my motives like never before. Sadly, I realized that I didn't need a larger car now that Dave and I would not be adding to our family. Also, I felt it was wise to be frugal, and I was reluctant to make such a large purchase without cause.

In the past, I had always driven used cars and didn't think anything of it. But while I liked my Santa Fe, it had been in and out of the shop and the costs were adding up. Since Dave wasn't here to do routine maintenance, I needed something safe and reliable, with no inherent problems.

I didn't want people to make assumptions or think I was being irresponsible with my money; however, the cost of the vehicle was only one factor. Where fear would have led me to buy a cheaper car just to get by, grace showed me God's provision. My worth to the Lord was far greater than the value of any car. So finally, after weighing all the pros and cons, I chose a new Subaru Outback.

Even then, I could see God's hand working on my behalf. Months before, I had been worried about our vehicles, but now, I could see Him lining up people to help me. My parents encouraged me to get something that would last. Cynda test drove vehicles with me in July. Friends helped me decide between features, such as all-wheel drive and navigation systems.

Then, on August 5th, at the car dealership, I traded in two of my three vehicles and put that money toward my Outback. I had hoped to sell Dave's

1965 Chevelle but wasn't able to include that in the deal. I still took out a small loan, but it felt good to let go of the emotional weight of those other vehicles. My sister and brother-in-law had come to visit, which turned out to be perfect timing. Livi distracted Lydia while Paul and I finalized the financial information with the dealers.

I didn't mind holding onto the Chevelle for a little longer, but I was adamant Dave's truck had to go. To me, Dave's truck symbolized his character. For instance, his servant's heart prompted him to carry tools in his truck so that he could help people on the side of the road. He could change a tire, check engine fluids, or tow someone to safety. The truck reminded me of who Dave was, and all I had lost.

On the other hand, the Chevelle represented Dave's dreams—all the car upgrades he wanted to make and the future that never came to pass. It was sad, yes, but I was less attached to the car because he had bought it before we were married. The Chevelle was not Dave's 'daily driver,' so it caused me less emotional pain, at least initially.

A week later, on August 12th, I celebrated my first birthday without Dave. Livi and Paul had returned to their home in Illinois, but thankfully, I had more company. My parents, along with Charlie and Mamie, came to visit. We sat on the deck Dave had built. We told stories and ate meals together, talking about how much we missed him. Lydia was excited about all the attention she received; I was grateful not to be alone. It was bittersweet.

Since Dave died on May 15th, I posted an update to Facebook on the fifteenth of each month. On August 15th, I thanked people for their warm wishes on my birthday and gave a brief recap of the last month. I mentioned one card that said, "May you be overwhelmed with God's grace, love, and comfort." Those words perfectly summarized how I felt with all the support people had shown. Even though my worst fears came true, I saw God's hand at work through the love of those around me. Life had given me lemons, but He had helped me make lemonade.

Later in August, Lydia and I took a quick trip to Illinois. During that time, I met with a family friend, Craig, whose company specialized in financial planning. I was thankful for his input and laughed at the irony. Money, to me, is a rather private subject. Yet, it seemed God had been preparing this personalized solution over many years.

Craig and Jan's daughter, Katie, was my college roommate (who also had visited me earlier that summer). As such, I had spent tons of time with them through family dinners, soccer games, sleepovers, holidays, and trips to Wyoming. This included many discussions about wise stewardship. Because of this, I felt comfortable with Craig's company knowing my financial information. I trusted them because I knew them so well.

Together, we made a plan for how to invest the life insurance settlement. Since I was nowhere near retirement age, it seemed wise for me to continue working to earn money and not depend on the life insurance payout. Instead, by investing the money, I was also investing in our future. I was immensely grateful for the Lord's provision and didn't want to take it for granted or squander it.

My financial life seemed to be falling into place, but that doesn't mean each day was easy. Lydia was the number one reason I kept moving forward, but it was rough handling temper tantrums and other parenting issues on my own. After one particularly tough day, I broke down. It was relatively late, and for some reason, Lydia was still awake. I sat in the dark with her, rocking her back and forth, with tears running down my face. I didn't know how I was going to make it as a single mom.

At twenty-one months, Lydia required so much hands-on care, and I felt worn down. Feeling desperate, I prayed, "Lord, I need wisdom! How am I supposed to discipline, train, and care for Lydia on my own?" I certainly needed help and a new perspective. As my tears dried, I slowly felt the Lord's peace surround me. Truthfully, I still didn't know how I was going to make it—but I did know I could rely on Him.

All summer, I sensed God surrounding me with what felt like a protective cocoon. I had felt Him secluding me with His peace and safety. But as summer turned into fall, I felt Him gently prod me to step out of my comfort zone and try something new. During cancer and the early stages of grief, we avoiding doing extra activities, but now I sensed the need to get involved again. This time, however, I was more selective about which activities to include. I needed to challenge myself but didn't want to get in over my head.

Thankfully, I had gained clarity on what mattered most to me and who I was meant to be. Life is way too short to constrain my life with random events, distractions, and other peoples' expectations. So, instead of automatically saying yes to every request for my time, I prayerfully rebuilt my life to match my God-given strengths and suit our needs. This may sound selfish at first, but I still had a lot of healing to do. And, I knew I could help others best if I were in a good place, too. I cannot give what I don't have.

In September, I signed Lydia up for a toddler gymnastics class once a week, which seemed manageable. Then, I signed up for a Mothers of Pre-Schoolers (MOPS) group, which met twice a month. Paul's wife, Kristen, had regularly invited me when Dave was sick. I hadn't been able to commit to MOPS then, but now, it seemed like a good thing to do. It was helpful that childcare was available during the meetings.

As I introduced myself the first night, many faces lit up in recognition. Kristen had shared my story with them, and they had been praying for us all this time. It was heartwarming to see their compassion. I immediately felt welcome and am so glad I joined! Indeed, that year's theme, "A Beautiful Mess," was quite fitting for how I felt. It was great to meet other fun ladies, and the theme helped me embrace God's grace for my imperfections.

At MOPS, I made many good friends who listened to me, prayed for me, and encouraged me. Some ladies also had older children, so I was able to learn from them. Others had children around the same age as Lydia, and we shared parenting strategies and resources. As we compared funny stories or asked for prayer, I saw that all moms have rough days—not just me as a single mom. Instead of feeling sorry for myself, I noticed we were all in this life stage together. Regardless of our backgrounds, we all had similar triumphs and trials.

One night, I mentioned I had been crying out to the Lord for help a few weeks before. One of the moms said, "You might be a single parent, but you don't have to do it alone." That simple revelation hit home, and I felt new courage rise within me. They were there to listen and help me—just like I was there for them.

A few days later, I was still contemplating how to discipline Lydia as a single mom. Suddenly, I realized if Dave were here, I still would have most likely been the one to discipline Lydia. I was with her most often, and besides, he had been wrapped around her little finger! I enjoyed a good laugh then decided to do my best and deal with each problem head-on. Knowing I had some local moms a phone call or email away was a relief.

In time, as a result of joining MOPS, I finally met a new friend who could relate to what I was going through. Amy didn't attend MOPS, but we had mutual friends there. She was a widow with three children, the youngest about a year older than Lydia. At the time Dave died, I didn't know any widows in my age group, so I was grateful for Amy's friendship. She had lost her husband a couple of years before me, and we were able to support each as we walked through the healing process together.

When it comes to the initial stages of grief, each season brings new burdens to address and new opportunities to heal. In September, Caterpillar held the first annual "David White Memorial Car Show." They used the event as a charity fundraiser in Dave's honor. A few employees (friends) came to my house to prepare his Chevelle for the show, while others grilled hamburgers and sold t-shirts to raise money. Both the turnout and emotions were high.

I did my best to stay cheerful and greet everyone. Having family there was helpful. Each car was entered in a contest, and at the end of the day, awards were given out based on everyone's votes. It was humbling when Dave's car won the People's Choice Award. Back home, we took a picture of Lydia and me with the huge trophy in our matching t-shirts from the event. Lydia's shirt was like a dress on her, but the whole day was a reminder of the legacy Dave had left.

When dealing with grief, some people either prefer to avoid the intense emotions that come, while others prefer to dwell on them. For me, where cancer had been a refining process, grief revealed an inner strength I had never noticed before. I had shown courage when Dave was sick, but I didn't appreciate it until much later.

While I attribute the source of my strength to Jesus Christ working in me, I also purposely chose strength and bravery as my new default. When faced with a new situation, instead of choosing the safe, easy option out of fear, I decided to do what needed to be done, even if it made me uncomfortable. After Dave died, it seemed I had nothing left to lose, and so I decided to start living my life with less hesitation.

Also, I never gave myself a timeline to grieve or go through Dave's belongings. I just handled each task when it felt right. One day in September, I finally felt empowered to go through more of Dave's belongings, specifically, his clothing. Each morning, I woke up with a view inside the walk-in closet. As my life moved forward, I acquired more memories—and more stuff that had no reference to Dave. As time went on, seeing his clothes each day was a sad reminder of his absence.

So one morning, I removed all of his clothes off the upper rack and put mine there instead. I felt a burden lift as I donated most of Dave's work clothes, feeling they could make a positive difference in someone else's life. I also felt compelled to box up some of my favorite items for Lydia. She was so little when Dave died that I wanted her to understand how tall he was or what his style was, for example. Thus, I kept a few of his shirts, a pair or two of pants, and a couple of pairs of shoes for future reference.

After I boxed up those items, there was another stack of shirts that seemed too personal to donate. Yet I didn't have emotional space for them, either. In the end, I decided to send close friends and family each a shirt by which to remember Dave. It was healing to see it as not getting rid of his stuff, but simply passing items on or sharing them with others.

In addition to going through the clothes, I also wanted to clean up the garage. Dave had so many tools! Generally he was very organized, but the garage had fallen into disarray when he had grown sick. It was overwhelming for me, and I asked my friends, Dean and Jackie, for help. Dean suggested an informal auction, so I could sell what I didn't need. It seemed like a good idea, and I was grateful for this solution.

I extended an invitation to five men, including Dean, Paul, Mike, and Deven from Caterpillar. The other man, Dee, had been helping me maintain the Chevelle. All of these men were quite handy and appreciated the opportunity. Before they came over, my parents visited again. My dad helped me decide which tools to sell and which to keep. Then, we held the auction in late September. I ordered some food and chatted with a couple of the Caterpillar wives while the men went through the tools.

The men tracked which tools were sold to each man and the final total owed. As a group, they decided what the cost of each item was new—and then started the bidding at a percentage of that price. In the end, each man walked away with quality tools, and I also benefited. They each thanked me and said they were pleased to have some of Dave's prized possessions. I felt that they went above and beyond to honor me.

Then, in October, Sam, and his brother, Andy, came again for the harvest season. We all reminisced about fun times with Dave, and it felt good to have these friends present. Sam and Andy completed a few house maintenance chores for me, too. I appreciated their support, and it was helpful to hear their thoughts on how or why Dave made decisions. In a few instances, when I was uncertain, these friends reminded me of what he would've done.

Though I lived in North Dakota, I still kept up with many aspects of life and news in Illinois. On November 18th, 2013, the town of Washington, Illinois, suffered losses due to an EF-4 tornado. To me, this was significant because Dave had looked for a job in nearby Peoria just before applying for the one in West Fargo. The fact that we had considered living in Washington was not lost on me.

My friends, Mike and Becca, knew some Caterpillar families directly impacted. I was emotional as I explained my thoughts to Becca, "Can you imagine if we lived there now? I would have lost not only my husband but also my entire house and all our belongings!" This stunning realization left me in awe that God had not only directed our steps to North Dakota, but in effect, had spared me of even greater tragedy. He had us safely tucked away in Fargo.

Time kept moving along. In late November, I celebrated Lydia's second birthday with a few close friends locally. But to my surprise, people all over the world remembered her special day! I was amazed at the outpouring of cards, gifts, and phone calls that she received. It was humbling to see how many people went the extra mile to encourage and celebrate Lydia. Their thoughtful support brought comfort on an otherwise bittersweet day without her daddy.

Truthfully, each holiday season without Dave has been an emotional challenge—though it has gotten better over the years. For us, several events occur back-to-back. In November, there is Lydia's birthday and Thanksgiving. Dave's birthday is in December, followed by Christmas. Then, we celebrate the New Year and our wedding anniversary in early January.

For that first grieving holiday season, I set no expectations. I could not bear traveling to Illinois without Dave, yet I didn't want to be alone in North Dakota. It was a big adjustment, but overall, I wanted to create new memories for each holiday, giving me something positive to look back upon each year. So, we went to visit friends and family elsewhere. For Thanksgiving, we flew to visit Katie and her family in Montana. We had a fun time hiking and hanging out together. We missed Dave, but it was easier since he had never been there.

Then, for Dave's thirty-fifth birthday, I decided to stay home. A small group of ladies from church came over for a Bible study, and I surprised them by making some of Dave's favorite foods. To me, this was better than feeling sorry for myself. Ironically, most of the ladies had never met Dave, but they said I was brave in my intention to celebrate him. Then, we enjoyed simple hors d'oeuvres and peppermint ice cream!

Other traditions were trickier. For example, that season, the thought of putting up our beloved Christmas tree made me too sad. Yet, on a whim, I decided to buy a small three-foot artificial tree and decorate that instead. I put it in another location, in hopes it would cheer me up. Looking back, I see resiliency, and I am proud that I was able to make a good compromise.

Then, for Christmas itself, we went to Ohio to visit my aunt, uncle, and cousins. On Christmas Day, we called our loved ones in Illinois. While they certainly missed us, they understood and graciously let me cope in my own way. I was doing my best, and I really appreciated the gift of their support!

Regarding the Christmas message, I felt telling Lydia about Jesus and Dave were linked. I wanted her to understand their love for her and see them both in Heaven someday. While I have nothing against Santa Claus, I didn't want Lydia to confuse make-believe ideas with what I was teaching her about Jesus and Dave. Basically, I did not want her to feel I had lied to her. So, I focused on telling Lydia all the beautiful things about Jesus and her daddy and kept Santa on the periphery. I have never regretted that decision.

At two years old, Lydia loved babies. So for Christmas, it was easy to highlight Jesus as a baby. She couldn't take in the entire gospel message, perhaps, but this approach worked well for both of us. She received many presents from others, but I kept Jesus the main idea.

That year, Christmas had even more meaning for me because Jesus stepped into our lives, not just as a baby, but in a personal way when Dave entered Heaven. Jesus didn't have to come and rescue us, but His love for us compelled Him to do so. Seeing Lydia's joy not just for presents, but also for Jesus as a baby was adorable! Her joy reinforced my strong desire to keep on this healing journey and live each day to the fullest.

On December 31st, we attended a wedding for one of Dave's coworkers. Deven, and his bride, Kimmy, wanted to start off 2014 together. To get into the party mood, Lydia and I each wore special dresses. Her dress was black-and-white with hot pink polka dots. I wore a beautiful purple cocktail dress that Dave had bought me shortly after we were married. Practically speaking, the dress wasn't the wisest choice, given that the temperature was near zero degrees!

After the wedding, I put Lydia to bed. I had mixed emotions as I ushered in the New Year on my own. Just like lemonade, I simultaneously tasted both sour and sweet. But despite my world turning upside down, God had been faithful. His grace had changed my whole perspective.

On Facebook, I mentioned the fun wedding celebration and how spending time with Caterpillar friends was reassuring. I thanked everyone who had supported us and shared a photo of Lydia and me in our dresses. I also wrote how it felt so foreign to be starting a new year without Dave. It almost felt like I was leaving him behind.

On the other hand, I was excited. The New Year symbolized a new start and an ongoing opportunity to be brave and trust the Lord. That night,

I wrote: “I know that God is with us, and for us. Joshua 1:9 says, ‘Have I not commanded you? Be strong and courageous. Do not be afraid; do not be discouraged, for the Lord your God will be with you wherever you go.’”

I had left so much behind in 2013, some by choice and some not. As I wrote my update, I was reminded of Dave’s enthusiasm when he had said it had been “a phenomenal year!” With that same approach, I decided to make the best of 2014 and see what else God had in store for us.

Chapter 22

"For the word of the Lord holds true,
and we can trust everything he does."
Psalm 33:4 NLT

On January 7th, 2014, I celebrated what would have been our sixth wedding anniversary. At first, it seemed awkward to celebrate something that wasn't my reality anymore. "Should I acknowledge the special day or not?" I wondered. "Is it still appropriate to commemorate special events Dave and I shared? Will people understand or think it is weird? Do people even care at this point? How long can I (or should I) keep bringing up special moments like these?" I was conflicted because I didn't want peoples' sympathy or to appear like I needed attention.

Finally, I decided to just be thankful for our time together and the memories we created. Dave and I had often gone to see a movie on our anniversary. So, I invited some friends to join me. Oddly enough, they all had other plans, and I nearly talked myself out of going several times! I wasn't sure whether going to the movie theater alone was brave or pathetic.

Nevertheless, I sensed the Lord wanting me to trust Him and not fear, so at the last minute, I went to the movies solo! I chose a matinee because it seemed like a more reasonable time to take Lydia to daycare and not affect her bedtime. Each time I decided to do something for myself, I had to think of who was going to watch her. It was an adjustment for me, and often, staying home was more convenient.

As I walked into the dimly-lit theater, I went up the stairs and sat toward the back half of the raised area. I sat in the middle of my row to allow space if someone else needed a seat. However, I was the only one in the theater. I chose to see "The Secret Life of Walter Mitty," which had been recommended to me. The breathtaking scenery of Iceland inspired me, but the plot also pulled on my heart. I saw a few parallels to my own life.

The main character lives a very timid life at first. But then, he goes on several adventures and transforms into a bolder person as the story progresses. Of course, I could relate to that! And then, I noticed something more amazing. As I sat in the theater, several other people came in late and sat in my area. Suddenly, there were couples and even other singles all around me!

As I sat in the dark, I smiled with tears in my eyes. Even though I had gone to the movies on my own, I was not alone. It was as if God had provided people to sit with me! Grateful, I saw it as one more way the Lord was taking care of me. He had surrounded me with His love!

When I returned home, I felt comfortable commemorating my anniversary and the movie experience with another social media update. I was grateful for the positive experience and wanted to praise God for His help. It was a blessing to see that my bravery, one step at a time, was becoming both a habit and a path. Each time I made a difficult or fearless decision, the Lord empowered me and encouraged me to keep moving forward. It felt liberating!

The following Sunday at church, I resumed teaching the PLACE class again. I had filled in for someone in November, but by the time January came, no one else was available to teach. So, I volunteered to lead the classes by myself on a regular basis. I found it just as rewarding as before, and I still learned more about myself in the process.

I also had the opportunity to continue sharing my story from time to time. It was good for me to meet others who could relate to my pain, even if they hadn't experienced the same trauma. Talking about all I had been through helped me process my grief further. And, seeing how my story impacted others gave me more courage to keep discussing it.

For my monthly Facebook update on January 15th, I shared how Lydia had been talking more about Dave. I had done my best to point him out in pictures: "Look, Lydia, there's Daddy!" Now eight months later, she still recognized him but had started noticing Dave's absence as well. We often spent time with other families, and Lydia noticed most of her friends had dads who were very involved.

It was heartbreaking for me, though I never wanted her to feel left out or know the anguish it caused me inside. Thankfully, many of these men stepped up and treated Lydia similarly to how they treated their own kids. It felt very natural how they included her. They played dolls and other games, colored pictures, and read books to her. One friend even let Lydia put barrettes in his hair! I enjoyed seeing her have fun, and I was grateful she adjusted so well.

Still, I was unsure how to explain Dave's absence in ways a two-year-old could understand. Naturally, I did my best to anticipate Lydia's needs and address her doubts. To start, I pointed out ways she was like Dave. If I noticed a similar character trait or physical trait they shared, I would say something like, "Lydia, you are a good helper, just like your daddy. He would be so proud of you." I wanted her to be able to relate to him and have a good idea of who he was.

I sought out grief resources for children, but I could not find anything substantial. So, I decided to keep my answers honest and straightforward, though Lydia did not need to know all the details right away. I also printed many of the pictures I had taken of Dave and Lydia together. I put them in several small photo albums so she could have something to hold and review. Even now, she enjoys showing her friends the pictures when they come over.

Then, in February, I had an opportunity to meet some older widows from church for a little encouragement. We met at the local Olive Garden restaurant, and I certainly was the youngest one there. However, I was happy to be included, and it felt good to be with these ladies. The host asked each of the ladies if they had any words of wisdom for me. Each of them briefly shared her story, and I jotted down notes to review later. I enjoyed what they had to say.

A lady named Elaine said, "When we focus on our pain, it is easy to feel sorry for ourselves or to compare our lives to those of others. Instead of becoming depressed by our circumstances, we can serve others with joy." In a similar vein, Marian said to keep on giving—to the church, other people, or special causes. She explained how God had always met her needs, and the more she gives of her time, energy, and resources, the more He continues to fill her life with good things and beautiful people. With a big smile, she said,

"You can't out-give God!"

Lorraine exhorted me to "keep praying and relying on the Lord." She had depended on Him to help her make big decisions and encouraged me to do the same. Another lady, Sharon, said to stay in touch with friends and family. "They are a built-in support system and can help us on those really tough days."

As I listened, I was pleased with my choices along the way. I realized that I had already been doing the same things these ladies suggested. It made me glad to know I was on the right track. Each month that passed brought a new level of healing and confidence.

Similarly, I also had more opportunities for growth. For instance, over time, several people in our support system moved away for work or to be near loved ones in other states. It was emotional for me because each family had been quite helpful to us. They understood the details of what Dave and I had been through, and I had relied on them. Now I had to learn to cope without them, too!

Around that time, I began subconsciously categorizing people into two groups: those who had met Dave and those who had not. With new friends, I found myself explaining who Dave was, but, I found particular comfort in those who already knew our story. It was a relief that I could just be myself around them and not have to start all over. So, it was especially sad anytime these friends moved away. It was another level of loss and adjustment.

For Valentine's Day, my parents came to visit again because they didn't want me to be alone for that special holiday without Dave. It was sweet of them to consider how I might be feeling, and we all had fun together! Interestingly, this holiday wasn't as painful for me. Because it was relatively close to our anniversary, Dave and I usually celebrated in a low-key manner.

However, through this, I saw that some everyday activities or places made my grief feel worse, some brought peace and healing, and some had a neutral effect emotionally. I also realized that I didn't want to avoid going somewhere special, just because it now made me sad. Instead, I decided to create new, happy memories in those places that would make me laugh and smile again.

For example, in March, Lydia and I met Uncle Charlie and Aunt Mamie in San Diego, California, for a little getaway. Dave and I went there in April 2007 for a friend's wedding. We went to the San Diego Zoo, and Dave later proposed to me while we watched the sunset on the beach. That trip was exceptional, but now it was only a memory.

With Charlie and Mamie's help, our mission to make new memories was a success. We visited the same zoo and took funny pictures. We ate yummy food and introduced Lydia to the Pacific Ocean! As she squealed with delight, I considered all that had happened since my first time there. Before, it was just Dave and me anticipating our life together. Now, Lydia and I were piecing together a life without our beloved husband and father. This trip was relaxing, and I was able to rest, soak up the sun, and continue moving forward emotionally.

In the spring of 2014, I continued to teach the PLACE class at church. I enjoyed keeping busy and helping others. But in April, when asked if I was available to teach the following month, I hesitated. I knew the timing conflicted with the next child dedication ceremony. Dave and I had never been able to do this together because he had been so sick.

Yet, when faced with going through with it on my own, I grew nervous. I would have to stand up on the stage without Dave. I was afraid, and my imagination started running wild. I envisioned not being able to speak clearly (to introduce Lydia) or that people I didn't know would be judging me as a single mom. This situation felt like a test.

I had already dealt with strangers' opinions of me at the park months before. I thought I had grown beyond that! But now I wondered, "Could I find the courage to do it on my own?" Then, someone reminded me there would be several families up there with me—and likely some other single moms. I was also encouraged to invite some friends if it was too far for my family to come. So, I bravely took a small step by filling out the one-page form. Next, I invited some of our Caterpillar friends to join us on May 11th.

That dedication Sunday also happened to be Mother's Day, the third one from the time Dave grew sick. I dressed Lydia and me in two of our prettiest dresses, taking extra care to look put-together that day because

I wanted to feel more confident. For me, the entire ceremony felt like a metaphorical line in the sand. With conviction, I was taking a stand for my family. We had been battered and bruised, but God had been faithful to us.

In many ways, it was an "as for me and my house, we will serve the Lord" moment (Joshua 24:15). We had made it thus far, just a few days short of the first anniversary of Dave's death. Surviving all the trauma of the previous two years was a victory in and of itself. But, I also saw it as me taking the lead as the head of my household, determined to raise Lydia to know Jesus and honor Dave's memory.

I felt so much love that day at church, and later, at the small gathering Dean and Jackie held for us at their house. Mike and Becca also attended the dedication, and they joined us for lunch, too. After lunch, Lydia and I each opened a gift from these friends. Lydia received a *Jesus Storybook Bible* from Mike and Becca. Then, Jackie presented me with a beautiful necklace.

Of course, I was probably extra emotional that day. There were many factors involved— the dedication, the gifts, the nerves, Mother's Day, and the upcoming anniversary of Dave's death. But, I was grateful for the support and for having survived my first year of being a widow and single mom. Of course, we took some cute photos to commemorate the day.

Later that week, my family visited us for the anniversary of Dave's death. Instead of moping around, we decided to do fun things to celebrate his life! On May 15th, 2014, we went to Nichole's Fine Pastry for lunch and gourmet desserts. In my usual way, I tried to connect this somewhat sad day with something positive for Lydia. She was over-the-moon excited!

Yet, just before my family came, I made an important decision about my wedding rings. I put away the engagement ring and moved the small wedding band to my right hand. I had never gotten them soldered, which ironically made my decision a little easier. I wanted to honor Dave's memory but didn't want to immortalize him. Surprisingly, I felt free: I had finally accepted my status as a widow and single mom and let go of what others might think of me.

As I reflected upon all my experiences over the last year, I was proud of myself for growing through my grief. I was no longer the new widow or single mom seeking approval from strangers in the park. Now my role had changed. I was the leader of my family, and I no longer cared if people judged me incorrectly!

I was empowered and felt lighthearted after taking this big step forward. During their visit, my family noticed the difference in me even before I told them about my decision. They were quite supportive. Later, I explained my reasoning to my new friend, Amy, as we met regularly to support each other through our grief. She soon made a similar decision, as well.

I could see God continuing to provide for us, and though I still faced challenges, He sent friends to encourage and help me. For instance, people at Caterpillar and church still periodically checked in to see if I needed anything. In May, two pastors organized a team of men to help me with some house maintenance and yard work.

As a result of their kindness, my garage was reorganized, my flower bed received fresh mulch, and my deck got its first coat of stain. Since Lydia required my full attention, the deck had sat unfinished for a year-and-a-half. What these young men accomplished in five hours would have taken me weeks to achieve otherwise.

Also, my Caterpillar friends continued mowing my lawn each week (for a third summer). I was grateful for how well God was taking care of us through all these friends. It was a bittersweet week, with the child dedication, guests coming to celebrate Dave's life, and men from church working around the house. But, all in all, I was proud of how well we had come through that first year of grief.

After Dave died, I had given myself one year to concentrate on dealing with my grief. (It is an ongoing process, but it doesn't require my constant attention now.) There were many times when I had wanted to skip ahead and avoid the tough emotional work. However, as the first year came to a close, I was glad I had not bypassed it after all. I had learned so much about God and myself.

As I looked back, I saw that God's faithfulness had never wavered. Some people may think God let me down because Dave died. Yet, I saw Him do so much more than we could ever dream! He answered big, audacious prayers and small, silent ones. It was an awful situation, no doubt. But, God was so kind and generous. Already Stage IV at diagnosis, Dave's prognosis wasn't great from the start, but God gave us those 364 days anyway. God used these extreme circumstances to prove He is bigger than my fears. He set me free, indeed!

I am genuinely grateful to have learned so many valuable life lessons at the age of thirty instead of much later down the road. Now, I can focus on what is most important, including walking out God's purposes for me. I prioritize spending time with Lydia and all the other people I love. I don't feel the terms 'widow' and 'single mom' define who I am. I simply live my life doing the best I can and seek God's sweet and refreshing grace along the way.

The journey from gripping fear to a deeper, stronger faith has not been easy, though God is redeeming my pain. He has rebuilt my life from the ashes. I choose to be brave and walk by faith, knowing the best is yet to come. With Jesus, there are always exciting adventures ahead!!

Epilogue

"So then, just as you received Christ Jesus as Lord,
continue to live your lives in him."
Colossians 2:6 NIV

Over the years, I have learned that grief is not just reserved for the loss of a loved one. Grief, in many ways, is wrestling with the emotions that come with loss. Grief can come with divorce; a child born with medical issues; a change in jobs or financial status; or moving across the country. Grief can occur when there is a loss of independence or ability, and there is even grief with survivor's guilt. Some of the examples listed above come together, which only compounds the emotional burden. Yes, grief requires a great deal of time, effort, and adjustment. It's not something we "just get over," but with God's help, we can move forward into a full life.

As such, Lydia and I have done our best to keep moving forward, too. A few years after Dave died, I sold his Chevelle to a local family friend. When it happened, it was God's perfect timing because Lydia was old enough to remember it and take a short ride in it! It was fun to see her joy as she sat in "Daddy's car." Otherwise, we still have the Subaru, and with a little routine maintenance, I hope to have it for a long time.

I have learned so much about the importance of self-care over the years. Health is not something to be taken for granted. I still don't always get enough sleep, but I am working on it. I try to be a good example for Lydia in eating well, exercising, etc. Thankfully, I feel better than I have in years!

As I have shared my story with others, I have realized spiritual doubt is common and can be a healthy part of growth. Doubt can lead us either to deeper faith or unbelief. It's easy to have faith and trust God in good times or when prayers are answered as we desire. We can clearly see His goodness then! But when everything falls apart, and our faith is tested, we have a choice.

In those times, we can either draw near to God or run away. When we draw near, we see His goodness does not depend on our circumstances. God never changes; He is always good (Malachi 3:6 and Hebrews 13:8). While praising Him feels effortless when things are going well, it can be a real struggle when we face difficult times.

Yet, I have come to realize God's goodness shines most in our dark moments. It is in our trials that He sits with us, carries us, and holds on to us. Sometimes He uses other people to comfort us, and sometimes we sense His presence in a personal way.

God's love is constant, and doubts do not disqualify us from His grace; He is not put off by our questions. If we let Him, He will patiently lead us to the answers we seek. And if there are questions left unanswered, He will give us the grace to trust Him with the unknown. Still, the choice to trust God is left with us. At first, it is a conscious decision, but over time, drawing near to Him becomes a beautiful habit.

Once, a friend asked me how she could prepare to go through challenges and not lose her faith. I didn't have a succinct answer, as God works with us individually. Still, I said we should seek Him daily in the good times and soak up His love and grace. Then, it will be easier to turn to Him as Father and Sustainer when times get rough.

Additionally, we should use those peaceful times to develop our faith through consistent Bible reading, praying, going to church, giving, cultivating gratitude, etc. We can't expect to start those 'spiritual disciplines' amid chaos when we are more prone to distraction, doubt, and despair. Besides, if we only seek our greatest Friend in times of trouble, what does that say about our relationship?

Similarly, most, if not all, of my family and friends in this book have gone through their own trials in recent years. With the tables turned, I've had the honor of praying for them, standing with them in faith, and offering practical hands-on support, too. In those heart-wrenching moments, I have reminded them of God's love and faithfulness as they did for me. God is always for us and with us. His plans for us are sure. He always comes through for us—we can trust Him!

Interestingly, cancer and grief exposed not only my tendency to fear but also my strengths and weaknesses. God helps me deal with fear as soon as it comes now, and my faith in Him has grown even more as I rely on Him. I have learned to trust His voice, whereas, before cancer, I often questioned if I heard Him correctly. Now, I have confidence in what He says. I don't expect perfection from myself. I know God will redirect me as needed.

For instance, for years I felt prompted to write, but I didn't know how to go about it or even what to write. Thus, I discounted that calling until I couldn't ignore it any longer. I'm thankful I decided to obey God and trust Him more fully. As such, He used writing this book to help me process my grief. He brought healing as I wrestled with putting my thoughts on paper. It was a great relief as I unloaded my burdens, and I have been able to bless others, too.

While this book helps explain 'how we got here,' in 2015, I started a blog, called Grace and Lemonade (www.graceandlemonade.com), to document our journey forward. The blog has also helped me to trust God and grow, while my readers keep me accountable for the message of grace and making the best of our circumstances. Blogging every week has had the added benefit of tracking Lydia's growth.

By God's grace, she has proven to be quite resilient. She has started her school years and is well-adjusted. We talk about Dave often, but we don't make him our focus. Lydia still enjoys looking through all the pictures of her with Dave. When other children ask about her dad, Lydia takes it in stride. Without missing a beat, she tells them he is with Jesus in Heaven. It seems her confidence helps the other children accept her story, and then they continue with whatever else they are doing at that moment.

Over the years, Lydia and I have had many conversations about Dave, cancer, death, grief, Jesus, Heaven, Hell, etc. Sometimes, the conversations happen at awkward times. For example, one Fourth of July, she was unusually excited about the ashes from the evening's campfire. This converged with her thoughts about a funeral we had recently attended.

At 11:00 p.m. that night, she had many questions about Dave's urn (which I keep out of sight). When I showed it to her, she took it much better than I expected. "That's so cool!" she exclaimed. For years, I had prayed about when to have this conversation, and when it finally unfolded, it felt like perfect timing. I'm grateful God keeps leading us!

At this time, we are living in the same house. I try my best to keep it well-maintained. I mow the lawn and clear snow, and my neighbors and friends help as needed. Along the way, I acquired a smaller snow blower, though shoveling snow remains good for refining my character! Last season, I hired a company to help me with the driveway and sidewalks, so that was a huge timesaver, especially with blizzards.

A few years ago, I did a little redecorating and made some updates around the house. It still has a warm and welcoming atmosphere, but feels a little more like 'me.' That year, with a bit of help and encouragement from my neighbor, I was finally able to put up our Christmas tree and decorate it. It felt like a huge milestone because it had previously caused so much heartache.

Overall, our holidays have improved each year. Generally, I look forward to them now because Lydia gets so excited. We still celebrate Dave's birthday and the anniversary of his death by doing something special or serving others. Sometimes I give Lydia a gift, such as a necklace or a book or puzzle, because I want her to associate those days with positive things, not sadness. We focus on how proud Dave would be of us, and we often invite others to join us.

We still attend the same church, and I still serve as a volunteer. It has been rewarding to see our relationships deepen over the years. I am also glad for the spiritual foundation Lydia is receiving. To me, the lessons she is learning are invaluable. I hope to instill the same lessons at home and train Lydia to follow Jesus from a young age. Then, when she faces her own trials, her faith will sustain her. She is free to follow her own path, of course, but I want to teach her to choose faith over fear.

Our friends at Caterpillar still offer support from time to time. We don't see them as often now, but occasionally, Lydia and I stop by to say hello and take a tour. As she gains more understanding of our story, it helps her get a better sense of who Dave was and the impact he had. She always points out his picture on the wall commemorating former workers who left their mark. I'm grateful for the legacy Dave left there.

I work for a different company now, and God led me through that transition, too. I've continued to make financial adjustments over time, but He has been gracious to meet our needs. In many ways, my experiences with cancer and grief have helped me professionally. I better understand the struggles people face and see the effect stress can have on their eating patterns. I've even had patients tearfully thank me for listening to them without making assumptions.

In terms of grief, it has slowly gotten better every year. There were many times when I didn't know if my pain would ever go away. But, God is faithful, and we could not have survived without His help and guidance. Occasionally, something will trigger a wave of grief, but it no longer knocks me over. I let those feelings have space or time as needed, and God's strength keeps me standing.

As I think about all the problems we have faced, I am grateful for how far the Lord has brought us. What was meant for evil, God has turned for good. Indeed, He has used my pain for greater purposes, far more than I could have imagined. I know He will continue doing so.

I pray others find hope and encouragement in my story. Life brings us many challenges, but God is here with us. We can trust Him as He empowers us to move forward, from fear to faith. He always leads us to Victory!

One Final Note

"For God so loved the world that he gave his one and only Son, that whoever believes in him shall not perish but have eternal life."
John 3:16

Dave spent many hours waiting during his treatments. This gave him a lot of time to come to terms with life, and ultimately, he did not want his suffering to go to waste. Dave was both a planner and someone who always thought of others. So, I would be remiss if I did not share these final thoughts.

Dave often talked about 2 Peter 3:9, which says, "The Lord is not slow in keeping his promise, as some understand slowness. Instead he is patient with you, not wanting anyone to perish, but everyone to come to repentance." While Dave meditated on that verse, his heart ached for everyone to be saved and understand God's love for them. He wanted us all to be prepared for the life to come!

If you would like to learn more about what this means, I recommend connecting with a local Bible-preaching church. You can also email me at nat.grace.lemonade@gmail.com; I'd love to share more information. God bless you!

Acknowledgments

While this book serves as a record for Lydia and a giant thank you note to those who have assisted us, it would not have been possible without valuable input from many people. Many thanks to Denis Ledoux at The Memoir Network in Lisbon Falls, Maine. He listened to me process my story and helped me find the courage to write it for others. He also helped shape all the details into a comprehensive work. I appreciate his professional feedback!

Several people provided valuable advice during various phases of writing and editing. Thanks, Livi and Katie, for being my first readers. Thanks to others God provided along the way, such as Devin, Gwen, Laurie, Lisa, Lolly, Melissa, Naa, and Sally. They helped in a variety of ways, including clarifying my message, walking with me through the publishing process, and praying for me. I owe a special thanks to Patrick Yeagle of Iconic Images for helping with my book cover and Mark How of How 2 Creative Services for piecing everything together in the final stages!

Thanks, Jackie, for watching Lydia for hours on end during the early drafts of this book. So many other people listened to me share my ideas and encouraged me, usually just when I needed it. Thanks for the little accountability checks along the way! As always, thanks to my family—especially my parents and Lydia—for your patience and prayers! Without their support, this would be an entirely different book. Thank you to Caterpillar, Inc., and all the employees represented in this book. I am continually humbled by how good you all have been to us. Thanks for being a part of our story. Finally, all thanks, praise, and glory to Jesus Christ, the great Author and Perfecter of my faith.

CPSIA information can be obtained
at www.ICGtesting.com
Printed in the USA
FSHW022312211121
86377FS